POLITICAL
Communication

in *ACTION*

POLITICAL
Communication
in *ACTION*

From Theory to Practice

David L. Helfert

LYNNE
RIENNER
PUBLISHERS

BOULDER
LONDON

Published in the United States of America in 2018 by
Lynne Rienner Publishers, Inc.
1800 30th Street, Boulder, Colorado 80301
www.rienner.com

and in the United Kingdom by
Lynne Rienner Publishers, Inc.
3 Henrietta Street, Covent Garden, London WC2E 8LU

Library of Congress Cataloging-in-Publication Data
Names: Helfert, David L., author.
Title: Political communication in action : from theory to practice / by
   David L. Helfert.
Description: Boulder, Colorado : Lynne Rienner Publishers, Inc., [2017] |
   Includes bibliographical references.
Identifiers: LCCN 2017018649| ISBN 9781626376809 (hc : alk. paper) | ISBN
   9781626376816 (pb : alk. paper)
Subjects: LCSH: Communication in politics—United States. |
   Rhetoric—Political aspects—United States. | United States—Politics and
   government.
Classification: LCC JA85.2.U6 H45 2017 | DDC 320.97301/4—dc23
LC record available at https://lccn.loc.gov/2017018649

British Cataloguing in Publication Data
A Cataloguing in Publication record for this book
is available from the British Library.

Printed and bound in the United States of America

The paper used in this publication meets the requirements
of the American National Standard for Permanence of
Paper for Printed Library Materials Z39.48-1992.

5   4   3   2   1

For Kathy

Contents

Acknowledgments

I don't know if many books are written start to finish by one person sitting alone at a keyboard. This one sure as heck wasn't! I've been blessed to have many friends and colleagues review it. Some actually went through and edited the text. Longtime friend and colleague Bill Emory—scholar, teacher, pollster, and political organizer—tore through it with a sharp blue pencil, caught mistakes, and made many suggestions to improve it. Dave Tully, a former student, congressional communications director, and now legislative affairs strategist, also read through the whole thing and made numerous suggestions.

I was very fortunate to have several distinguished professors of communication studies review the text in its early stages and counsel me on the value and realistic possibilities of finding a publisher for a textbook written by an academic outsider. Natalie (Talia) Jomini Stroud in the University of Texas (UT) Department of Communication Studies, author of *Niche News*, which I cite extensively in this book, was kind enough to sit down with me several times. Her colleague Sharon Jarvis, who teaches political communication at UT, was also very gracious. Another UT communication studies professor, John Daly, friend and author of *Advocacy*, which I use in all my classes, went above and beyond as well. I am very honored and grateful that Ralph Begleiter, professor emeritus and founder of the Center for Political Communication at the University of Delaware, took time to review the text. Another review was written by old friend and former colleague Mark McKinnon, who was communications director for the George W. Bush presidential campaign.

Several of my Washington, DC, teaching colleagues have also been incredibly helpful. Bob Lehrman is a former Al Gore speechwriter, fellow adjunct professor at American University, and author of *The Political Speechwriter's Handbook*—another text I use in every class I teach. Bob first finagled me into writing surrogate speeches in the 2008 presidential election and has become a dear friend. He reviewed the text, especially the chapter on political speeches, and chewed me out for not going into enough depth about the speechwriting process. Okay. Okay. He was right.

Alan Rosenblatt, a recognized authority on social media and a teaching colleague at Johns Hopkins University, reviewed that chapter in the book to make sure I sounded like I knew what the heck I was talking about. Dave Petts, partner in Normington, Petts & Associates, a nationally respected public opinion research firm, was kind enough to review the chapter on the types and uses of research in political campaigns and public affairs communication and make very helpful suggestions. Mike Larabee, opinion editor of the *Washington Post,* reviewed the chapter on communicating through the news media and made suggestions to sharpen and improve the text. Monica Davis, longtime friend, colleague, and principal in the Davis Group, an Austin-based media planning and placement firm, provided up-to-date radio and television advertising rates in numerous markets across the country.

I did my absolute best to put my Democratic bias aside while writing this book. And I was most fortunate to have good friends of the Republican persuasion willing to share their perspectives and experiences. Ken Spain, former communications director for the National Republican Congressional Committee and now partner in the CGCN Group, an advocacy and strategic communications firm, shared insights into what was happening on the other side of the aisle while we were both working in Congress. And Republican communications guru Dave Winston explained to several of my classes the development of many remarkably effective messaging strategies.

Over the several years I was writing, rewriting, re-rewriting, and re-re-rewriting *Political Communication in Action*, I was blessed to find some consummate professionals to review, edit, and offer numerous criticisms and suggestions to help improve the expanding manuscript. Christina Mueller helped me to pull many pieces of the story together and put them in an order that made sense. Later in the process, I worked with professional copyeditor Jan Fitter, who helped me to transform some of my political gibberish into words and paragraphs that people might actually understand. Another coat of polish was applied by the pros at Lynne Rienner Publishers, including acquisitions editor Carrie Broadwell-Tkach, project editor Shena Redmond, and copyeditor Sonia Smith. I will always be grateful that Carrie and Lynne Rienner herself were willing to take a chance on me and my "real world" approach to teaching the process of political communication.

And finally, I need to express eternal profound gratitude to the person who has been unfailingly supportive, endlessly patient, and amazingly long-suffering, who has read and heard every syllable of this book thousands of times and has made helpful and positive suggestions about it more times than I can count: my best friend, my partner, and the love of my life, Kathy Ledbetter Helfert.

1

Political Communication in Action

This is not a conventional textbook. It isn't written in scholarly language or style and doesn't rely solely on academic research and scholarly works to authenticate its conclusions. It does assuredly contain citations and references to academic research to help explain certain important considerations in political and public affairs communication. But it also relies on observations and conclusions, along with citations and references, from communication professionals and journalists who cover, analyze, and write about the process.

I believe this more comprehensive approach is appropriate because political communication is an active, dynamic professional field in addition to being an area of academic inquiry. By exploring both perspectives, we can better understand how each step of the political communication process actually works, how it's done, and what it looks like. And we can better investigate and understand why the steps in the process work and what makes them effective.

The Origins of Political Communication

Political communication in its broadest form did not suddenly appear in 1952 in a black and white TV spot with a musical chorus of "I Like Ike." As long as people have lived together in societies and created structures—governments—to establish and maintain some semblance of order, there has been communication from, to, and about those governments; about rules, roles, and responsibilities for citizens; and eventually about new and theoretical concepts of societal structures called democracies.

Over the millennia, as societies evolved and the rudiments of democracy began to be imagined and discussed, elemental political communication emerged. People attempted to influence the thoughts and actions of others, to propose and discuss principles for societies, and to motivate people to take certain actions.

Less than sixty years after the death of Socrates came one of the first recorded examples of the effective practice of political communication. In 342 B.C.E., Athenian statesman and general Demosthenes, considered one of the greatest orators of all time, used his rhetorical skills to rouse fellow Athenians to stand up to Phillip II of Macedon, whose army was moving aggressively into the Ionian Peninsula. It worked. After Demosthenes' stirring speech, people cried out, "To arms! To arms!" and rushed off to defend their city from the invading Macedonians. That was indeed effective messaging.

The world was a stage for Roman political communication for centuries. One of the best-known examples of political communication occurred in 33 C.E. in Roman-occupied Judea. Biblical scripture tells us that the Roman prefect of Judea, Pontius Pilate, was pushed by the influential Sanhedrin to imprison Jesus of Nazareth. Pilate made a highly political decision and gave the assembled crowd the choice of freeing either Jesus or Barabbas, a notorious criminal. "Give us Barabbas," chanted the crowd. Acceding to "public opinion," Barabbas was released and Jesus was condemned to death by crucifixion. Then, Pilate publicly and ceremonially washed his hands, sending the absolutely political message, "This isn't on me."

Despite these examples of early messaging, the written word has been the primary medium for political communication. It has evolved and developed over the centuries, sometimes enriching and aspirational, and sometimes proffering a much darker view of society.

Contemporary Political Communication

The reach and impact of political discussions in literary form have been transformed in today's world. Books still have great power, but with near-instantaneous and omnipresent media presence in our lives, the nature and practice of political communication have also been transformed. Today, we're all consumers, whether from a candidate for public office, from a politician or other government official talking about a public policy, or from an outside interest group trying to win the public's agreement with them on a particular issue. Political communication is nearly impossible to escape. We see, hear, and read it every day. Much has been written about how it works and how it affects people, and more scholarly research is being conducted, analyzed, and interpreted all the time.

Putting the Pieces Together

Most of the academic literature on political communication is based on scholarly research. And because conducting accurate and meaningful research on a broad topic is practically impossible, it is nearly always tightly focused. Consequently, very little research explores or describes the broader process of political communication. And much of the literature is focused or theoretical and does not readily connect with the general public. Additionally, very little of this knowledge appears in a form or forum easily accessible to the public.

That realization was the seed for this book. I wanted to take a different approach, exploring the use of the broad communication process rather than focusing on one distinct element. I wanted to use real world cases to illustrate what many of the conceptual and theoretical aspects of political communication look like in actual practice. And I wanted to write in everyday language that was aimed more at political communication students than at their professors, perhaps even making it interesting to a broader audience of people who follow our political processes.

We all very much need to be interested in how political communication is designed and used. That politicians and political consultants try to play us like a Stradivarius is not exactly news, nor should it set off any alarms as long as people are fully aware and understand the process. If we're better informed about the art and science of political communication, we can be a more critical and sophisticated audience, even a bit skeptical. And we'll be better prepared to make informed decisions about what and who to believe.

This book's approach has its foundation in nearly forty years of working every day in local, state, and national political and governmental communication. Layers of content and context have been added by constant and continuing interest in academic and public opinion research into communication processes. And—I hope—my insights have been sharpened by more than a dozen years of teaching upper division and graduate classes to amazingly bright and motivated students, many already working in government and politics.

Most of the classes I teach in political and governmental communication last about three hours, but preparing to teach them took me many years because very few of the operative principles behind the skills I teach can be found in textbooks. They weren't taught in any of the journalism or communication classes I took as an undergraduate. Even in graduate school, the theories and concepts behind the skills were only addressed tangentially.

My education in political communication began with learning to translate the language of everyday government into everyday English as a news reporter covering Austin city hall and the Texas capitol. After four years as public information director helping members of the state legislature communicate with their constituents, I moved full-time into the business of political campaign media and governmental consulting. I worked on issues in city, county, and state government for over seventeen years. I wrote and produced media and communications in more than 120 election campaigns, from local, county, legislative, and statewide offices to US congressional and senatorial campaigns across Texas, New Mexico, and Arizona.

Upon joining the Bill Clinton administration in 1994, I had a front row seat for Newt Gingrich's Republican Revolution and the message wars with the Clinton White House. I became an avid student of Washington political messaging and paid rapt attention to every word and phrase, every attempt to frame a hot political issue and get the American public to see it a certain way.

My interest grew. By then, I'd been a practitioner in political-governmental communication for nearly twenty-five years, but I wanted to learn more about the art and science behind it. What made some political messages more powerful than others? Why did some messages move people to take a stand on particular issues or policies? What motivated them to act: to sign petitions, rally, express their feelings to elected officials, to vote? What made some political messages memorable while others were total duds?

While I was working full-time in Congress, I went to graduate school, where I eventually conducted my thesis research on the selling of the Iraq War, which was unfurling before my eyes. What words and phrases did the George W. Bush administration use to move a skeptical American public from opposition to support for a preemptive war against a sovereign nation that had neither attacked nor threatened to attack the United States?

Working as a communication director in Congress at the same time provided amazing opportunities to watch and learn. I was first a participant and over time became a mentor and trainer in the daily world of competing political messages.

I ultimately wanted to pass along what I'd learned about the political communication process, so I jumped at the chance to teach. But I don't even pretend to have all the answers. I've never stopped watching and listening and asking questions and arguing and reading about political communication. I don't intend to.

What I've attempted to do here is integrate what I've learned as a student, teacher, and practitioner in political campaign media, governmental affairs, and advocacy communication with scholarly explanations—the research and conceptual theories about how and why contemporary styles of political communication work. I've tried to describe in plain English what a lot of that theory actually looks like when applied.

Putting the pieces together about effective government and political communication took me a while because I had to learn most of it by doing. And I continue talking with political experts and communication scholars to try to understand not only what works, but how and why.

The fundamental truth in my professional experience and my teaching is that political communication is a process, not an event. As a process, it's composed of a set of logical steps that lead us through it, and there is a principle that clarifies the need for each step. In this book, I've attempted to use those principles to mark a logical path through the process, to explain each one, to expand and put them into context, and, as much as possible, to do so in the sequence that the steps are used by practitioners.

Outline of the Book

Chapter 2, "Defining Political Communication," addresses the first principle:

Principle 1. The term *political communication* describes all public outreach from political campaigns, messages to the public about issues and policy matters from government, and messages aimed at government by individuals and organizations trying to influence decisions.

This chapter explains political communication, not just by describing its use, but by showing how it's used and how that use changes in the different venues for political communication. I include numerous case studies—many from my own experience—to illustrate what it looks like done well and what it looks like done poorly. I also explore the current political environment in Washington, DC, its origins and development, and the essential role that partisan messaging plays in communication at the highest levels of our government.

Chapter 3, "The Tools of Political Persuasion," focuses on the second principle:

Principle 2. Political communication has one overriding purpose—to persuade people to agree with the communicator in order to win an election or to win support for a position on a public policy issue.

This chapter describes and explains many of the techniques and devices used to make political communication persuasive, from the most basic—repetition and focus—to media effects, such as agenda setting, priming, and, particularly, issue framing. These methods can increase the likelihood that a political message is couched in the right words and phrases to have precisely the desired effect on exactly the intended audience or audiences. I have included numerous case studies to demonstrate their use by opposing parties and outside interest groups to define the issues in our national political dialogue.

In Chapter 4, "Making Political Communication Effective," I address the third principle:

Principle 3. To be effective, political communication has to be conveyed in words, phrases, signs, and symbols the audience understands, can relate to, and will accept.

I rely a great deal on scholarly and scientific research to further examine the idea that effective political messages have to connect to the intended audience to be effective. Communicators have learned that persuasion can only occur when the message touches or relates to things people care about, such as their family, their career, their financial security, their future, their community, their country, or their values. The chapter describes the importance of using simple, direct language, choosing words that will have maximum effect, and the impact of couching political messages in a narrative style. I also discuss the pitfalls of using numbers, statistics, and dollar amounts to try to make compelling arguments, all too common in policy communication.

The second part of Chapter 4 provides background and context on what researchers tell us occurs when people receive particular kinds of messages, how those messages are processed by the recipients' brains, and how that processing can lead to particular kinds of actions.

Chapter 5, "Political Issues," deals with political issues and the fourth principle:

Principle 4. Issues are vital tools in politics—to define yourself, divide the public, and provide ammunition against your opponent.

This chapter examines the essential role issues continue to play in effective political communication. I offer an in-depth look at the development of issues, again with numerous case studies, to demonstrate how issues often evolve along with their support or opposition by competing political interests and how they are used. I include numerous hot-button issues in today's news coverage and explores the ways in which opposing sides attempt to define an issue and lay out the best course of action.

Chapter 6, "Political Research and Communication Planning," addresses the fifth principle:

Principle 5. Without the most comprehensive and accurate information possible, the aim and content of a communicator's most costly and time-intensive activities would be based on complete guesswork. But even with the best information, effective political communication rarely occurs without careful planning.

The first part of Chapter 6 focuses on the essential nature of political research and communication planning. I walk through case studies that illustrate the need for sound audience research to guide a communicator in developing the most persuasive words and phrases, and I identify who the target audience is and what communication channels will be most effective in reaching them. There are detailed descriptions of different tools of quantitative and qualitative research, how each type of research is conducted, and how each is used.

The second part of Chapter 6 focuses on how political communicators use that research to develop a comprehensive media plan that lays out what message will be targeted to which audience, through what medium, when the communication needs to occur to have the most impact, and what that communication will cost.

Chapter 7, "Political Speeches," addresses one of the oldest and most basic tools in political communication, public speeches:

Principle 6. The spoken word has always been a primary channel for political communication. It still is.

This chapter explores the purposes and practice of political speaking, offers examples of American political oratory at its best and worst, and includes an analysis of the skills and techniques that made former president Bill Clinton such an effective public speaker. I then go behind the scenes and address the art of political speechwriting, detailing many of the rhetorical devices used to put words in politicians' mouths and discussing the role and responsibilities of professional speechwriters.

Chapter 8, "Political Advertising and Television," explores the world of political advertising, addressing the seventh principle:

Principle 7. Despite the digital media revolution and profound changes in media and media audiences, paid advertising by election campaigns and interest groups will continue to be an essential tool to reach target audiences with political messages.

The chapter discusses the overall consequence of advertising, different kinds of advertising in different media, and includes arguments about the continuing importance of radio and even television in election campaigns in our increasingly online world. I get into the effective use of emotional content in political ads, with case studies, and then analyze the debate over the question of the purpose and impact of negative ads in campaigns.

Chapter 9, "Political Communication in the Internet Age," takes us into one of the fastest developing areas of today's political communication—online communication—as we discuss the eighth principle:

Principle 8. The Internet and digital revolution have changed a lot of things, but not quite everything.

I recount the brief history of online communication in campaigns, and how it has quickly gone from a fairly static tool for communicating messages to a highly interactive and targeted medium that has become an essential part of fundraising, voter identification, and outreach. The chapter also discusses the growth and impact of data mining, with case studies from the 2004 and 2012 presidential campaigns.

I then get into the exploding use of social media in every aspect of political communication, from the campaign headquarters to the government press office to the interest groups' headquarters. The chapter includes a discussion and case study from the 2016 presidential campaign.

Chapter 10, "Communicating Through the News Media," looks at the continuing role of the news media:

Principle 9. One of the most effective ways to reach a lot of people with the same message at the same time is still through the news media.

This chapter explores the fact that, even in a time when political communicators have the ability to disseminate messages very quickly and target them almost individually, news media coverage of an issue or policy is often the most practical way to reach the broad public or even a more targeted audience. For many smaller local political campaigns not awash in money for extensive advertising or direct contact programs, the news media can be the only way to get a message or information out to voters. This chapter also explores the power relationship between political figures and the news media and illustrates the importance of having the media help convey messages to the broader public. I discuss the role and route to seeking editorial endorsement for a candidate or an issue and how important that can be in influencing public opinion.

Within this chapter is an extensive discussion of the news media's evolving role in political communication, some changes brought about by an evolution in media reporting in an online world, and other changes created by the media's response to transformations in the public's readership habits and the financial pressures that have resulted. This includes a lengthy analysis of media coverage of the 2016 presidential campaign and how the media's apparent fascination, particularly among television networks, with Donald Trump from the day he announced his candidacy exerted a profound impact on the Republican primary election campaign that continued into the general election.

Chapter 11, "Communication in an Age of Partisanship," addresses the challenges and realities of communicating political or policy messages in today's highly charged and highly competitive environment. The principle itself is cautionary:

Principle 10. Being a political communicator in today's highly partisan environment is like working near the mouth of a volcano. The challenge is doing your job well without falling in.

The chapter offers a case study of the limitations posed by the current partisan division in Congress and explores the broader effects on our society as this division has trickled down to every level of government and, ultimately, to the public.

Chapter 12, "Crisis Communication," deals with the near-inevitability for public organizations that some sort of embarrassing, possibly ruinous occurrence will threaten the future effectiveness of the organization:

Principle 11. In politics and government, something bad is bound to happen. The smart thing is to be as ready as possible when a crisis hits.

I suggest that crises are inevitable—that at some point, every public or private organization will need to respond to an internal crisis or external bad news that threatens the reputation, stability, success, or in extreme instances, the actual survival of the organization. And I point out that for political communicators and their organizations, the key to weathering a crisis lies in preparation. This chapter begins with several case studies describing crises in which communicators failed to rise to the occasion and then offers some guidelines for preparing to handle a crisis effectively. I lay out a crisis communication planning process and the steps in an effective plan. There is also a section on crisis communication in our digital world and how the profound changes in communication can make rapid and comprehensive response a matter of life and death for an organization and/or its leaders.

The final chapter, "The Ethical Line in Political Communication," discusses and describes the ethical lines in the practice of political communication, and it argues that crossing those lines is a decision that must be faced and made by the political communicator. I attempt to define ethical political and policy communication and provide definitions and a list of spin and propaganda techniques. The overriding principle is pretty simple and very direct:

Principle 12. Ultimately, whether political communicators are ethical or not is completely up to them.

I encourage political communicators to try to imagine a situation in which they may have to make a difficult choice before it actually occurs and decide how they will act and react if and when it does.

The steps and principles I've outlined here and explored in depth in the following chapters are a logical path through the process of creating effective political communication. Whether it is communication in an election campaign that is trying to persuade voters to back one candidate or another, from an elected or other government official trying to win backing or create opposition for a particular government policy, or by an outside interest group or advocacy organization trying to marshal public support to influence a decision by government, it's all political communication, and it plays an increasingly important part in our society. The more we know about how it works and why, and the more informed we are about the process, its uses and misuses, and its practitioners, the more prepared we will be to make informed and reasoned decisions about our own futures.

2

Defining Political Communication

Principle 1: The term *political communication* describes all public outreach from political campaigns, messages to the public about policy matters from government, and messages aimed at government by individuals and organizations trying to influence decisions.

Today's political communication may seem like the crazed by-product of an overly technological society, with twenty-four-hour cable and ubiquitous online outreach on various social media platforms. Some observers argue that the nature and volume of current political communication are creations of our often-shrill partisan political environment. In fact, even the shrillness is nothing new. At its best and its worst, political communication played a defining role in US life and governance long before our founding. Sometimes it was a message in carefully crafted prose intended to clarify and illuminate, such as in the Declaration of Independence:

When in the Course of human events, it becomes necessary for one people to dissolve the political bonds which have connected them with another, and to assume, among the powers of the earth, the separate and equal station to which the Laws of Nature and Nature's God entitle them, a decent respect to the opinions of mankind requires that they should declare the causes which impel them to the separation.

As Thomas Jefferson later wrote on May 8, 1825, he and the Continental Congress felt the need to devise a political message "to place before mankind the common sense of the subject, in terms so plain and firm as to command their assent, and to justify ourselves in the independent stand we are compelled to take."[1]

The Declaration of Independence set a pretty high bar for all political communication to follow. Rare cases have reached that bar; many cases haven't even come close. Political communication has always, and more than likely will always, range from sublime to sub-slime—from high-minded expressions of ideals and visions to the lowest and most dishonest attacks. But every phrase, every word, every syllable is intended to convince people to view a candidate, public official, issue, or political agenda in a particular way. Nearly all communication from advocacy and interest groups is aimed at government decisionmakers, some directly and some indirectly, by appealing to the public for support.

Communication scholar Richard Perloff points out,

Political communication involves the transfer of symbolic meanings, the communication of highly charged words that can arouse, agitate and disgust. Words convey different meanings to different groups. To conservatives, freedom conjures up immigrants' dreams of owning a business in the USA or practicing religion as they see fit. To liberals and minorities, freedom calls to mind the opportunity to display one's own creed publicly without fear of prejudice. It also conveys empowerment, the way a previously victimized group can throw off the shackles of oppression, openly expressing its own cherished values. Political messages inevitably call up different meanings to different groups, an inevitable source of friction and conflict in democratic societies."[2]

The Steps in Political Communication

There are three common environments for political communication: election campaigns, public policy debates, and issue advocacy. The different settings may have different audiences, but they share a common process. Even the simplest, most basic political appeal uses a wonderfully logical sequence of steps, sometimes formal, sometimes very informal:

- Communicators assess prevailing conditions to understand exactly the environment in which they are working and what challenges and opportunities exist.
- They conduct research, formal or informal, so they know what to say to whom.
- They use that research to develop an overall plan, including persuasive messages.
- They set specific goals, objectives, strategies, and tactics to achieve their plan.
- They set deadlines to meet overall goals and incremental timelines for each step along the way.
- They build a budget: How much money will they need and when will they need it?
- They conduct the campaign.
- They monitor, evaluate, and analyze. Are they winning? Is their message being heard? Is it being accepted or rejected? Are they making progress? Are they hitting deadlines? Do they need to change or adjust anything? And finally, afterward, did they win or did they lose?

Settings for Political Communication

Election campaigns, with their compressed time limits, require the most urgent attempts to persuade people to see things in a particular way and take a particular action. In today's highly partisan, highly competitive government policy environment, for better or worse, they have become the model for public policy and issue advocacy communication.

Policy communication describes messages from government entities or officials to win support for particular policies or decisions. The message can be from the White House, Congress, a federal agency, a governor or state legislature, or someone at the county courthouse or city hall. It can be aimed at winning the support of other government officials, but it nearly always includes appeals to the larger public as well, because demonstrated public support makes it easier to win over government officials.

Advocacy communication refers to attempts by individuals or organizations outside government to influence government decisions. Obviously, public policy and advocacy communication are closely related. Both public policy and advocacy communication try to influence government policy decisions, but, if they're going to be really effective, they also have to generate, retain, and demonstrate public support.

In all three venues, persuasive messages must try to create, shape, and move peoples' opinions. Remember the second principle in the preface, which is discussed in depth in the next chapter: "Effective public communication has one purpose: to persuade people to agree with the communicator." Everything that follows—all the research, planning, targeting, timing, message development, approaches, and techniques—exists to achieve that end.

Election Campaigns

In today's communication environment, with a growing reliance on e-mail, social media, and a wide variety of web sources for information, campaign communication strategy has become infinitely more complex. Buying advertising time on television and radio, holding an occasional news conference, making a speech, and putting out press releases and statements will no longer convey a campaign message to all the different demographic groups who need to hear or see it.

Every bit as important as crafting the right message is making sure the right message gets to the right audience, with enough repetition and reinforcement to persuade the undecided and motivate the committed. Among all the things an election campaign must prepare for, address, and deal with, four overriding imperatives have to be accomplished. An effective campaign must:

- create awareness of its candidate—what campaigns call generating name identification;
- create a positive image to reassure committed voters and persuade undecided voters (i.e., to give them a reason to support its candidate), create a negative image to give people a reason not to vote for the opposing candidate, or both;
- identify those who are likely to vote for its candidate and those who are likely to vote but have not yet decided for whom; and
- motivate identified voters to actually go to the polling place and vote. It's one thing to convince people you're right and the opponent is wrong, but it won't win an election unless you also get them to act on that belief.

Campaigns are an unbelievably intense form of marketing in a competitive environment, usually with finite resources, an absolute deadline, and an unconditional need to win more than half the market, except in very rare cases. (In the 1992 general election, Independent H. Ross Perot attracted 18.9 percent of the total vote; President George H. W. Bush, the Republican incumbent, wound up with 37.5 percent; and Democrat Bill Clinton became the forty-first president of the United States with a 43 percent plurality.) There are no do-overs in politics. If campaigns don't get it right the first time, they lose. At best, politicians have to wait a few years to try again, if they get a second chance at all.

Despite these unyielding imperatives, communication in successful campaigns follows the same logical steps as any other form of effective marketing. The technological changes in how, when, and where campaigns communicate do not change the essential responsibility of the political communicator: to create and disseminate persuasive, compelling, and memorable messages.

Public Policy and Advocacy Communication

After the campaign is over, there is not much letup in the flow of political rhetoric. But instead of advancing reasons to vote for a candidate, it appeals for support or opposition on a particular government policy or issue. Most of these appeals have traditionally been communicated through the news media to the ultimate audience, the public.

To become public policy, a position has to be adopted by elected officials or top-level appointed officials. Because the first priority for most elected officials is to continue to hold elective office, they tend to be sensitive to anything that might be politically unpopular. They're not likely to take a step unless they're comfortable that the public, particularly their constituency, either does or can support it.

For their part, appointed officials—top government administrators and agency executives—tend to be sensitive to what they perceive elected officials will support. Many of them are appointed by elected officials. In the federal government and in most states, the top-level appointed officials are part of the president's or governor's cabinet. Even career administrators—those who do not come and go with new administrations—will nearly always "consult" with elected officials before making significant policy decisions because, at all levels of government, elected officials vote on agency or departmental operating budgets.

In short, few government officials—elected or appointed—are going to stick their necks out and do something they think might be unpopular with most of the public. Demonstrating that the public favors or accepts specific policies can create a safe zone for officials to act. This safe zone can be validated by public opinion or membership surveys.

In issue advocacy, interest groups use demonstrations of support to influence government decisionmakers. They organize grassroots campaigns, which involve getting members or motivated citizens to participate in rallies, write letters or e-mails, make phone calls, or even set up face-to-face meetings to urge elected officials to take action.

Building public support for a proposed government policy requires a persuasive message that makes a convincing case, first, that there is a problem and a need for a policy to address it and, second, that the policy being advocated is the best way to deal with the problem. Savvy policy communicators know they need to inform people why they should care in order to convince them to focus on a government policy, not because people are ignorant, but because most people are focused on their day-to-day lives—their family, career, financial or physical security, interests, or community. If a policy can be connected to their world and it is very clear how they benefit, people are much more likely to take an interest, even to express support. If the policy does not connect, it remains an abstraction—something they are not likely to spend much time thinking about.

Communicators have to connect their message to attitudes people already have and information they use to form opinions: their concerns, fears, hopes, ambitions, pride, or values; their geographic, ethnic, age, or professional identity; their identification with a political party; and their support for or opposition to political figures or groups, policies, or issues. Successful communicators don't try to convey new sets of information their audience can't relate to easily. They make new information congruent with the opinions and attitudes already held by their audience (see Chapter 3). They don't make the audience come to them. They go to the audience.

One of the most basic yet often overlooked elements in going to the audience—in connecting—is communicating in words and phrases the audience understands. Generally, that means communicating in plain English. Yet, it is all too common to hear or read communication about public policy matters or government issues clad in rhetoric that might as well be a foreign language.

Attempting to communicate with the public in this kind of policy garble is all too common. Here is an excerpt from a Department of Health and Human Services memo explaining guidelines for determining the suitability of accessibility accommodation:

> In other instances, an accommodation would be the optimal solution when EI has been designed to interact with the user based on specific sensory user-input and interaction. For example, an on-line tool intended to gauge color blindness cannot be

made accessible to someone who is completely blind. An <alt-text> tag might read "color blindness test images," but that alone would be of little value. A similar case can be made for simulations that model physical objects. Again, one could create tags for such a system, such as <an interactive 3-D molecular protein modeling tool>. However, the user needs to interact with the visual output of the modeling tool in response to the variables being tested. A conventional 508 standard does little to provide accessibility in this situation.

Put more simply, an online tool that requires the user to be able to see cannot be used by someone who is blind.

Within a government unit, policy communication is frequently steeped in details of substance—fiscal impact, regulatory history, and data—not to mention jargon. That is to be expected in this venue. All the participants are operating on the same level of detail in government policy, dealing with the fine points of issues. They speak the language. Every field, every industry, every area of government has its own language, its own jargon, its own acronyms.

Case Study: Speaking Policy Garble Instead of English

"Great news! MilCon-VA hasn't been CBO scored yet, so we still have time to plus it up before full committee." A colleague in my congressional office gave me this good news one morning. For just a second, I wondered how many people would have any idea what we were talking about. In fact, we were discussing MilCon-VA Appropriations, the annual funding bill for Military Construction, Veterans Affairs, and Related Agencies appropriations legislation, produced by one of twelve subcommittees of the House Appropriations Committee. The twelve subcommittee bills make up the annual appropriations bill, which pays for every program, activity, and function of the US government for the year. MilCon-VA's budget is not chump change. For fiscal year 2015, it allocated $71.5 billion, a $1.8 billion cut from 2014.

What my colleague was so excited about was that the Military Construction–Veterans Affairs appropriations bill had not yet been scrutinized and received a statement of its budgetary impact by the Congressional Budget Office. That meant we still had an opportunity to increase funding for existing items or add additional items within the bill before it was considered and voted on by the full House Appropriations Committee. After that vote, it would have been much more difficult to add funding—to "plus it up."

Problems occur when policy professionals try to explain a policy to the public and fail to adapt their message to that audience. Effective communicators speak and write about their issue in more conversational English. They use short declarative sentences. They avoid acronyms, jargon, and obtuse phrases. They understand the need to convince their audience about a policy idea in terms their audience will readily recognize and understand.

Over the years, several veteran political and government communicators have disagreed with the need for this. They insist that communictors can completely rely on evidence-based persuasion to make the case for a policy to the general public. "They'll figure it out," they've told me. "The public isn't stupid." They were confident that all you need to do is give people the facts: research data, history, legal precedents, or the CBO estimate of fiscal impact in trillions of dollars over ten years. In fact, I was once admonished by a fellow Appropriations Committee staffer for using the phrase "committee hearing" in a news release rather than the more esoteric if technically accurate "mark-up."

To be sure, communicators need well-presented, convincing evidence to have a truly credible message. But it has to be set forth in language the public will listen to and accept, which ultimately makes it easier for Congress to go along. Sometimes it's done effectively, couched in words and phrases that most people understand and that help make a case for the policy or expenditure.

Case Study: The Navy's "Strike Fighter Shortfall"

Since the mid-2000s, the US Navy has projected a date far in the future when it thinks it may not have enough F/A-18 Super Hornet or F-35 Joint Strike Fighter aircraft for ten aircraft carrier air wings. The number of aircraft they are supposedly short and the date on which they will have the shortfall change every year. However, the term "Strike Fighter Shortfall" is used in all the budget materials and testimony they present to Congress.

The details of the so-called shortfall are debatable. There is, in reality, no such "shortfall" under the most generous planning assumptions. For example, the navy hasn't deployed ten aircraft carrier air wings at the same time since World War II, which calls into question the urgency of having ten air wings of aircraft in the first place. There are only ten aircraft carriers in the navy, but at least three are usually undergoing long-term maintenance and not deployable anyway.

The real reason behind the "Strike Fighter Shortfall" is the navy's desire to continue F/A-18 Super Hornet production. Many in the navy don't think the F-35 stealth fighter aircraft, with a price tag of somewhere between $85 million and $116 million each, are affordable and would like to see the navy skip it entirely. To do that, they have to keep building F/A-18s. For the past two years, this "Strike Fighter Shortfall" has helped the navy make the case with Congress to keep F/A-18 production going, even though the Department of Defense budget didn't have any funding for them. In both 2015 and 2016, Congress added more than $1.2 billion for continued production of the F/A-18.

The navy developed the term "Strike Fighter Shortfall," which sounds bad and is difficult to debate since the specific number changes year-to-year. The navy has also avoided directly mentioning the F-35 program, which has a lot of congressional support. Instead, they are basically arguing against the F-35 program, without directly attacking it, and have thus avoided pitting Boeing and Lockheed-Martin aircraft manufacturers against each other with Congress.

Sometimes, however, the communication effort gets lost in buzzwords and phrases that are completely unintelligible to the average person:

Case Study: The Army's Future Combat System

The Future Combat System (FCS) was at the heart of the US Army's transformation efforts in the early 2000s. The Boeing Company and Science Applications International Corporation (SAIC) acted together as prime contractor, or "lead system integrator," coordinating more than 550 individual contractors and subcontractors in 41 states. The $340 billion multiyear program was supposed to be the Army's major research, development, and acquisition program. It included fourteen manned and unmanned systems tied together by an extensive data network.

Since the beginning of its development in 2003, however, the program had undergone significant adjustments, mostly budgetary. Problems included large cost overruns in a time of economic recession, growing mandatory federal spending, and two wars.

At the time, I was communication director for the Chairman of the House Armed Services Subcommittee that authorized and oversaw programs for the US Army and

continues

Case Study: continued

Air Force. I tried repeatedly to understand exactly what FCS did so I would have something credible to say when the media asked questions and so I could let people back in my boss's district know what he was working on. I attended a number of briefings by the Defense Department and the Army and read everything I could find on FCS, but I found few recognizable nouns in their explanations, just acronyms and specialized jargon. Here, from one information piece, was their simple explanation about the Future Combat System:

> FCS was networked via an advanced architecture, called System of Systems Common Operating Environment (SOSCOE) that would enable enhanced joint connectivity and situational awareness (see Network-centric warfare). SOSCOE targets x86-Linux, VxWorks, and LynxOS. The FCS (BCT) network consists of five layers that when combined would provide seamless delivery of data: *The Standards*, Transport, Services, Applications, and Sensors and Platforms Layers. The FCS (BCT) network possesses the adaptability and management functionality required to maintain pertinent services, while the FCS (BCT) fights on a rapidly shifting battlespace giving them the advantage to take initiative. FCS would network existing systems, systems already under development, and systems to be developed:
>
> • XM1100: Intelligent Munitions System
>
> • XM501 Non-Line-of-Sight Launch System
>
> • AN/PSW-2 Common System Controller (CC)
>
> • Unattended Ground Sensors[3]

Got all that? Boeing, SAIC, and the Army never did figure out how to tell the FCS story effectively. They never made a convincing case that the Future Combat System could play an essential role on the battlefields of the future and save American lives. In fact, they got downright defensive when people asked questions about it. They conducted a series of multiroom, multiscreen multimedia briefings for congressional staff with videos, models, and uniformed pitchmen. One trooper finished his presentation by telling us, in a rhetorical leap, "If FCS isn't funded, soldiers will die." How FCS would prevent those deaths was never made clear enough.

But what most people did know, including many of the people who would vote on its continued funding in Congress, was that this "system of systems" was going to cost some $340 billion and its precise function was unintelligible. It certainly was not something a senator or congressperson would enjoy trying to justify to people back home. There is a chain of communication the Army and its FCS contractors ignored. So, when budget choices had to be made between continuing to develop FCS or quickly deploying mine-resistant armored vehicles to Iraq, which kept US troops from being blown up by roadside bombs, guess which one got the ax.

The Washington Political Communication Environment

Nowhere are political considerations and approaches to public policy more visible—or audible—than in the unending, no-holds-barred free-for-all over national public policy among the White House and Republicans and Democrats in the House and Senate. Frequently others join the squabble: the Republican and Democratic National Committees and their suborganizations, Washington think tanks aligned with one side or the other, random interest organizations, media outlets, and the occasional candidate for Congress, statewide office, or the presidency.

"Casus Belli" for Today's Public Policy Message Wars

The hyper-partisan atmosphere in Washington and across the country has had an overwhelming impact on the nature and substance of political communication from statehouses to the national capitol. Communication has been every bit as rancorous at different periods in our history, but rarely has it been so well-orchestrated, carefully crafted, and deeply divisive.

I would argue that the great partisan divide defining today's national debate has its modern roots in President Lyndon Johnson's push for passage of the Civil Rights Act of 1964 and the Voting Rights Act of 1965. Those pieces of landmark legislation alienated generations of conservative white southerners from the Democratic Party. LBJ reportedly remarked to his press secretary Bill Moyers after signing the Civil Rights Act into law, "I think we just delivered the South to the Republican Party for a long time to come."[4]

The 1964 Barry Goldwater and 1968 Richard Nixon presidential campaigns both used a "Southern Strategy," appealing primarily to disaffected white southerners and other states' rights advocates to bring them into the Republican Party and oppose the "liberal elites" in Washington, DC; New York; and California. Both campaigns carried most of the old Confederate states.

The partisan divide grew during the two terms of Ronald Reagan. It may or may not have been happenstance that in his 1980 campaign, he spoke at the Neshoba County Fair, just down the road from Philadelphia, Mississippi, where three civil rights workers had been murdered in 1964. In that speech, Reagan promised to "restore to states and local governments the power that properly belongs to them."

His constant references to the evils of the federal government helped implant that mindset as bedrock in conservative orthodoxy, along with cutting taxes and spending on social programs. "Government isn't the solution to the problem. Government is the problem," said President Reagan, ironically while he was the chief executive officer of that government/problem for eight years.

Yet through the Reagan and George H. W. Bush administrations, Democrats remained firmly in control of the House and

Senate. And very importantly, communication between the two sides remained occasionally testy but fairly cooperative for a few more years, and the business of governing continued. It was not until 1995 and the ascension of Rep. Newt Gingrich of Georgia from congressional back-bencher to Speaker of the US House of Representatives that the landscape began to change significantly

The Republican Revolution

Gingrich has written about the frustrations of being in the minority party in the US House: you show up every day and vote with little or no chance of ever actually winning; you get few chances to actually lead—let alone prevail—on any significant issues. Gingrich wanted to pursue a new plan for achieving Republican ascendancy.

Gingrich is hardly responsible for causing what longtime *Washington Post* congressional reporter Juliet Eilperin characterized as "the story of how the House of Representatives became the House of Unrepresentatives." In her book, *Fight Club Politics: How Partisanship Is Poisoning the House of Representatives*, Eilperin said, "House Republicans are not the only ones responsible for this modern predicament. Their Democratic counterparts have balked at legislative compromise and have crafted election-proof districts across the nation, as well. Both parties have used hardball tactics that have polarized Washington."[5]

In *The Broken Branch: How Congress Is Failing America and How to Get It Back on Track*, noted congressional scholars Thomas Mann of the Brookings Institution and Norman Ornstein of the American Enterprise Institute for Public Policy Research stated that "it would be a mistake to suggest that all the problems facing Congress are the result of the actions or misjudgments of a handful of Republican leaders." They found, "Many of the larger problems plaguing Congress, including the demise of regular order, and growing incivility, began years ago, when Democrats were in the majority. Their roots, and the reasons they have gotten demonstrably worse, are firmly implanted in larger political dynamics."[6]

They described in detail the prevalent attitudes among House Democrats following forty years in the majority, and the profound changes in the way communication was used and business done in the nation's capital following the 1994 election. The "Gingrich Election" took partisanship to unprecedented levels and for the first time implanted it in the structure of the institution and in the working and social relationships among Republican and Democratic representatives.

As a communication specialist working in the middle of Gingrich's revolution, I was interested in identifying the guiding procedures used to exercise party control and discipline:

1. Gain and hold a majority in the US House by running the institution like a political campaign all the time, year round, always maintaining the attack.

2. Point out the differences between "us" and "them."

3. Use sophisticated market research techniques, including extensive public opinion polling and focus groups, to develop and hone your political agenda and your message; to find out what issues people care about and what framing—how those issues are labeled (see Chapter 3)—grabs the public's attention and helps move them to agree with your point of view.

4. Come up with a compelling name for your political agenda, such as a "Contract with America." Keep it simple. Celebrate it. Have your congressional members and candidates all pledge to support it.

5. Put out talking points based on your market research, so that everyone in your party can repeat the same audience-tested words and phrases to the public in speeches, statements, and interviews.

6. Establish and enforce message discipline, so that all your people stay on the same points. Tell your folks, "This is what we are going to say. If you're not saying this, then you're not saying anything at all."

7. Do not look for opportunities to work across the aisle. Finding common ground with the other party does not help you win elections. As conservative activist Grover Norquist once put it, "Bipartisanship is another name for date rape."

8. Do not be afraid to use hyperbole. If you are a national official, claim that what you oppose is the biggest, worst, stupidest,

most corrupt or costliest undertaking in the nation's history and dare anyone to argue. If anybody does argue, keep saying it anyway.

9. Attack the news media, especially when they question or disagree with anything you say. Constantly refer to the main-stream news media as the liberal media and media elites. Always try to tie them to East Coast elites or Hollywood elites.

10. Always remember that one of the slowest, fattest, easiest-to-hit targets in American politics is the US government. Blame everything on Washington bureaucrats.

Did these strategies and techniques work? The "revolution" changed the working relationship between the two political parties and, over time, the culture of Congress. Gone was the tradition that "we can disagree on policy all day but go to dinner together in the evening." More and more, the legislative process became about winning, and winning itself was redefined from making decisions and accomplishing policy goals that benefit the country to accomplishing a party's political agenda or, alternatively, blocking the other party from accomplishing theirs.

The Gingrich approach took root and spread—some say metastasized—as Republican revolutionaries in the House began to run for and win election to the Senate. A new generation of highly partisan and ideological candidates were also elected to the "World's Greatest Deliberative Body," shaking the US Senate to its stately roots. University of Texas professor of government Sean Theriault researched, described, and analyzed this phenomenon in *The Gingrich Senators: The Roots of Partisan Warfare in Congress*. He provided the following example:

On December 4, 2012, the U.S. Senate rejected a United Nations Treaty that drew its inspiration from the Americans with Disabilities Act. In his advocacy for it from his wheelchair on the Senate floor, Bob Dole (R-Kansas), a former five-term senator and 1996 Republican presidential nominee, argued that the treaty was an attempt to make the rest of the world as hospitable as the United States for people with disabilities, including disabled veterans like himself. One hundred fifty-four countries—including Russia, Mongolia, China and Paraguay—signed the treaty, which was negotiated by President George W. Bush and supported by President Barack Obama. In the end, the treaty was rejected when 18 senators voted against it. Although Republicans John Barrasso (R-Wyoming), Dick Lugar (R-Indiana), and Kelly Ayotte (R-New Hampshire) voted for it, they were joined by only one of the 21 Gingrich Senators (Republicans who were first elected to Congress after 1978 and had previously served in the House).[7]

Pushing Buttons Instead of Information

For the four years between 2010 and 2014, with a Republican-led House of Representatives and a Democratic-led Senate, we saw in session after session that the first order of business for each side was to block the agenda of the other, which means very little, if anything, of substance was accomplished. In addition to the grid-lock that is created in Congress, the situation shortchanges the public because they seldom get to hear much substance behind differing viewpoints on national issues. The hot rhetoric is aimed at winning political support by pushing buttons rather than offering real information.

We see this when one or both sides in the national debate are more concerned with "firing up the base" to elicit emotional, even knee-jerk reactions than in helping people really understand issues. Because the goal is to get the public riled up, the communication is filled with dire warnings about threats to things people favor or value:

- "Democrats are willing to kill millions of jobs to stop the XL Pipeline."

- "Republicans are trying to cut Social Security and Medicare to pay for more tax cuts for the wealthy."

Sometimes it's done by suggestion:

- "The latest in a series of White House scandals. . . ."
- "Senate Republicans continue to block efforts to help. . . ."
- "Some observers say. . . ."

Or innuendo:

- "In what could be the most expensive. . . ."
- "Democrats have not denied. . . ."

Or flat-out lies:

- "The fact is we know that Saddam Hussein has weapons of mass destruction and we know where they are."
- "If you like your doctor, you can keep him."

Today, more than twenty years after the Republican Revolution, communication continues to reflect a Congress in which the main consideration is how an issue can be used for political gain; how it will play to a partisan political base; how it can be used to make the other side look bad.

While I was a communicator in Washington, I was asked many times by friends why Republicans always seemed to get the better of Democrats in the perpetual political messaging war. I developed several theories over the years:

1. The Republican message process uses a marketing approach: find out what the public wants and tell them that's what you're doing. Aim your message at the people you're trying to win over.

2. Democrats use a marketing process during campaigns, but after the election, they revert to a public information approach: Just give everybody the facts, budget figures, or statistics. They'll know what it all means.

3. Republicans have been "more creative," even willing to bend and stretch the truth when necessary to make their version of the story better.

4. Republicans have been highly adept at framing issues with their definitions to influence how the public sees them. Simply adding the word *reform* or *relief* lends a certain nobility to a position, even if the intention is to totally gut a program.

The Affordable Care Act became "Obamacare," tying a bill completely devised by Congress to the president. The ability of a business, an individual, even a government employee to refuse to provide service to people in same-sex marriages became a matter of protecting religious freedom.

5. Democrats have occasionally come up with effective issue framing: on welfare reform, "Mend it, don't end it," and "The Republican War on Women," for example. In 2005, George W. Bush attempted to "reform" Social Security by creating individual investment accounts to replace the traditional Social Security retirement benefit. Democrats framed it as "privatization," and it died a quick death. Democrats have out-messaged Republicans a few times, but not many.

Case Study: New Direction Congress

A week or so before the 2007 August congressional recess, House Democratic chiefs of staff and communication directors were summoned to a message meeting in the Ways & Means Committee Room, a huge, ornate chamber in the Longworth House Office Building across the street from the Capitol. On the riser at the front were the Speaker's chief of staff, communication and press staff, a group from the Majority Leader's office, and a highly respected Democratic pollster. We had seemingly been summoned to receive the word from on high: The Message. We had been given the results of the latest research along with talking points on Democratic issues and suggestions for different kinds of press events we could devise for our bosses while they were home in their districts. It was all about getting the message out, and we were about to get that message.

We walked through the research methodology and findings, which indicated that after six years of the

Bush administration, Iraq, Afghanistan, and a weakening US economy, the American public was primed for a new direction. Then we waited for the message: the essence of the new direction the public wanted Congress to take, boiled down to a few compelling words that would be a dagger in the hearts of Republicans. We waited. And we waited.

Finally, we were told that "New Direction Congress" *was* the message. That was it! Every utterance, every statement, every news release, and every speech would be built around the phrase "New Direction Congress." We were assured that when the words "New Direction Congress" rolled out, the other side would run for cover and the public would flock to our banner.

There was a hush. Seriously? New Direction Congress? That was the message? That was it? The message gurus had skipped a step in the process—they forgot that research does not provide answers; it provides *information*. You have to use the information to develop creative answers—in this case, a catchy, memorable political message. As I remember, New Direction Congress was never raised as a battle cry.

Issue Advocacy

Advocacy communication is used by individuals and organizations outside of government to try to influence government decisions, for example, when Mothers Against Drunk Driving, the Nature Conservancy, or the National Rifle Association holds a rally on the Capitol steps, organizes a phone or e-mail campaign, or buys advertising time on Washington, DC, stations; or when interested individuals or organizations speak at public meetings or submit testimony to federal or state agencies responsible for implementing, administering, or enforcing a law or policy, usually by enacting specific rules or regulations.

The Nature of Advocacy Communication

Washington and every state capital are home to many organizations that represent and advance particular points of view. They include interests and businesses competing for state contracts or pursuing some of the more than $1 trillion appropriated by Congress every year. However, the more active practitioners of political communication are the major professional and industry associations, issue nonprofits, and think tanks with a stake or interest in the domestic and international laws, rules, regulations, and policies enacted or administered by federal or state governments. They all attempt to cut through competing viewpoints as they disseminate persuasive messages to identified targeted audiences.

What do their messages sound like? To begin with, they have to find the "sweet spot" between two distinctly different styles of communication: they must incorporate data, statistics, history, and information upon which to formulate a policy and give it credibility and authority, and they must include persuasive elements that tell the broader audience why the policy is needed and why they should care about it. This requires a well-integrated form of expression. The advocacy message has to have substance. Advocates could promise that adopting their policy will make every man taller, every woman more beautiful, and every child smarter, but why would anyone believe them? Conversely, if they speak or write like a "policy expert," their audience may fail to understand the message or to remain attentive.

Targeting the Advocacy Message

In political communication, whatever the medium, the goal is to get the right message to the right audience. Advocacy and interest organizations have learned that developing and sending the right message is critical, but having the right messenger for a particular target audience is also crucial. It's true whether the message is delivered by letter, e-mail, telephone, social media, carrier pigeon, or face-to-face.

Advocacy organizations in Washington and all fifty state capitals find that one of their most effective techniques is personal communication with decisionmakers in targeted visits. Sending armies of citizens through legislative offices like trick-or-treaters can certainly stir things up, but not nearly as much and not nearly as effectively as having constituents from an elected official's home state or district make an appointment or knock on the door. Nothing gets a politician's attention quite like hearing from folks back home, whether from local leaders, a business group, seniors, environmentalists, public school parents, or other groups of everyday citizens who are potential voters.

Effective organizations not only organize the visits, but also make sure visitors are educated or briefed on the specifics of an issue or policy, particularly on its impact back home. These meetings almost always include key staffers who handle or work on the advocates' issue for the elected official. And frequently, the staffers will ask questions or seek technical information that the attendees cannot answer on the spot. When this occurs, effective advocacy organizations know how important it is to provide the requested information fully and quickly. They realize that the meetings and a prompt follow-up can transform them into trusted resources on the issue, which can make them effective advocates.

Visitors often have been provided "leave-behind" materials by the organization with which they are working. A 2012 survey conducted by the Congressional Management Foundation found that leave-behind pieces can be very important. In the survey, 94 percent of the House chiefs of staff said a one- to two-page issue summary was quite helpful, 86 percent liked getting follow-up e-mails with information attached, and 18 percent said they liked getting more detailed research reports of five pages or more. Leave-behind pieces and follow-up information can continue communicating long after the meeting has ended.

Conclusion

Principle 1: The term *political communication* describes all public outreach from political campaigns, messages to the public about policy matters from government, and messages aimed at government by individuals and organizations trying to influence decisions.

Political campaigns, public policy communication, and issue advocacy use three distinct styles of communication to achieve three different purposes. Yet they all involve the development and transmission of persuasive messages to create, shape, and move peoples' opinions. And they all employ elements of the same process because they share one overriding purpose: to persuade people to agree with the communicator.

Notes

1. Thomas Jefferson, Letter to Henry Lee, May 8, 1825.
2. Richard Perloff, *The Dynamics of Political Communication: Media and Politics in a Digital Age* (New York: Routledge, 2014), 31.
3. *Army Acquisition, Logistics, and Technology* (January–February 2004), http://asc.army.mil/docs/pubs/alt/archives/2004/Jan-Feb_2004 .pdf, 6.
4. Bill Moyers, "Second Thoughts: Reflections on the Great Society," *New Perspectives Quarterly* 4, no. 1 (Winter 1987), http://www .digitalnpq.org/archive/1987_winter/second.html.
5. Juliet Eilperin, *Fight Club Politics: How Partisanship Is Poisoning the House of Representatives* (Lanham: Rowman and Littlefield, 2006), 5.
6. Thomas Mann and Norman Ornstein, *The Broken Branch: How Congress Is Failing America and How to Get It Back on Track* (New York: Oxford University Press, 2006), 11.
7. Sean Theriault, *The Gingrich Senators: The Roots of Partisan Warfare in Congress* (New York: Oxford University Press, 2012), vii.

3

The Tools of
Political Persuasion

Principle 2: Political communication has one overriding purpose—to persuade people to agree with the communicator in order to win an election or to win support for a position on a public policy issue.

When government officials, candidates for office, or interest and advocacy organizations engage in discussions about legislation, public policy, regulation, or the allocation of public resources, they are usually attempting to generate support or opposition by individuals or groups. But problems occur when the communicators confuse techniques of persuasion with some of the darker communication arts, like spin, propaganda, and deception.

Judging by his essays, such as *Politics and the English Language*, and his classic novel *Nineteen Eighty-Four*, George Orwell had a very dark view of government and its persuasive techniques. "In our time, political speech and writing are largely the defence of the indefensible. . . . Thus political language has to consist largely of euphemism, question-begging and sheer cloudy vagueness."[1]

He was a champion of clear, precise language and warned that vague language can be a powerful tool of political manipulation because it can mask the truth and thereby shape public perception. In fact, his novel's descriptions of a totalitarian government's use of propaganda, misinformation, and doublespeak to control people's language, thoughts, and actions have led to the term *Orwellian* being used when accusations are made of government manipulation and control.

How does acceptable persuasion differ from propaganda and spin? It's essentially a matter of the honesty of the message and the communicator. The tactics of spin and propaganda are explored in detail in Chapter 13. In short, the difference is in the extent to which a communicator is willing to go to make a message credible. Persuasion can include placing an authentic message in a context that maximizes its chances to be received, considered, and accepted by the audience. Spin resorts to the use of artifice or manipulative tactics to focus the audience on certain aspects of the message. Propaganda crosses the line into creating deceptive or dishonest messages, or putting messages into completely fabricated contexts to generate a reaction.

Communication scholar Richard Perloff defines persuasion as "a symbolic process in which communicators try to convince other people to change their attitudes or behaviors regarding an issue through the transmission of a message in an atmosphere of free choice."[2] The atmosphere of free choice is essential. Convincing someone to do something they really don't want to do isn't persuasion—it's coercion. People persuade *themselves* to change their attitudes or opinions. Effective communication just provides the arguments.

In the effort to persuade, whether in election campaigns or in public policy and advocacy communication, the communicator— an elected or appointed official or an interest group—first has to break through the clutter of competing messages to get the public or target audience to pay attention to a particular issue. Then the communicator must persuade the audience to view the issue through a certain perspective, then to agree with the communicator, and, frequently, to take an action: vote for a candidate, call an official, send an e-mail, sign a petition, or send a contribution. This chapter discusses some of the basic persuasive techniques most often used in political communication.

One Message at a Time: A Rifle Shot, Not a Shotgun Blast

Did you ever try to tell someone about four different things at the same time? How well did it work? They probably didn't remember any of them. It's a matter of focus.

Like effective commercial ads, effective political messages are usually focused on one and only one major point. They can start off with a headline, something to grab the reader's, viewer's, or listener's attention. That way, even in a thirty-second television or radio spot or a brief news release, the message has time to back up the headline a bit with facts or other supporting information.

The challenge is in finding words that might refer to several different issues, but sum up a position or attitude in one memorable phrase. In 2008, the Barack Obama presidential campaign used the slogan, "Change We Can Believe In," conveying a very positive, empowered feeling. Ads and messages took on a variety of specific issues, but the messages always came back to "Change We Can Believe In." In 2016, every message from Donald Trump, in rallies, speeches, and other public statements concluded in one way or another with the phrase, "Make America Great Again."

When communicators try to cram too many topics into one message, they wind up with a list instead of a message. Which topic is most important? Why? What's next? Why? It's a lot more effective and usually not much more expensive to produce a series of messages, each focused on a single point or issue. Then the messages can be run in rotation or in sequence, and each message can promote the others, as in, "This is the second in a five-part series of reasons why voters should . . ."

The importance of strong focus can apply to a single statement, speech, or television commercial, or to an entire agenda. In December 2009, *New York Times* commentator John Hardwood cited criticism of President Obama, then in office for less than a year, for having too scattered a program, which therefore scattered his messaging. "On Tuesday, he will lay out his agenda for creating jobs for the 15 million Americans out of work. Then he travels to Oslo to accept the Nobel Peace Prize, even as he seeks support for sending 30,000 more troops to Afghanistan. And next week he heads to Copenhagen in search of a worldwide deal to curb climate change by reducing carbon emissions."[3]

"It is a very real problem," said Republican pollster Jan van Lohuizen, who advised President George W. Bush. "Not just that attention is scattered, but the message is scattered as well."[4] Noted conservative author David Horowitz has said, "Lack of focus will derail your message. If you make too many points, your message will be diffused and nothing will get through. The result will be the same as if you made no point at all. . . . One message is a sound bite. Many messages are a confusing noise."[5]

A 2007 case study at Penn State University's College of Communication found, "One notable lesson learned from the 2004 presidential campaign is the importance of key messages. Political pundits have at times made fun of the Bush camp's incessant use of talking points, but their message comes across loud and clear. On the other hand, at best, Kerry was inconsistent. At worst, the Democratic candidate did not appear to have a message to share."[6] The *Los Angeles Times* observed, "While he is deft at fielding audience questions with thoughtful and detailed responses, his stump speech—a long catalog of his policy positions—often sounds rambling and unfocused."[7]

Repetition

One of the simplest and most effective ways to persuade people is to say something, then say it again, then say it again, over and over. In 1885, Thomas Smith wrote about the need for an audience to be exposed to an advertising message multiple times before it really sank in and received serious consideration:

> The first time people look at any given ad, they don't even see it.
> The second time, they don't notice it.
> The third time, they are aware that it is there.

The fourth time, they have a fleeting sense that they've seen it somewhere before.

The fifth time, they actually read the ad.

The sixth time they thumb their nose at it.

The seventh time, they start to get a little irritated with it.

The eighth time, they start to think, "Here's that confounded ad again."

The ninth time, they start to wonder if they're missing out on something.

The tenth time, they ask their friends and neighbors if they've tried it.

The eleventh time, they wonder how the company is paying for all these ads.

The twelfth time, they start to think that it must be a good product.

The thirteenth time, they start to feel the product has value.

The fourteenth time, they start to remember wanting a product exactly like this for a long time.

The fifteenth time, they start to yearn for it because they can't afford to buy it.

The sixteenth time, they accept the fact that they will buy it sometime in the future.

The seventeenth time, they make a note to buy the product.

The eighteenth time, they curse their poverty for not allowing them to buy this terrific product.

The nineteenth time, they count their money very carefully.

The twentieth time prospects see the ad, they buy what is offered.[8]

Numerous psychological studies since then have confirmed that messages, particularly advertising messages, have an increased chance of being remembered, accepted, and considered when they are seen or heard multiple times. In everyday life, no radio or television commercial is intended to be seen or heard just once. Advertisers have learned that the more times an audience is exposed to a message, the better the chances it will penetrate—that is, break through the clutter of all the other messages confronting people and sink in. In fact, in advertising media planning, two primary considerations are reach and frequency. *Reach* is a measure of how many people in a target audience will be exposed to a message. *Frequency* measures how many times those people will see or hear the message. Advertisers have learned that a message typically needs to be seen or heard between three and five times to sink in.

In one psychological theory, the power of repetition is based on the illusion-of-truth (or illusory truth) effect. Research finds that people are much more likely to believe a familiar statement than an unfamiliar statement. In other words, if they've heard something before, they're more likely to believe it when they hear it again.

It works in advertising. It works in political rhetoric. Repeating the same thing over and over, using the same words and phrases to describe an issue, an action, or an agenda, adds to the impact of what has already been said. Every iteration reinforces previous iterations. This assumption underlies message discipline, and Chapter 2 described how effectively the approach was used in the Republican Revolution in Congress. Once a message was researched, developed, and approved, everybody said it or said nothing at all.

Talking points are now routinely circulated on controversial policy issues by the White House, the House and Senate Democratic and Republican leadership, and their respective political party structures, laying out the words and phrases everyone is supposed to use in speeches, statements, news conferences, news releases, and interviews. You will hear those same words and phrases in the Speaker or Majority Leader's press briefings, speeches on the House or Senate floor, responses to media questions, and eventually on cable television from elected officials and respective party "strategists."

Media Effects

Three major communication theories, or effects—agenda setting, priming, and framing—have for many years been the topic of significant research and learned articles as scholars have sought to better understand how people are influenced by the messages they receive. They are categorized as media effects because they are seen as ways the news media influences or affects audiences, intentionally or not, by the choice of the individuals, topics, and issues being covered and the context in which they are covered. They are discussed here in a political communication context.

Agenda Setting

The agenda-setting theory was developed by Max McCombs and Donald Shaw. The premise of *agenda setting* is not that the media tells us what to think, but that they exert a strong influence over what we think about by what they choose to cover. For example, in the 2016 Republican presidential campaign, it would defy logic to suggest that the amazing amount of news media coverage and commentary focused on Donald Trump did not create and sustain his equally amazing level of public visibility, which in turn prompted the media to continue focusing on him and his candidacy. The media did not tell people what to think of Donald Trump, but it was unlikely that many people failed to think *about* Donald Trump. The same thing happens when the news media chooses to cover particular issues, which leads to the public perceiving those issues as newsworthy and therefore important. The corollary is also true: if the media chooses not to cover particular issues, then for many people, those issues simply do not exist.

The Priming Effect

The priming theory is largely drawn from the political science research of Shanto Iyengar, Mark Peters, and Donald Kinder.[9] Political media *priming* is usually associated with agenda setting because both deal with people's recollection of information in almost a one-two sequence. Once agenda setting has created and raised the audience's awareness of a political figure or issue, the amount and tone of media coverage influences how the audience perceives that political figure or issue.

Priming occurs because most people do not focus intently or remember every detail about a political figure or issue, so they tend to reach judgments based on what they do recall. If media coverage has emphasized certain aspects or characteristics of the political figure or issue, especially in repeated coverage, then those aspects or characteristics will be at the forefront of many people's memory and form the basis for their evaluation, even if other aspects and characteristics are just as relevant or important. The more prominent the media focus, the more the public's memory is primed.

Case Study: A Little Slip Can Sink Your Ship

In the 2012 presidential election campaign, Republican Mitt Romney was secretly videotaped telling a group of wealthy contributors that 47 percent of the public was dependent upon government and believed that they were victims, that the government had a responsibility to care for them, and that they were entitled to health care, food, and housing. He said that his job was not to worry about those people. Those comments were played over and over again in news media coverage and, despite all the other issues, became the criteria for many people to evaluate Romney's candidacy.

During the 2016 presidential campaign, it was revealed that as US secretary of state, Democrat Hillary Clinton sent and received official communication, as well as private messages, on a private e-mail server. It became a major issue and continuing focus throughout the primary campaign and into the general election. A State Department inquiry, followed by eight separate Republican-led congressional investigations, concluded that she had used poor judgment in using a private e-mail server for official business. However, no violation of law or breach of security was found. The director of the Federal Bureau of Investigation stated publicly that he would not recommend any sort of prosecution. Yet the issue became and remained a major focus throughout the campaign. Even though the details of Clinton's actions were largely unknown and widely misunderstood, her Republican opponent Donald Trump began calling her "Crooked Hillary," and a frequent chant at Trump campaign rallies was "Lock Her Up!"

Framing

Framing is the third theory of media effect most often studied by communication scholars for its role in persuasion and the formation of public opinion. The broader framing theory is usually attributed to the work of Erving Goffman, who focused primarily on economics.

The framing effect has been called a cognitive bias, in which people react to a particular choice in different ways depending on how it is presented. Researchers find that people tend to avoid risk when a positive frame is presented, but seek risks when a negative frame is presented. Amos Tversky and Daniel Kahneman described how different phrasing affected participants' responses to a choice in a hypothetical life and death situation in a 1981 article in the journal *Science*. Their research found "predictable shifts of preference when the same problem is framed in different ways."[10]

Participants were asked to choose between two treatments for 600 people affected with a deadly disease. Treatment A would result in 400 deaths, whereas treatment B had a 33 percent chance that no one would die, but a 66 percent chance that everyone would die. This choice was then presented to participants either with positive framing: "How many people would live?" or with negative framing: "How many people would die?"

When presented with positive framing—"200 lives will be saved"—72 percent chose Treatment A. Yet when the same choice was presented with negative framing—"400 people will die"—only 22 percent chose the same treatment.

Tversky and Kahneman's study found the same effect in other contexts:

- When a penalty fee for late registration was emphasized, 93 percent of doctoral students registered early, but only 67 percent did when it was presented as a discount for earlier registration.

- More people support an economic policy if the employment rate is emphasized than if the associated unemployment rates are highlighted.

Applied to media, framing refers to a focus or environment in the content of a story that influences how an audience will understand or evaluate it. News reporting may convey, deliberately or not, a particular context—a frame of reference—which affects the story's interpretation. A certain candidate has been called too ideological for his or her party's mainstream; a news story on a particular piece of legislation includes the charge that the measure will benefit special interests. Those frames often set a baseline for the audience's understanding and interpretation of all future reporting on that subject.

Political Framing

In political communication, framing is more than a theory. It is a deliberate, calculated technique that can significantly increase the impact of certain communication. Framing in this sense is more easily explained by what it does than what it is: it attempts to make a message more persuasive to its audience by suggesting how or in what context the message should be perceived. Framing is the packaging. It doesn't tell you what the message is, but what the message is about.

Political scholar Robert Entman writes that framing is the absolute bedrock in political communication. "Frames call attention to some aspects of reality while obscuring other elements, which might lead audiences to have different reactions."[11]

Political communicators commonly use framing to try to define issues—to get the audience to view the message through the lens the communicators want them to. Effective framing is critical to the communicators' success because they are appealing to an audience usually faced with choices among candidates, political philosophies, parties, policy, and legislative solutions. In the real world of politics and policy, there are frequently two or more opposing ways to view the same issue, and just as frequently, both or all sides are framing the issue in a way intended to persuade the audience(s) to "see it their way."

"Framing operates at different levels," writes Richard Perloff. "Political elites harness framers in an effort to advance a particular definition of a problem, hoping this will propel a bill into law or appeal to voters during an election campaign. Journalists use frames when they employ broad themes to structure factual details. Citizens interpret political issues in terms of broad principles that help them structure and organize the political world. The relationship among elite, media and citizens' frames are complex, just as relationships among these actors' different agendas are complicated."[12]

Professor John Daly agrees, "Wise proponents seek agreement on the problem before discussing possible solutions."[13] He says this accomplishes several things:

1. It makes the proponents more influential;

2. If people accept the proponent's definition, they're more likely to see things the same way and will be more open to the proponent's solutions; and

3. It limits discussion to problem solutions that fit the accepted definition.

Daly sums up the ultimate goal: "Whoever defines the problem wins."[14]

How do political communicators decide on political frames? Conventional wisdom and traditional political commentary have told us that politicians use public opinion research like a drunk uses a lamppost—for support rather than illumination. In their frames, do communicators simply echo prevailing public opinion and attitudes and restate them in a catchy phrase?

The answer appears to be "not always." Lawrence Jacobs and Robert Shapiro write that this conventional wisdom has been dead wrong on several major policy issues in the past decade. They highlighted and analyzed the Clinton administration's attempts to "reform" the nation's health-care delivery system and the Republican Contract with America that emerged just before the 1994 election, providing the conservative philosophical agenda for the 1995 Republican Revolution in Congress, and they analyzed the 1998 impeachment of President Clinton.

According to the authors, the political actors sought to shape rather than react to public opinion. They conducted extensive polling, not to measure public opinion or see which direction people were heading but to determine what arguments might be effective in manipulating public opinion to support a predetermined policy or political goal. "Public opinion research was used by politicians to manipulate public opinion. Their words and presentations were crafted to change public opinion and create the appearance of responsiveness."[15]

This approach has been used with particular effectiveness several times in recent US history to justify and build broad public support for one of the most costly actions on the planet: going to war in a foreign country. Half a century ago, it led us to spend nearly twenty years and hundreds of billions of dollars, to squander the lives of 58,000 Americans and as many as 3.3 million indigenous soldiers and civilians fighting in a country more than 8,500 miles away in a place called Vietnam.

It was a lesson apparently forgotten less than twenty-five years later.

Case Study: Framing the War in Iraq

As a student of communication theory in graduate school in 2002, I became fascinated by what I was seeing and hearing in the news every day. I was very familiar with the old axiom, "Where the public leads, our leaders will follow." Yet, as I listened to a growing drumbeat for a US invasion of Iraq, I realized that the George W. Bush administration was not following public opinion. It was changing it. It was shaping it.

To determine exactly how, I conducted two different types of academic research: (1) a textual analysis to identify particular words and phrases intended to frame issues and get the public to accept a certain perspective and view the issues a certain way, and (2) a content analysis to measure the frequency of use of those words and phrases.

I examined twenty-five different speeches, statements, and interviews by President Bush, Vice President Dick Cheney, National Security Advisor Condoleezza Rice, Secretary of Defense Donald Rumsfeld, Secretary of State Colin Powell, and other administration spokespeople over a seven-month period.

I was able to identify a number of classic propaganda techniques used by the administration: fear, association, the bandwagon effect, inevitable victory, oversimplification, and testimonials. (These techniques are explained in Chapter 13.)

All these were used to make the case for invading Iraq and deposing Saddam Hussein. Hussein was always framed as the "Dictator" or the "Evil Dictator," as if the epithets were part of his official title. According to the Bush administration, he had amassed huge stockpiles of biological, chemical, and nuclear weapons and was on the brink of using them. Most alarming, all the administration spokespeople claimed that Iraq was prepared to supply those weapons to terrorists, who could easily transport them and use them against the US homeland.

Administration officials also constantly asserted that Saddam Hussein enjoyed close relations with al-Qaeda, suggested that he was somehow complicit in 9/11, and repeatedly declared that the invasion of Iraq was a critical step in the War on Terror. President Bush, Vice President Cheney, and National Security Advisor Rice all said over and over again that the United States had to take action before, as Rice put it, the "smoking gun took the shape of a mushroom cloud."

Evidence indicates that this framing effort was effective. Numerous Pew Research opinion surveys found that when the administration began to talk seriously, in August 2002, about the possibility of war with Iraq, most Americans were

continues

Case Study: continued

ambivalent about a unilateral US offensive. There was a strong preference for allowing UN weapons inspectors, already on the ground in Iraq, enough time to continue searching for Hussein's weapons of mass destruction (WMDs). However, by the time combat operations were actually launched in March 2003 with "shock and awe," public opinion had moved to the president's position.

Without the slightest bit of evidence, the public accepted that Hussein had direct involvement in 9/11 and had consorted with al-Qaeda for years. Public opinion supported the Bush administration through three weeks of combat, while searches for WMDs turned up nothing and serious questions about the administration's rationale were being raised. Only when it became clear that Iraq had not possessed any sort of WMDs in many years, and that the entire justification had more to do with a predetermined agenda than with defending the United States from terrorism, did public opinion begin to turn.

Even then, the administration came up with an effective frame that glossed over the nonexistent WMDs and the fact that no connection has ever been established between Iraq or Saddam Hussein and any international terrorist activities, particularly the events of 9/11. In the words of President Bush, the framing message was now, "Iraq is the central battleground in the war on terror." It was also referred to as a "strategic battleground in the war on terror," "a key battleground in the war on terror," and the "main battleground in the war on terror."

It may be a testament to the skill of the Bush communicators that loss of public support occurred slowly. A series of polls conducted six months after the invasion, found the following:

- 22 percent of the public still believed weapons of mass destruction had been found in Iraq.

- 25 percent believed world public opinion favored the United States going to war with Iraq.

- 13 percent believed they had seen conclusive evidence that Iraq was directly involved in 9/11.

- 48 percent of the American public believed links between Iraq and al-Qaeda had been found.

- 33–36 percent believed that Iraq had given al-Qaeda substantial support.

Congressional Framing Wars

Partisan combatants in our national public discourse are continually drawing lines in the dirt. You're either on one side or the other. You're either in favor of raising taxes on job creators and stifling economic growth or you're in favor of tax giveaways to the rich at the expense of working families. You either support a government takeover of health care or you favor allowing millions of low- and moderate-income Americans to continue without proper health care because they can't afford it. You either favor a bloated, intrusive federal government that makes it tougher and tougher for US businesses to succeed or you support uncontrolled crony capitalism in which giant corporations can do whatever they want.

The stark either/or choices emanate mainly from the Democratic and Republican leadership in Congress and the White House, and they are used in speeches, statements, interviews, news releases, and Twitter feeds. Other representatives, senators, and administration officials repeat them using the same platforms. Then they are picked up and repeated by political pundits and various media outlets, and the two-party organizations disseminate them in communications to state organizations and opinion leaders across the country. Interest groups use them in their messaging, which frequently includes television ads.

Political parties and their candidates fight these framing wars to define the problems, and they do so with good reason. William Gamson, who directs Boston College's Media Research and Action Project, writes, "Policy controversies inevitably involve battles over meaning. Think of them as framing contests. On most issues, there is typically a conventional, dominant frame that most people use without thinking since much of it is taken for granted. Controversy is created when one or more challengers offer an alternative way of framing the issue."[16]

For a number of years, it wasn't really a fair fight. Congressional Republicans had learned how to frame issues effectively and use those frames to influence the public dialogue; the Democrats, not so much. As former *New York Times Magazine* reporter Matt Bai noted:

> Of course, the idea that language and narrative matter in politics shouldn't really have come as a revelation to Washington Democrats. Bill Clinton had been an intuitive master of framing. As far back as 1992, Clinton's image of Americans who "worked hard and played by the rules," for instance, had perfectly evoked a metaphor of society as a contest that relied on fairness. And yet despite this, Democrats in Congress were remarkably slow to grasp this dimension of political combat. Having ruled Capitol Hill pretty comfortably for most of the past 60 years, Democrats had never had much reason to think about calibrating their language in order to sell their ideas.[17]

Does it really matter? Does it make that much difference how you define an issue? Ask yourself:

- Is the abortion issue a matter of protecting women's reproductive rights and freedom? Or is it a fight to protect the rights of the unborn baby?
- Are numerous state laws attempting to put severe limitations on the availability of health-care coverage for birth control part of a Republican War on Women or are they intended to protect the religious freedom of the employer?

- Do we have a Federal Death Tax that places an onerous burden on family farms and small businesses, or an Estate Tax assessed on only the wealthiest one half of one percent of all estates in the country to ensure they pay their share?

- Should we look at Benghazi as a White House failure to take prompt action and the ensuing cover-up the tragic death of four Americans in Libya, or in an unforeseeable terrorist attack?

- Are all the problems with wait times at VA hospitals and clinics a matter of the Veterans Health Administration system being denied proper funding by Congress? Or are they in place to cover up inadequate medical care of our military veterans?

- Are Environmental Protection Agency regulations an example of federal overreach that kills jobs and slows economic recovery, and part of the Democrats' "War on Coal," or do the regulations cut back on toxic emissions by coal-fired power plants to address a health threat that also contributes to global warming?

- Are attempts to impose limits on campaign contributions by establishing maximums and requiring more disclosure following the US Supreme Court's *Citizens United* decision an effort to place badly needed limits on the ability of large corporations and millionaires to buy elections? Or are they attempts to restrict our constitutional right to free speech?

How you feel about these issues and how you receive and process messages about them depends to a large degree on which political issue frame, on which definition of the "problem," you accept. Getting people to view an issue in a certain way can be as simple as attaching a label to an issue or action, and then repeating it over and over and over:

- tax cuts or tax relief?
- oil-well drilling or energy exploration?
- marriage equality or religious liberty?
- global warming or climate change?

In another example, in the decades after the 1972 Watergate scandal, which led to the resignation of President Richard Nixon, every time one side in a partisan debate attempted to brand the other as corrupt or untrustworthy, the issue at hand was dubbed "_____ gate": Billygate, Debategate, Irangate, Troopergate, Travelgate. In the 2016 Republican presidential primary campaign, New Jersey governor Chris Christie was still dealing with Bridgegate. These were attempts by Republicans and Democrats to frame a political controversy as scandalous. The term has become so commonplace, it is now used in other countries and other languages.

Similarly, particularly during the Obama administration, Republican communicators began to refer to issues or actions with which they disagreed as a crisis or scandal. We have heard about dozens of them, although none has yet proved substantive. The use of such labels is aimed more at firing up a political base than persuading people who have not made up their minds. The problem with this technique, though, is that overreliance on such labels eventually dulls the impact. If every issue or action is a crisis or scandal, most people eventually tune the label out.

Occasional shortcomings in certain techniques notwithstanding, public policy debate and political campaigns have largely become issue-framing contests. Both sides try to frame the issues, frame themselves, and frame the other side. The side that wins the framing contest—that convinces more of the public to view the situation through their frame—usually wins the political debate.

Case Study: Religious Liberty or Legalized Discrimination?

In 1996, following a state supreme court decision in Hawaii that same-sex marriage opponents feared might open the door to requiring other states to recognize same-sex marriages, Congress passed the Defense of Marriage Act (DOMA). The legislation passed by large, veto-proof majorities in both the House and Senate and was reluctantly signed into law by President Bill Clinton. Under the law, marriage was defined for federal purposes as the union of one man and one woman, meaning that same-sex spouses were not eligible for federal marriage benefits, including insurance benefits for government employees, social security survivors' benefits, immigration, bankruptcy, and the filing of joint tax returns, as well as protection for families of federal officers and eligibility for financial aid. Under DOMA, individual states were allowed to refuse recognition of same-sex marriages granted under the laws of other states. In most places in the United States, bans on same-sex marriage were the norm and seemed generally to reflect public sentiment.

However, beginning in 2009, attitudes began to change rapidly and dramatically. Public opinion polling across the political spectrum showed growing acceptance—even support—for same-sex unions. By 2015, thirty-seven states had legalized same-sex marriage: twenty-six by court decisions throwing out bans, eight by state legislative action, and three by popular vote.

Much of the rapid change was attributed to a new generation of voters, the Millennials, whose attitude toward same-sex unions, even among 18- to 35-year-old Republicans, seemed to be, "So what? It's none of my business."

This attitude change energized LGBT rights groups to organize and push for state legislation around the country to legalize same-sex marriages everywhere, granting to gay or lesbian unions the same legal rights and protections enjoyed by "straight" marriages, and for more states to legally recognize same-sex marriages performed in other states. Activists and progressive forces began to frame the issue as "marriage equality."

In response, opponents of the trend began to push state legislation to deny legal status to same-sex marriages and prevent their recognition by any level of government. These forces framed their efforts as "protecting religious

continues

Case Study: continued

liberties," intended only to protect those who oppose same-sex unions on religious grounds from being required to provide services for such marriages. This framing was actually adapted from earlier opposition to requirements that health-care insurance providers include coverage of birth-control measures.

Then in June 2015, in *Obergefell v. Hodges*, the US Supreme Court ruled 5 to 4 that the Constitution requires that same-sex couples be allowed to marry no matter the state in which they lived, and that no state had the right to limit marriage only to heterosexual couples.

In several states, some elected clerks and lower-level judges voiced opposition on religious grounds. In Texas, the state attorney general initially claimed the ruling did not apply there. In Alabama, the state supreme court's chief justice made a similar claim, and in other states, officials initially refused to issue licenses to anyone, gay or straight. Notably, in Kentucky, Rowan county clerk Kim Davis refused to issue same-sex marriage licenses, claiming that doing so would violate her religious freedom. When she refused to follow a federal court order to do so, the judge found her in contempt and she spent six days in jail.

The issue of same-sex marriage created strong issue frames with strong moral appeal for both proponents and opponents. Same-sex marriage supporters argue that gay and lesbian couples have the same constitutional rights to the privileges and protections of legal marriage as any straight couple. And, they claim, any attempt to prevent such unions is legalized discrimination. Opponents, however, argue that nobody with sincerely held religious convictions opposing same-sex marriage should be forced by law to participate in or support them in any way.

In the 2016 presidential election campaign, which unfolded in a highly partisan environment, political framing neither stopped nor slowed. Efforts by Congress and a number of state legislatures to curtail the existence of women's clinics offering legal abortion services and to curb requirements that employee group health insurance policies cover the cost of birth control along with other prescription drugs have been framed as failing to "protect women's health." At the same time, opponents of abortion were framing their position as "protecting the rights of the unborn.

Within days of the death of US Supreme Court Justice Antonin Scalia in February 2016, the Republican Senate leadership announced that they would not hold hearings or vote or even meet with President Obama's nominee to fill the vacancy. They said the country should leave the seat open for nearly a year and wait for the next president, who took office in January 2017, to nominate a candidate. They framed the issue as "letting voters decide what kind of Supreme Court they want by whom they elect as president."

In *Words That Work: It's Not What You Say, It's What People Hear*, Republican framing guru Frank Luntz writes, "You can have the best message in the world, but the person on the receiving end will always understand it through the prism of his or her own emotions, preconceptions, prejudices and pre-existing beliefs. It's not enough to be correct or reasonable or even brilliant. The key is to take the imaginative leap of stuffing yourself into your listener's shoes to know what they are thinking and feeling in the deepest recesses of their mind and heart."[18]

His stated purpose is to cause audiences to react based on emotion. "Eighty percent of our life is emotion, and only 20 percent is intellect. I am much more interested in how you feel than how you think."[19]

There is also a language and framing guru on the Democratic side, George Lakoff, professor of linguistics and cognitive science at UC Berkeley and a founder of the progressive Rockbridge Institute. Lakoff has been speaking and writing about the importance of words and phrases for years, and has written extensively on political rhetoric.

"Political framing is really applied cognitive science. Frames facilitate our most basic interactions with the world—they structure our ideas and concepts, they shape the way we reason, and they even impact how we perceive and how we act," writes Lakoff in *Thinking Points: Communicating Our American Values and Vision.* "Just as frames structure and define social institutions, they also define issues. An issue-defining frame characterizes the problem, assigns blame and constrains the possible solution."[20] He provides an example of effective issue framing: the War on Terror.

Case Study: War on Terror

"In the immediate aftermath of 9-11, there was a brief discussion of treating terrorist acts as an international police problem," Lakoff writes. That idea, however, didn't last long. The Bush administration started promoting a "War on Terror," which Lakoff suggests created certain semantic roles: armies, a fight, a moral crusade, a commander in chief, the capture of territory, the surrender of an enemy, and patriots supporting troops. War implies the necessity of military action. When we're in a war, all other concerns are secondary. And when the word *terror* is added to *war*, a metaphor is produced in which terror becomes the opposing army. As in any war, the enemy must be defeated.

"However," writes Lakoff, "terror is not actually an army—it is a state of mind. As such, it cannot be beaten on the field of battle. It is an emotion. Moreover, the 'war on terror' frame is self-perpetuating. You cannot permanently capture and defeat an emotion."[21]

Lakoff and Luntz may disagree about most policy and political issues, but they are in complete agreement about the impact of issue frames in public policy debate.

Framing Elections

Accompanying the attempts to define specific issues and agendas in our national elections are highly effective efforts to frame the elections themselves. Midterm elections often become framing contests between the party in the White House and the opposition party. The "in-power" party usually attempts to focus voter attention on specific issues, particularly those on which they can tell a positive story: "Look at what we've done for you. Look how much better off you are."

Meanwhile, the opposition party tries to nationalize the election and make the case that voters should express their feelings about broad national issues and the president, even though the president is not on the ballot. This is often accompanied by a campaign to create public discontent or anger or even fear about the state of the country or the world, sometimes questioning the administration's competence.

In 1994, two years after the election of President Bill Clinton, the big issues were allegations of ethical shortcomings by the administration and "Hillarycare," the Clinton's unsuccessful attempt at health-care reform. Republicans ran on the Contract with America (as was chronicled in Chapter 2) and took control of the House for the first time in forty years.

The next midterm election that brought a big change was in 2006, two years after George W. Bush's reelection, and nearly four years after the US invasion of Iraq. Democrats focused their message on the war, which most Americans were growing tired of, both in loss of US lives and its expense. Democrats won thirty-one seats and recaptured a majority in the House.

The 2010 midterm came two years after Barack Obama's election and followed the rancorous, extremely noisy congressional passage of the Affordable Care Act, or as the Republicans branded it, Obamacare. During this time, the country also saw the emergence, in various forms and versions, of the Tea Party, ostensibly an independent, unstructured, even spontaneous grassroots effort, yet actually highly organized and financed in large part by the ultraconservative Freedom Works, a super political action committee. In the 2010 midterm election, Republicans gained sixty-three seats in the House to take the majority and picked up six Senate seats.

Case Study: Fear Beats "Feel Good"

In November 2014, midway through Barack Obama's second term, most Democratic candidates for the US House and Senate had issues to talk about in their campaigns. There were positive developments in the economy: the unemployment rate was the lowest in years, there had been fifty-six straight months of job growth, the national deficit had been cut in half since 2008, US manufacturing was growing, and the United States was close to becoming an energy exporter, producing and generating more energy than the country uses. And all of this took place with little to no support for the administration's policies from congressional Republicans.

Republicans effectively turned the election into a referendum on President Obama, and many Democratic candidates, especially incumbents in "red states," ran as far and fast as they could from anything tied to the White House. The Republican message was successful in appealing to public fears: fears of Islamic militants; fears of little children from Central America flooding across the US border, porous due to the Obama administration's refusal to make it "secure"; fears of the Chinese, the North Koreans, and the Ebola crisis in Nigeria. Democrats allowed the Republican message—"Be afraid. Be very afraid"—to frame the election. Republicans, who already had a majority in the House, won nine Senate seats, all in states carried by Mitt Romney in 2012, and gained a majority in both houses of Congress for the first time since the Democratic wave in 2006.

For Democrats, the carnage from the 2014 midterm election was not limited to Washington, DC. Republicans won majorities in sixty-seven of the nation's state senates and houses, and thirty-one governorships.

Means-End Theory

Another persuasive communication technique used in political debate is the means-end theory. It was developed by University of Southern California marketing professors Jonathan Gutman and Donald Vinson in the late 1970s. It is a construct most commonly used in product and service marketing and advertising. The point is to connect whatever you are selling with positive consequences for the buyer and, ultimately, the buyer's values. Applied to politics and government, means-end links policy choices with voters' personal values, which certainly has strong emotional appeal.

I first heard means-end theory used in political communication in House Appropriations Committee hearings back in 2005, when Republicans were attempting to extend the Bush tax cuts of 2001 and 2003 and pass additional tax cuts. I did not fully appreciate the art behind what I had heard until a year later. Dave Winston, a leading public opinion researcher and communication advisor who has helped House and Senate Republicans develop effective political messages for many years, spoke to one of my classes. He illustrated the application of the means-end theory, and it sounded familiar:

1. If we pass more tax relief, the average working family will have more money.
2. If they have more money, they can spend more on their children's education.
3. If they spend more on their children's education, the children have a better chance of success.
4. If their children are successful, it means taxpayers were good parents.
5. Therefore, cutting taxes allows people to be better parents.[22]

A means-end ladder has three steps: product–consequences–values. Used effectively, it accomplishes the same things as other forms of persuasive political communication; it links the action the communicator wants to take to the things the public cares about.

This theory could have been used as effectively by Democrats in the debate over health care, and it would have looked something like this:

Product

1. More than thirty million US families can't afford decent health care.

2. Many families are faced with making a choice between paying for health insurance and paying the rent or buying groceries and clothing.

Consequences

3. If health care is more affordable, we're putting money in the pockets of millions of US families.

4. If families have more to spend, demand for consumer goods and services grows.

5. If demand for consumer goods and services grows, US businesses can prosper.

6. When our businesses grow, they create jobs and our economy grows.

7. As our economy grows, the United States becomes a stronger nation.

8. A stronger nation means the American people are more secure and more prosperous.

Values

9. Therefore, passing the Affordable Care Act leads to a more secure and prosperous United States.

Conclusion

Principle 2: Political communication has one overriding purpose—to persuade people to agree with the communicator in order to win an election or to win support for a position on a public policy issue.

To persuade effectively, communicators must break through the general clutter of the other messages the public hears with a political message that will have the best chance of being accepted. In pursuit of these goals, effective public affairs communicators use a variety of approaches described in this chapter: maintaining a strong focus on a single point in each message; using repetition; and employing issue framing and the means-end ladder. We see issue framing, in particular, nearly every day in nearly every utterance from political communicators.

Notes

1. George Orwell, "Politics and the English Language," April 1946, http://www.orwell.ru/library/essays/politics/english/e_polit/.

2. Richard M. Perloff, *The Dynamics of Persuasion: Communication and Attitudes in the Twenty-First Century* (New York: Routledge, 2010).

3. John Harwood, "As Obama's Poll Numbers Fall, Criticism of Multitasking Rises," *New York Times*, December 6, 2009.

4. Ibid.

5. David Horowitz, *Take No Prisoners: The Battle Plan for Defeating the Left* (Washington, DC: Regnery Publishing, 2014).

6. Penn State University College of Communication, "The Downfall of John Kerry's 2004 Presidential Campaign," Public Relations Problems and Cases Blog, 2007, http://psucomm473.blogspot.com/2007/04/downfall-of-john-kerrys-2004.html.

7. Matea Gold, "Students Give Kerry Mixed Grade," *Los Angeles Times*, April 18, 2004, http://articles.latimes.com/2004/apr/18/nation/na-youth18.

8. Thomas Smith, *Successful Advertising*, 7th ed. 1885, https://www.brandingstrategyinsider.com/2010/08/advertising-frequency-theory-circa-1885.html#.WTHCb4WcHIU.

9. Shanto Iyengar, Mark Peters, and Donald Kinder, "Experimental Demonstrations of the 'Not-So-Minimal' Consequences of Television News Programs," *The American Political Science Review* 76, no. 4 (1982): 848–858.

10. Amos Tversky and Daniel Kahneman, "The Framing of Decisions and the Psychology of Choice," *Science* 211 (1981): 453–458.

11. Robert Entman, "Framing: Toward Clarification of a Fractured Paradigm," *Journal of Communication* 43, no. 4 (1993): 51.

12. Perloff, *The Dynamics of Persuasion*, 159.

13. John Daly, *Advocacy: Championing Ideas and Influencing Others* (New Haven, CT: Yale University Press, 2011), 51.

14. Ibid.

15. Lawrence Jacobs and Robert Shapiro, *Politicians Don't Pander: Political Manipulation and the Loss of Democratic Responsiveness* (Chicago: University of Chicago Press, 2000).

16. William Gamson, "Framing Social Policy," _Nonprofit Quarterly_, September 21, 2000, https://nonprofitquarterly.org/2000/09/21/framing-social-policy/.

17. Matt Bai, "The Framing Wars," _New York Times Magazine_, July 17, 2005, http://www.nytimes.com/2005/07/17/magazine/the-framing-wars.html?_r=0.

18. Frank Luntz, _Words That Work: It's Not What You Say, It's What People Hear_ (New York: Hyperion Books, 2007).

19. Ibid.

20. George Lakoff, _Thinking Points: Communicating Our American Values and Vision_ (New York: Farrar, Straus and Giroux, 2006), 25.

21. Ibid.

22. Dave Winston, in-class presentation, American University, 2008.

4

Making Political
Communication Effective

Principle 3: To be effective, communication has to be conveyed in words, phrases, signs, and symbols the audience understands, can relate to, and will accept.

It is important to keep in mind a point at the beginning of the previous chapter: with all the technological changes in how, when, and where campaigns communicate, the essential responsibility of the political communicator is still to craft and disseminate persuasive, compelling, and memorable messages. Persuasion can only occur when the message sufficiently connects with things the audience cares about in order to be received, considered, and accepted.

This chapter explains practices that help make the communicator's message effective. These practices are informed by research findings, and the second part of the chapter offers background on some of what researchers have learned about what happens when people receive a message.

Use Plain Language:
Simple, Direct, and Lots of Impact

One of the fundamentals in communicating effectively with people is to talk the way people talk. That does not mean talking down or "dumbing" down. It simply means you need to describe issues and political agendas in plain language that will be clear to ordinary folks. Most people are not stupid. But most people don't live and work in the world of politics and policy, and they aren't glued to C-SPAN waiting for an in-depth analysis of the latest Senate vote.

As explained in Chapter 2, what speaking plainly requires is good writing. One of the foremost advocates for good, clear writing is William Zinsser, whose book, *On Writing Well*, has achieved near-biblical status in graduate and undergraduate journalism, communication, and any other classes involving writing. Zinsser said, "The secret of good writing is to strip every sentence to its cleanest components. Every word that serves no function, every long word that could be a short word, every adverb that carries the same meaning that's already in the verb, every passive construction that leaves the reader unsure of who is doing what— these are the thousand and one adulterants that weaken the strength of a sentence. And they usually occur, ironically, in proportion to education and rank."[1]

Zinsser cites an example of government communication vastly improved by simplifying. During World War II, an order requiring blackout curtains on the windows of government buildings was issued: "Such preparations shall be made as will completely obscure all Federal buildings and non-Federal buildings occupied by the Federal government during an air raid for any period of time from visibility by reason of internal or external illumination." The order was brought to the attention of the ultimate government editor, President Franklin D. Roosevelt, who said, "Tell them that in buildings where they have to keep the work going to put something across the windows."[2]

Sometimes, however, a government official's attempt to clarify falls short. In February 2002, Secretary of Defense Donald Rumsfeld explained to reporters the ins and outs of intelligence reports about Iraq's purported weapons of mass destruction: "Reports that say something hasn't happened are always interesting to me, because as we know, there are known knowns; there are things we know we know. We also know there are known unknowns; that is to say we know there are some things we do not know. But there are also unknown unknowns—the ones we don't know we don't know."[3]

Occasionally, even the simplest statement doesn't quite mean what it was supposed to mean. Democratic Speaker of the House Nancy Pelosi talked in March 2010 about the content of the 1200-page legislation enacting the Affordable Care Act: "But we have to pass the bill so that you can find out what is in it, away from the fog of the controversy."

Tell a Story

> Five years ago, Gladys Ndiema lived in fear during ethnic cleansing in her village of Kitalale, Kenya. She was scared to leave her home, since guerrillas had taken over her land and the village [was] plagued with violence. Gladys' brother and husband had been victims of torture. Shortly after the violence in Kitalale died down, a program funded by a U.S. corporation worked with local groups to restore the dairy industry and help reconstruct the economy. Today, Gladys is president of the Meeboot Dairy Farmers Cooperative Society.

That was the lead-in for a student's op-ed assignment in one of my public policy writing classes. The student demonstrated one of the most powerful approaches to grabbing the reader's attention. She told a story.

This approach is hardly new. Storytelling has been an essential part of the transfer of values and traditions in cultures throughout history, and narratives can be highly effective for today's policy advocates.

Telling a story has become a modern tradition in political communication at the highest level. In Ronald Reagan's 1982 State of the Union speech, he told the following story relating to an aircraft that had crashed into the Potomac River on take-off:

"Just two weeks ago, in the midst of a terrible tragedy on the Potomac, we saw again the spirit of American heroism at its finest, the heroism of dedicated rescue workers saving crash victims from icy waters. And we saw the heroism of one of our young Government employees, Lenny Skutnik, who, when he saw a woman lose her grip on the helicopter line, dived into the water and dragged her to safety." Then he introduced Lenny Skutnik, who was in attendance.

Since then, every president has introduced individuals and their stories as part of the nationally televised address, using the stories to underline and illustrate policy issues. From civil rights icon Rosa Parks, US Olympic heroes, foreign leaders, highly decorated military personnel to a ninety-two-year-old woman forced to wait in line for four hours to vote in the 2012 election, all their stories made powerful points and put a human face on government policies and decisions.

But the story does not have to be about a heroic individual to grab the audience's attention, and the setting does not have to be grand to make the story effective. Narratives are used effectively in communication as mundane as news releases. If a news release focuses on a compelling individual or event to help tell a story, there is a good chance that the news media will pick up that perspective and include it in their coverage. When a communicator can find a person whose story illustrates the need for a policy or the policy's impact—like Gladys Ndiema in Kitalale, Kenya— they have a much better chance of getting the audience to take enough interest to read or watch the rest of the story.

Millions, Billions, and Trillions

In a national government with an annual budget of $3.77 trillion, it's easy to stop thinking about it as real money and just deal with numbers. Even in smaller chunks like the 2014 defense budget—a paltry $615 billion or so—every budget figure and expenditure has more zeros than most of us are used to dealing with. I know what a hundred looks like. I've seen a thousand, and I can imagine a million. But a billion or a trillion? Those are just concepts.

Effective political communicators translate those galactically large numbers into terms people can more easily relate to. Sometimes they do so by breaking large quantities into monthly or weekly expenditures, or they might talk in per-person numbers, or they might even describe what some huge amount might buy: seventeen middle-class homes, twenty-three jumbo jets, a new car for every resident of Illinois.

Large dollar figures are sometimes translated into more comprehensible concepts by focusing on what the money will provide. Rather than talking about the $16 million my boss got into the Military Construction-VA Appropriations bill for the Pearl Harbor Naval Shipyard, we would talk about how many jobs would be created, how many new dry docks, how it would maintain Pearl Harbor as one of the nation's most vital military facilities—a big factor in the state's economic security. We tried to put things in terms that most people could relate to, and we tried to connect them to things people cared about.

Make Connections

A critical step in effective political and government communication is to connect the audience with the message, and persuasion cannot occur without doing so. Communicators need to let people know why they should listen to the message. They should connect what they are talking about to their audience's lives by telling people how an issue or a candidate's political agenda is going to touch them—how it will affect their job, their family, their community, their kids' school, or their financial security. If they hear what a candidate or policy interest wants to do and understand how it will make their lives better, it will increase the chances that they pay attention. If they hear how the opponent's agenda or government policy will make their lives worse, they will be more likely to pay attention to that, too. As Benjamin Franklin put it, "If you would persuade, you must appeal to interest rather than intellect."

To have the desired impact and really reach people, political communication has to connect with information, attitudes, and values that people already have. It has to connect with information that forms their opinions and attitudes: their concerns, fears, hopes, ambitions, pride, standards, and cultural mores or values; their geographic, ethnic, age, or professional identity; their identification with a political party and support or opposition to political figures or groups or issues. Successful communicators do this not by trying to teach the audience to understand and accept entirely new sets of opinions and attitudes, but by making new information fit with opinions and attitudes they already hold. Much of that depends on agreeing about what the problem is in the first place. Sometimes everyone agrees on the problem. Sometimes not.

Case Study: You Have to Walk a Mile in the Other Person's Boots

Competing definitions of issues are usually rooted in competing perspectives. According to the Congressional Research Service (CRS), "Charging fees for grazing private livestock on federal lands is a long-standing but contentious practice. Generally, livestock producers who use federal lands want to keep fees low, while conservation groups and others believe fees should be increased."[4] As CRS noted, the hearings tend to be contentious.

The late Bob Armstrong, former state representative, gubernatorial candidate, and longtime Texas Land Commissioner, was assistant secretary of the Department of the Interior in the Clinton administration. Among his many responsibilities were public hearings over grazing fees on public lands required by the Taylor Grazing Act of 1934. The Department of the Interior's Bureau of Land Management oversees all federally owned lands in the nation and conducts periodic hearings with ranchers to set fees for livestock grazing.

At one particular hearing in Wyoming, after a great deal of heated rhetoric over fair fees, a woman representing a nature conservation organization stood and proclaimed, "The real problem is that we eat too much meat. If people didn't eat so much meat, we wouldn't have these disagreements about grazing cattle on public lands. Everyone simply needs to eat more vegetables."

To which one grizzled cattle rancher stood up and responded, "Lady, vegetables ain't food. Vegetables are what food eats."[5]

Clearly, the two speakers did not share much in the way of perspective on the nature of the problem, which made the government's responsibility for setting fees and communicating a rationale a bit more challenging.

UCLA Professor John Zaller in *The Nature and Origins of Mass Opinion* wrote: "Every opinion is a marriage of information and predisposition: information to form a mental picture of the given issue, and predisposition to motivate some conclusion about it."[6] Much of the recent study of political influence and public opinion is built on Zaller's work. One of his fundamental conclusions is that predisposition is most often based on information already assimilated and opinions already held. In other words, most people learn by stacking new information on top of existing information. The more that new information relates to or is associated with existing information—the more it connects—the more likely people are to pay attention, consider, and retain the new information. In other words, the more that what the communicator is telling people connects to things they already know or feel, the more likely the new information is to stick.

The late Tony Schwartz will always be remembered for his role in creating the best-known political television ad in history, the "Daisy" spot for Lyndon Johnson's 1964 presidential campaign (see Chapter 8). Schwartz said, "Commercials that attempt to tell the listener something are inherently not as effective as those that attach to something that is already in the voter. We are not concerned with getting things across to people as much as getting things out of people."[7]

His point is that successful political communicators spend less time talking about what they think and more time talking about what the public thinks. That message is implied in words to undecided voters: "I'm like you. I share your values. I care about the same kinds of things you care about. I want the same kinds of things you want." Sometimes the connection is stated outright as a slogan or tagline: "One of our own. One of our best." "He works for me." "I grew up here." "You work hard. So should your governor."

Cognitive Research: How Political Messages Are Received and Processed

Strategic political communicators try to understand how different kinds of messages are received and processed. More specifically, are different kinds of messages received and processed differently by different kinds of people? What determines which messages break through the clutter of communication to be received and considered? What kinds of messages are most likely to cause changes in opinion or belief and motivate people to act? In other words, what works?

These questions have been poked, probed, and examined by political and communication scholars and cognition researchers for decades. They have conducted significant neurological and physiological research. Their work strongly suggests that different kinds of political messages are considered in different ways depending on established attitudes and predispositions. And in the last few years, we have learned a lot more about actual physical differences in the way people receive and process information, and the role different lobes of the brain have in determining how and which messages are more likely to be processed. We are learning that the ways our brains are wired can be a major factor in our openness to considering new information.

Back when I began to learn about writing and producing effective political messages, there were no formal classes or how-to manuals on the effective use of emotion in campaign television spots. What practitioners knew about it they learned mostly through trial and error. Occasionally—but only occasionally—there were opportunities to conduct the most primitive form of research: individual follow-up conversations with voters who could recall particular radio or television spots and remember their reactions to them. Even then, the spots people remembered, the ones people said got their attention, were those with some level of emotional context. It was not until years later that I learned there were sound scientific explanations for this.

Neurological Research

Drew Westen is neither a political scientist nor a communication researcher. He teaches in the Departments of Psychology, Psychiatry, and Behavioral Sciences at Emory University, and he has conducted and participated in extensive clinical research into the way the human brain receives and processes different kinds of messages.

In the November 2006 *Journal of Cognitive Neuroscience*, Westen described research using functional magnetic resonance imaging, or fMRI, to measure brain activity by detecting changes in blood flow. It relies on the fact that when an area of the brain is in use, blood flow to that region increases. Westen wrote, "The findings provided the first neuroimaging evidence for phenomena variously described as motivated reasoning, implicit emotion regulation, and psychological defense. They suggest that motivated reasoning is qualitatively distinct from reasoning when people do not have a strong emotional stake in the conclusions reached."[8]

In his book *The Political Brain: The Role of Emotion in Deciding the Fate of the Nation*, Westen further explained the heightened impact of emotion over pure logic in political messages. He concluded that emotional messages have more impact primarily because of the way our brains are wired. He described an almond-shaped group of neurons called amygdalae, located in each of the brain's medial temporal lobes. The amygdalae process emotional messages and are where our emotional memories are stored. They are an evolutionarily older part of the brain where the "fight or flight" response was activated in early humans.

According to Westen, emotional messages are processed more quickly because there are more receptors and neural pathways to the amygdalae from the body's various sensory organs than there are to the prefrontal lobes that process "reasoning" information and stimuli. As a result, messages with an emotional element reach the cerebral cortex with more urgency and impact than messages based on reasoning.[9]

Left Brain, Right Brain

Other neurological studies seem congruent with Westen's findings. In the 1980s, pop psychology began to describe people as either left or right brained and suggested that the characteristic determined whether they tended to be more artistic, sensitive, thoughtful, creative, emotional, or analytical, depending on which lobes of the brain dominated their thought processing and behavior. The theory that everyone is either one or the other has been roundly disputed in recent years. Now, however, it appears there may be something to the basic idea after all, and that the unique characteristics of the left and right lobes of the brain may have consequences in political communication.

Journalist and author Chris Mooney has written extensively on how different kinds of political messages are received and processed by different people. Mooney has built on Westen's research about neurological differences in processing varying kinds of messages. In his 2012 book *The Republican Brain: The Science of Why They Deny Science—and Reality*, he points to research that finds the predisposition to process stimuli in one lobe of the brain or the other is due to an actual physical difference in the size of the respective lobes.[10]

Some people, says Mooney, actually have a larger right brain lobe, including the limbic system, which supports emotion, behavior, motivation, and long-term memory. Other people, he says, have a larger left brain lobe and tend to process most information through their prefrontal cortex, the lobes that help in reasoning and logical processing.

Mooney suggests that this neurological difference can reflect political tendencies. In *The Republican Brain*, Mooney describes "a recent magnetic resonance imaging (MRI) study of 90 University College of London students that found on average, political conservatives actually had a larger right lobe, including the amygdalae, while political liberals had more gray matter in the anterior cingulated cortex (ACC)," part of the brain's frontal lobe, with many links to the prefrontal cortex.[11]

This seems consistent with studies conducted in 2013 by Darren Schreiber, a researcher in neuropolitics at the University of Exeter in the UK, and colleagues at the University of California. Their research was described in "Red Brain, Blue Brain: Evaluative Processes Differ in Democrats and Republicans" in the international online journal *PLOS ONE*.[12]

The study used data from a previous experiment in which a group of people were asked to play a simple gambling task. Schreiber's team took the brain activity measurement of eighty-two people and cross-referenced them with the participants' publicly available political party registration data. They found that Republicans tended to use their right amygdala, the part of the brain associated with the body's fight-or-flight system, when making risk-taking decisions; Democrats tended to show greater activity in their left insula, an area associated with self and social awareness.

Schreiber claims the insula/amygdala brain function model offers an 82.9 percent accuracy rate in predicting whether a person is a Democrat or Republican. In comparison, the longstanding model using the party affiliation of parents to predict a child's affiliation is accurate about 69.5 percent of the time. Another model based on the differences in brain structure distinguishes liberals from conservatives with 71.6 percent accuracy.[13]

Mooney cites other academic research findings indicating that people whose limbic system is more involved in processing information are less likely to change their minds. Once they have arrived at a position on an issue that is congruent with their belief system and values, they are unlikely to change their minds even when presented with irrefutable evidence to support a different viewpoint. They will actually reject or discount facts or attempt to discredit the source of facts that conflict with their position.

Motivated Reasoning

A series of related behavioral concepts could shed light on why different people seem to react differently to various political messages. One of the best known concepts is *motivated reasoning*, which is based on research findings, such as that described by Mooney, that some people tend to process most information through the prefrontal cortex of their brains while others tend to receive and process information through the limbic system.

Other research has found that subjects who tend to process information through the prefrontal lobes of the brain tend to be more open to new information, and to be more politically liberal. Those subjects who tend to process information through the emotion-centers in the brain tend to be more politically conservative.

Several recent studies have explored various aspects of the apparent differences in how people perceive the same events and issues. An extensive 2012 international research project involving five different studies, thousands of participants, and two different cultures was coordinated by scholars from the University of Virginia and two universities in China. The study's report was published in *Personality and Social Psychology Bulletin* in 2014. It concludes that basic cultural thought styles may help explain why liberals and conservatives see political issues differently—that political differences and divisions are partly cultural divisions.

These researchers argue that liberal culture tends to be more individualistic, with looser social bonds, more emphasis on self-expression, and a priority on individual over group identities. They also conclude that liberalism is associated with cities, which are centers of self-expression and nonconformity. Conservatism, on the other hand, tends to be associated with rural areas, with more tightknit communities. Conservatism is also associated with interconnected groups, such as churches, fraternities, and the military.

"This study shows that the two sides in the 'culture war,' conservatives and liberals, really approach the world as if they came from two very different cultures," said study leader Thomas Talhelm, a University of Virginia doctoral candidate in cultural psychology. Of course, partisans on both sides believe different facts, use different economic theories, and hold differing views of history. But might the differences run even deeper? Do liberals and conservatives process the same set of facts with different cultural thought styles?

Yes, the study concludes. And it indicates that "political differences and divisions are partly cultural divisions, and they can be studied—and perhaps bridged—as such."[14]

Other behavioral research has found that certain emotions are more powerful than others and tend to lead to stronger reactions. Generally, negative emotions, such as fear, distrust, and anger, are stronger motivators than positive emotions, such as hope or pride. Even among negative emotions, researchers found that, while fear is one of the strongest motivators, anger is more likely to generate action. Fear causes many people to seek more information before they take action. Anger frequently moves people to act without seeking further information.

Another 2013 study, "Fear as a Disposition and an Emotional State: A Genetic and Environmental Approach to Out-Group Political Preferences," found that fear can play a very real role in influencing political attitudes on hot-button issues like immigration. The summary, published in the *American Journal of Political Science*, indicates that individuals genetically predisposed toward fear tend to have more negative opinions of people from other races and ethnic groups and tend to hold attitudes that are more anti-immigration and pro-segregation.[15]

Research and the Practice of Political Communication

None of this is to suggest that an effective political communicator needs to be an expert in behavioral science or cognition research. But the people who develop political messages are learning how to say things in a way that has the best chance of prompting their audience to do what they want. Research findings like those just discussed provide part of the background for the practices communicators use to be effective.

These are just a few theories and concepts to explain why certain words and phrases evoke predictable emotional responses in voters or potential voters, and to explain scientifically the impact that emotion has in political messages. But does this research—or any research—find that everyone who responds to certain stimuli in a certain way is a liberal or a conservative? Does it mean that all conservatives or all liberals will respond to certain kinds of messages in certain, predictable ways? Does it mean that all conservatives are more right-brained and that all liberals are more left-brained? Hardly.

Which brain lobe a person activates to process information is not a conscious decision, nor is it an innate and permanent physiological condition like the color of your eyes. Most people routinely use both the left and right lobes of their brains at different times. Yet people do tend to process more information in one side of the brain or the other. And Westen's neurological research indicates that different kinds of messages are more likely to be processed by different lobes of the brain. In terms of political communication, understanding what such research finds can provide insight into why certain kinds of political messages tend to be more resonant with particular individuals, and especially why political messages infused with emotional appeals seem to have more impact and memorability than messages relying on factual information alone.

Think about the messages we see and hear from different political perspectives. Are they intended to have particular impacts with particular people? Does understanding the way people receive and process information help political communicators develop more effective messages for target audiences? There's a phrase sometimes thrown around that certain political messages are "dog whistle" communication—only intended for certain people to hear. That may be an exaggeration, but let's take another look at the 2014 midterm (nonpresidential) election, described in more detail in Chapter 3. Although Republicans took control of both houses of Congress with huge margins and started talking about a "clear mandate from the American people," they benefited from the lowest voter turnout since 1943. Just over one-third of the voters—36.9 percent—came out to vote. It was what is called a "base" election, when turnout is dominated by the base of a party—activists and other highly motivated voters. In this election, Republicans targeted their base voters, and judging by the results, their base turned out. The Democratic base stayed home in droves. By and large, Democratic candidates ran away from their best potential issues and left the field to the Republicans' message: "Be afraid! Be very afraid!" Democrats allowed the Republican message to frame the election. Fear was an effective motivator for the voters.

In 2012, however, the dominant messages were about class warfare and suppression of voting rights. Democratic voters turned out and President Obama won reelection by five million votes.

Conclusion

> **Principle 3**: To be effective, communication has to be conveyed in words, phrases, signs, and symbols the audience understands, can relate to, and will accept.

Political communication has to break through the clutter of all the other messages most people receive in the course of a day so that it will be noticed and considered. It has to connect with the life of the average voter. And it has to touch on or relate to things people care about, such as the welfare of their family, their career, their financial security, their future, their community, or their values.

Notes

1. William Zinsser, *On Writing Well*, 7th ed. (New York: Harper-Collins Books, 2006), 7.
2. Ibid.
3. Donald Rumsfeld, Department of Defense news briefing, February 12, 2002.
4. "Grazing Fees: Overview and Issues," Congressional Research Service Report, June 2012.
5. Ibid.
6. John Zaller, *The Nature and Origins of Mass Opinion* (Cambridge, UK: Cambridge University Press, 1992).
7. Tony Schwartz, *The Responsive Chord* (Garden City, NY: Anchor Books, 1974), 96.

8. Drew Westen, "Neural Bases of Motivated Reasoning: An fMRI Study of Emotional Constraints on Partisan Political Judgment in the 2004 U.S. Presidential Election," *Journal of Cognitive Neuroscience* (November 2006): 1947–1958.

9. Drew Westen, *The Political Brain: The Role of Emotion in Deciding the Fate of the Nation* (New York: PublicAffairs, 2007).

10. Chris Mooney, *The Republican Brain: The Science of Why They Deny Science—and Reality* (Hoboken, NJ: Wiley, 2012).

11. Ibid., 111.

12. Darren Schreiber, Greg Fonzo, Alan N. Simmons, Christopher T. Dawes, Taru Flagan, James H. Fowler, and Martin P. Paulus, "Red Brain, Blue Brain: Evaluative Processes Differ in Democrats and Republicans," *PLOS ONE* (February 13, 2013).

13. Ibid.

14. T. Talhelm, Jonathan Haidt, Shigehiro Oishi, Xuemin Zhang, Felicity F. Miao, and Shimin Chen, "Liberals Think More Analytically (More 'WEIRD') Than Conservatives," *Personality and Social Psychology Bulletin* 41, no. 2 (2014): 250–267.

15. Peter K. Hatemi, R. McDermott, L. J. Eaves, K. S. Kendler, and M. C. Neale, "Fear as a Disposition and an Emotional State: A Genetic and Environmental Approach to Out Group Political Preferences," *American Journal of Political Science* 57, no. 2 (April 2013): 279–293.

5

Political Issues

Principle 4: Issues are vital tools in politics—to define yourself, divide the public, and provide ammunition against your opponent.

Cynics claim that elections are not about issues but instead are popularity contests, about who people like and do not like. Those cynics are wrong. Issues play a role in virtually every election. In fact, University of Washington professor of communication and political science W. Lance Bennett says issues become symbols, and symbols are "the basic units of most human communication." He says politicians and interest groups are preoccupied with how to represent real situations in the most favorable strategic terms. "Through the skillful use of symbols, actual political circumstances can be redefined."[1]

The Role of Issues

It is true that elections are mainly about intangibles and voter perceptions of the candidates. Can I trust them? Are they up to the responsibilities of office? Do they have any relevant experience?

Do they see things the same way I do? Such perceptions, however, are often shaped by what an official or candidate has done or said about issues. Will she act on issues as she says she will? Do we agree with her priorities? Does what he says convey intelligence and common sense? Is he serious and thoughtful? Issues grab people's attention. They give people something to rally around—either for or against. Governments exist to make decisions and act on issues. But in political communication, issues are just as important for what they tell the public about a candidate or elected official.

In an election campaign, the issues smart candidates talk about are products of their record, their familiarity with their constituency, and good public opinion research. Knowing and staying in touch with what is on people's minds in the district or state is indispensable. Communicators learn about and keep up with trends and public sentiment through informal research. If the public is focused on particular issues, trying to redirect their attention or introduce a new topic is at best an uphill battle. If the campaign is in a coastal area and the public is concerned about flooding and beach erosion, trying to get them to rally around legislation to save the desert tortoise is probably not going to bring people flocking to events.

Talking about an issue that a candidate or elected official has worked on or taken a position on before is easy. It is a lot tougher to introduce a new topic into the public dialogue, and it is seriously risky to start favoring something previously opposed or opposing something previously favored. People can have epiphanies, but changing positions on a hot issue can make the public skeptical and a candidate look shallow and opportunistic.

On broader issues, including national or international affairs, polling can tell the campaign or interest group how much the public knows about an issue and how they view it. That information is essential in crafting an effective message on that issue and searching for ways to connect the issue to the target audience or constituency.

Truly effective political communicators also use research to probe for weaknesses or potential weaknesses in their own issues and arguments. By identifying a weakness, they can often avoid pitfalls and, just as importantly, be prepared with effective responses or even deflections should the opposition attempt to exploit the weakness. Political support for issues can slowly erode. Issues themselves often evolve over time and in a number of ways. Sometimes the issues themselves change. Sometimes the issues don't change but support or opposition does. And, of course, perspectives on an issue can change with successes, failures, and other apparent indicators of effectiveness. Mounting cost figures can have a corrosive effect on support for an issue, especially if there are not accompanying markers of success.

Case Study: The War on Terror Becomes America's Longest War

Three days after the September 11, 2001, terrorist attacks on New York City and Washington, DC, Congress, reflecting suddenly massive public support, overwhelmingly passed an Authorization for the Use of Force in Afghanistan, aimed at defeating or destroying the al-Qaeda organization, which had used the country as a base, and at defeating the Taliban, who had given al-Qaeda sanctuary. Then, reflecting a slower evolution in public opinion, Congress passed a similar authorization in October 2002 for the invasion of Iraq, a country that had nothing to do with the 9/11 attacks but had been subsumed by the Bush administration into what it called the "Axis of Evil," a group of three nations that were fomenting terrorism and deserving of US invasion.

Chapter 3 explored the effective use of issue framing by the Bush administration to move public opinion on this issue from suspicion to support. Suffice it to say that backing for the war in Iraq waned markedly, if more slowly than might be expected, with the inescapable conclusion that the primary justification for invading—Saddam Hussein's Weapons of Mass Destruction—had not existed in nearly twenty years. Added to that, 4,500 US troops had been killed and the United States had spent more than a trillion dollars with no clear end in sight. The Iraq war became very unpopular, and the 2006 midterm election, in which Democrats made major gains in House and Senate elections, was largely a referendum on the Bush administration.

Issues as Cues

In today's political environment, highly partisan messages about issues are constantly being framed and inserted into the national dialogue by Republicans and Democrats in Congress, their respective party organizations, partisan or ideological interest groups, and the White House. These messages are then repeated and amplified as much as possible. According to a 2014 research study by Pew Research (described in more detail later in this chapter), the public is more polarized than it has been in twenty years, and this shift has changed the function of issue messages. No longer are they intended to convey information or focus public attention on the substance of government policy. The primary role of issue messages is to provide a cue about an individual's political alignment with one side or the other. Issues are litmus tests of loyalty. They indicate whether a particular politician is "with us or against us."

The time is long past when a Republican could be prochoice, favor even the least intrusive restrictions on air pollution from power plants or petrochemical refineries, or think that small steps to keep automatic weapons out of the hands of people with mental disabilities might be a good thing. The expression of such beliefs or positions is simply not allowed. Similarly, any Democrat is immediately suspect who thinks the nation's largest employers might be too heavily taxed, that burdensome and confusing environmental regulations can make it tough to do business, or that unfettered access to firearms really is a constitutional right.

In the 2012 Republican presidential primary campaign, then–Texas governor Rick Perry was roundly criticized and lost significant conservative support because he favored allowing undocumented immigrants in Texas to pay in-state tuition at state universities if they had lived in the state most of their lives and graduated from Texas high schools.

Mitt Romney spent the 2012 presidential campaign trying desperately to distance himself from his own creation: "Romney-care." As governor of Massachusetts, he had been instrumental in developing and enacting that state's highly successful health-care system, but that accomplishment became poisonous several years later because the national Affordable Care Act (also known as Obamacare) was partly patterned after it.

Sometimes, an issue changes—for example, one that was popular or at least supportable is poisoned by subsequent events or circumstances. After a near-disastrous rollout, Obamacare appeared to be running fairly smoothly by 2012, attracting more people than predicted, helping bring down health-care costs, and making health-care insurance, and with it improved care, possible for millions of Americans who previously could not afford it. Yet in several southern states with apparent majorities of Republican voters, incumbent Democratic US Senators ran and hid at the mere whisper of Obamacare, even those who voted for it in 2010.

When issues become partisan touchstones, the discussion is not about the substance of particular issues or policies, and it has nothing to do with building support for or opposition to them. Seldom if ever nowadays is there a rational, fact-based discussion or debate on the substance of the issues. The message is simply about who does and does not support them, about who is with us or against us.

In *The Nature and Origins of Mass Opinion*, cited in Chapter 4, John Zaller defined two types of political messages: persuasive and cueing. "Persuasive messages are arguments or images providing a reason for taking a position or point of view; if accepted by an individual, they become consideration." And a cueing message, according to Zaller, "carries contextual information about the ideological or partisan implications of a persuasive message."[2] The cueing message suggests relationships between an issue and an audience's political predispositions. Do such partisan messages fall on fertile soil?

2014 Pew Research Center Report

From January through March 2014, the Pew Research Center conducted its largest ever telephone survey on US political attitudes—10,013 adults. The survey found that "Republicans and Democrats are more divided along ideological lines—and partisan antipathy is deeper and more extensive—than at any point in the last two decades."[3]

The Pew Report found divisions are greatest among those the most active in the political process. "Partisan animosity has increased substantially over the same period. In each party, the share with a highly negative view of the opposing party has more than doubled since 1994." Most of these intense partisans believe the opposing party's policies "are so misguided that they threaten the nation's well-being."[4]

The study found the rise of ideological uniformity much more pronounced among the most politically active. Nearly four in ten (38 percent) politically engaged Democrats were consistent liberals, up from just 8 percent in 1994. The change among Republicans was less dramatic—33 percent express consistently conservative views, up from 23 percent in the midst of the 1994 "Republican Revolution." But a decade ago, just 10 percent of politically engaged Republicans had across-the-board conservative attitudes.

However, Pew found that, while "ideological silos" are now common on both the left and right, and many on both the left and the right think the outcome of political battles in Washington should be that their side gets more of what it wants, these sentiments are not shared by all—or even most—Americans.

> The majority do not have uniformly conservative or liberal views. Most do not see either party as a threat to the nation. And more believe their representatives in government should meet halfway to resolve contentious disputes rather than hold out for more of what they want. Yet many of those in the center remain on the edges of the political playing field, relatively distant and disengaged, while the most ideologically oriented and politically rancorous Americans make their voices heard through greater participation in every stage of the political process.[5]

How has this played out? If opposition to particular legislation is part of the Republican agenda, and the party's spokespersons talk about how wasteful the legislation is, claim it will suppress business expansion and job creation, and perhaps characterize it as liberal or even socialist, Republican activists and true believers across the country have no need to analyze the detailed provisions of the legislation to make a judgment. They have their cue from party spokespersons. And they are prepared to appraise elected officials and candidates based on support or opposition to that legislation.

Conversely, if Democratic leaders extoll the virtues of that same legislation and talk about how it will help create opportunities for upward mobility for low and middle income families, and how it reflects the country's long tradition of ensuring that everyone gets a chance at success and financial security, those are cueing messages to the Democratic faithful. They do not have to read the Congressional Budget Office fiscal analysis to decide that they are for the legislation and that the candidates and elected officials they support should also be for it.

Often, it's not a political party or its elected officials that provide cues for support or opposition to particular issues. When highly visible interest groups announce positions on various matters, many people do not bother to learn details. They have received a very credible cue from the interest group. When the Nature Conservancy, Clean Water Action, or the American Federation of Labor and Congress of Industrial Organizations (AFL-CIO) take a position on an issue, that's an unmistakable cue for many people. If the National Rifle Association, the US Chamber of Commerce, or Americans for Tax Reform announce their opposition or support for an issue, that also sends a clear cue to the public.

Political Pressure and Changing Issue Perspectives

In each election cycle, issues often have more to do with providing cueing messages about the character of candidates who support or oppose them than they do with building support or opposition to the issue itself. Sometimes, the competition to frame or define the issue is not between opposing political parties, but within the same party.

Case Study: Comprehensive Immigration Reform Versus Secure Borders

In December 2015, fourteen people were killed and twenty-two injured in an attack in San Bernardino, California, by a US-born citizen of Pakistani descent and his wife, a Pakistani-born legal resident of the United States, who were then killed in a shoot-out with police. The couple was purportedly "inspired" by Islamic terrorist organizations in the Middle East, although such inspiration is nearly impossible to substantiate or disprove.

The tragedy occurred during a crowded and heated Republican presidential primary contest. Not surprisingly, the issue of tightening restrictions on or even closing down immigration into the United States, especially to Muslim refugees, many of whom were fleeing violence in Syria and Iraq, instantly became a headline topic. The argument became loudly framed as a choice between keeping Americans safe from terrorist acts in their own communities and instituting blatantly "un-American" prejudice by denying entry into the United States based solely on religious faith.

Most congressional Democrats have favored a more comprehensive approach on immigration reform that addresses border security but also takes steps against unscrupulous employers who exploit undocumented workers. Such reform would create a path to earn legal status and citizenship for undocumented workers while requiring that they pay penalties, pay their taxes, and learn English before they can get in line.

In fact, comprehensive legislation—the Border Security, Economic Opportunity, and Immigration Modernization Act of 2013—was written and sponsored by the "Gang of Eight" in the US Senate, which included four Democrats and four Republicans, one of which was Marco Rubio (R-FL), a candidate in the Republican presidential primary. The bill passed the Senate on a 68-32 vote, but was never introduced in the House.

In the intense heat generated by the issue, Senator Rubio's support for such immigration reform became a liability among very conservative voters, and he abruptly changed course from his bipartisan legislative history. He began to campaign on the massive deportation of the estimated eleven to twelve million undocumented immigrants in the United States, and a more dramatic solution to security along the nation's southern border, including construction of a wall and huge increases in border patrol and law enforcement personnel deployed to the area. This was despite the fact that the number of illegal immigrants entering along the southern border had recently dropped precipitously due to shrinking employment opportunities in the United States. In fact, in some months, more people were crossing the border into Mexico than crossing from Mexico into the United States.

Since the issue became such a hot-button topic for warring camps of Republicans, most Democrats have been smart enough to simply shut up and allow Republicans to fight each other.

An abrupt about-face on issues is not that unusual when a political figure decides to run for a different office. Organizations, too, sometimes change their positions on major issues.

Case Study: Gun Safety Versus Gun Rights

For many years, the National Rifle Association (NRA) supported wider background checks for gun buyers. But following congressional passage of the 1994 Assault Weapons Ban, the NRA began to oppose background checks or any legislative proposal the association viewed as limiting or threatening the right to own guns in any way.

continues

Case Study: continued

In 2000, I was coordinating press events in Milwaukee, Wisconsin, for the Al Gore-Joe Lieberman presidential campaign during the final two weeks before the election. The gun control–gun rights debate had not been that visible during the campaign, although there was a definite contrast between the presidential candidates. Texas governor and Republican presidential candidate George W. Bush had signed a permissive concealed carry law in his state. Vice President Gore had supported Clinton administration initiatives including the assault weapons ban in 1994, and during the campaign Gore had expressed support for background checks for all gun show purchases, steps strongly opposed by the NRA and other gun rights groups.

Out of curiosity, I attended an NRA rally along with about 1,200 other people. I listened to the actor and NRA president Charlton Heston and the executive vice pesident Wayne La Pierre tell the crowd that the Democrats, especially Al Gore, were determined to take their guns away— including their hunting rifles.

On opening day of hunting season in October in Wisconsin, a flood of armed citizens head to the woods. This crowd, in a highly unionized area of the country, viewed any interference with their ownership of hunting rifles as a primal threat. The NRA's anti-Gore campaign was framed "Vote Freedom First," all about protecting the Second Amendment. It was a brilliant frame. Follow-up polling revealed that a large proportion of union workers, whose economic interests had always been aligned with the Democratic Party, voted Republican to protect their gun rights.

The NRA's continuing campaign to convince the public that the federal government is intent on confiscating their guns has reached and persuaded a lot of people. Longtime Cable News Network (CNN) political reporter and analyst Bill Schneider tells a story about conducting focus groups in West Virginia during the 2004 election. He said the focus groups were discussing which of two issues was a more important consideration in the election, health-care insurance or Second Amendment rights. Many participants felt that protecting the right to bear arms was paramount. When Schneider asked a woman, "Don't you consider health insurance when you vote?" she replied, "Mister, guns are our health insurance."[6]

By the 2012 election, the NRA had gotten a bit more shrill. This time, La Pierre tried to convince anyone who would listen that he had unassailable proof of President Obama's intention to violate gun rights in his second term, even to the point of confiscation. When it was pointed out that neither Obama nor anyone else in the administration had uttered a syllable about gun control in the previous four years, La Pierre simply claimed that the silence simply proved how crafty and underhanded Obama was.

The heated issue of significantly changing our system for providing health care did not just appear with the inauguration of Barack Obama in 2009. Sixteen years before, the Clinton administration had attempted to win public and congressional support for major changes in national health care. And between 1993 and 2009, the positions of many elected officials and many organizations changed dramatically.

Case Study: An About-Face on Health-Care Reform

In 1993, the Clinton administration pushed passage of comprehensive national health-care legislation, the Health Security Act. Developed by a task force headed by First Lady Hillary Clinton, the plan was immediately dubbed

continues

Case Study: continued

"Hillarycare" by opponents. Republican opposition was prompted and captured in a 1993 memo to Republican leaders from the newly formed policy group Project for the Republican Future led by William Kristol, neoconservative strategist and former chief of staff to Vice President Dan Quayle: "The Clinton proposal is also a serious political threat to the Republican Party. Republicans must therefore clearly understand the political strategy implicit in the Clinton plan—and then adopt an aggressive and uncompromising counterstrategy designed to delegitimize the proposal and defeat its partisan purpose." Kristol outlined the proposal's threat to Republican political prospects:

> Its passage in the short run will do nothing to hurt (and everything to help) Democratic electoral prospects in 1996. But the long-term political effects of a successful Clinton health care bill will be even worse—much worse. It will re-legitimize middle-class dependence for "security" on government spending and regulation. It will revive the reputation of the party that spends and regulates, the Democrats, as the generous protector of middle-class interests. And it will at the same time strike a punishing blow against Republican claims to defend the middle class by restraining government.[7]

During the debate, the conservative American Enterprise Institute proposed an alternative approach that included mandates requiring the public to buy health insurance as a matter of personal responsibility.

Yet in 2009, when Congress cobbled together the Patient Protection and Affordable Care Act, conservative organizations, including the American Enterprise Institute, lambasted the inclusion in the law of healthcare mandates requiring the public to buy healthcare insurance as a matter of personal responsibility.

Occasionally, an issue will mutate from broad and credible acceptance to a highly partisan dispute. In such instances, facts can take a back seat to ideology, and political positions can be based more on which political figures or organizations support or oppose the issue rather than the merits of the issue itself.

Case Study: Global Warming Versus Climate Change

According to the National Aeronautics and Space Administration's Global Climate Change website, "Multiple studies published in peer-reviewed scientific journals show that 97 percent or more of actively publishing climate scientists agree: Climate-warming trends over the past century are very likely due to human activities."[8]

For years, there was not a lot of argument about the facts. Global climatic patterns are, in fact, causing significant changes in weather phenomena, such as continually warming temperatures across the globe and rising sea levels. The battles were over remedies.

Then, in a 2002 memo to President George W. Bush entitled "The Environment: A Cleaner, Safer, Healthier America," Frank Luntz, whose work is cited in Chapter 3, applied his market research tools to the issue and found the term *climate change* to be perceived as much more benign and less threatening than *global warming*. Based on his research, the Republican Party began to use *climate change* in all its messaging.

Over the past ten years, economic forces behind the Republican agenda have begun to push back directly against the idea that human activity plays any part in global warming, and more recently, they have started to deny that global warming itself even exists. Notwithstanding that 97 percent of the world's climate scientists

continues

Case Study: continued

agree on the issue, the deniers' talking points have tried to make it sound like a toss-up debate. Conservative stalwarts like US Senator James Inhofe (R-OK), radio personality Rush Limbaugh, and some of the commentators on Fox News back them up, pointing to unusually heavy winter snowstorms in Minnesota and Wisconsin as proof that fears about global warming are groundless. Over a number of years, a growing segment of the Republican base have become climate change deniers and accept instead that the whole notion of global warming is a conspiracy pushed by the green energy industry.

The US Environmental Protection Agency (EPA), created in 1970, is the federal entity responsible for implementing and enforcing provisions of the 1970 Amendments to the Clean Air Act of 1967. In 2015, as part of the Obama administration's Clean Power Plan (CPP), the EPA introduced a voluntary program to provide participating states with emission rate credits for reducing greenhouse gas emissions by investing in renewable energy or energy efficiency measures by 2021.

According to the National Conference of State Legislatures, the CPP has emerged as a contentious issue among states, industry stakeholders, and environmentalists. Various research shows that the CPP is the most heavily litigated federal environmental regulation in US history. Governors, attorneys general, and environmental regulators have differed on its legality and whether to engage in legal action. As of early 2016, twenty-nine states and state agencies are in legal opposition to the rule, while eighteen states and Washington, DC, have filed motions in support.[9]

The campaign to discredit the concept of climate change as a human-made phenomenon has been highly effective, creating doubt in the minds of much of the public about the urgency for remedial actions by government. Only in the past three years, as more glacial melt, coastal flooding, and other once-rare climatic phenomena become more commonplace have public opinion surveys indicated that the number of climate change deniers is dropping precipitously.

Typical results can be found in the University of Texas (UT) at Austin Energypoll, conducted online between September 1 and 15, 2015, among 2,019 US residents age 18 and older.[10] According to the poll, 76 percent of respondents agreed that global climate change is occurring, up from 68 percent one year ago. Meanwhile, 14 percent disagreed and 10 percent were not sure. The level of agreement is the highest since the poll started asking the question in 2012.

"Political ideology continues to be the single greatest determinant of Americans' views on climate change," noted UT poll director Sheril Kirshenbaum. "The poll, now in its fifth year, reveals sharp political divisions among Americans on several prominent energy issues. For example, 90 percent of Democrats say climate change is occurring, compared with 59 percent of Republicans (up from 47 percent six months ago); 29 percent of Republicans say climate change is *not* occurring, compared with only 3 percent of Democrats."[11]

Issues as Symbols

Issues often become symbols for larger, sometimes intangible concerns. In this way, issues frequently become symbols of what's right or wrong with a politician, a political party, or a presidential administration.

In 1976, Jimmy Carter said, "I'll never lie to you," symbolizing a restoration of honesty in government following the Watergate scandal.

In 1980, Ronald Reagan made an issue of the Panama Canal, claiming that the United States built it, paid for it, and wasn't going to give it away. Overlooking the fact that the Panama Canal was located in another sovereign nation, the issue symbolized a denial of the assertion that the United States had become a weak and defenseless giant in the wake of the Iranian hostage incident and a failed rescue attempt.

In 1988, George H. W. Bush made an issue of Willie Horton, who committed rape and assault after being granted a weekend furlough from prison in Massachusetts. Willie Horton became a symbol for "soft on crime" liberals. The Bush campaign's Willie Horton ads also became a symbol for absolutely ruthless, win at all costs, twist-the-truth—and even racist—campaigns (see Chapter 8).

In 1992, the issue-symbol was President George H. W. Bush's apparent inability to connect with the economic problems of the average American ("It's the economy, stupid").

In 2000, the issue-symbol, following President Clinton's impeachment, was restoring honor to the Oval Office.

In 2004, the issue was the need for strong, unswerving leadership in a time of war, and the symbol became Senator John Kerry's quote, "I was actually for it before I was against it," and the word "flip-flopper."

In 2008, after two wars, thousands of Americans killed, and billions of dollars spent, the issue was a change in national leadership and national direction, symbolized by the word *Hope*.

In the 2010 midterm election, the issue was a government too large and intrusive, symbolized by the Affordable Care Act, which had so galvanized the Tea Party.

The 2012 election was decided, more than anything else, on which candidate was perceived as best able to relate to the challenges facing the average American. Mitt Romney's comment that 47 percent of the American people were dependent on the federal government and would therefore support President Obama, along with an investment portfolio that put him in the top 1 percent of Americans, made it hard for his campaign to portray him as "one of us" (see Chapter 3)

In all these situations, issues were used effectively, more to tell voters something about the candidates than to try to win converts on the issues themselves. The issues were symbols. They did not have to touch the voters' lives directly, but they had to make connections between the candidates and things the voters cared about: honesty, national pride, personal and family safety, and the necessity for empathy from political leaders.

Case Study: Abortion—From Substance to Symbol

In June 1971 in St. Louis, Missouri, two years before the US Supreme Court's *Roe* v. *Wade* decision, the Southern Baptist Convention (SBC), one of the nation's leading pro-life voices, adopted a resolution on abortion concluding:

> That we call upon Southern Baptists to work for legislation that will allow the possibility of abortion under such conditions as rape, incest, clear evidence of severe fetal deformity, and carefully ascertained evidence of the likelihood of damage to the emotional, mental, and physical health of the mother.

In its June 1974 convention, a year following the Supreme Court's *Roe* v. *Wade* decision, SBC adopted a resolution that included this language:

> That we reaffirm the resolution on the subject adopted by the messengers to the St. Louis Southern Baptist Convention meeting in 1971, and
> Be it further RESOLVED, that we continue to seek God's guidance through prayer and study in order to bring about solutions to continuing abortion problems in our society.

The SBC's 1976 Convention resolution concluded with:

> Be it further RESOLVED, that we also affirm our conviction about the limited role of government in dealing with matters relating to abortion, and support the right of expectant mothers to the full range of medical services and personal counseling for the preservation of life and health.

continues

Case Study: continued

That language was reaffirmed in 1977, 1978, and 1979. But in 1980, the SBC changed its position on the proper role of government in the question of abortion:

> Be it finally RESOLVED, that we favor appropriate legislation and/or a constitutional amendment prohibiting abortion except to save the life of the mother.

In 2012 and since, the abortion issue has been used by both sides to reach different constituencies. Even those without direct or personal experience hold strong opinions and attitudes. It has become a symbol.

For many Republicans, abortion symbolizes a perceived loss of a traditional American value: protecting the unborn. For many Democrats, restrictions on abortion symbolizes a continuing attempt by mostly male politicians to define and dictate women's reproductive rights.

The political debate surrounding a controversial issue can often generate strong feelings about the issue, even among those with no personal equity in the issue itself.

**Case Study: Same-Sex Marriage—
Issues Can Take Root in Unlikely Places**

Same-sex marriage or marriage equality is an example of an issue that has veered in direction and impact in just a few years (see Chapter 3). Today, many states and a number of federal courts around the country have determined that laws preventing same-sex marriages are a violation of individual rights under the US Constitution, and those laws have been overturned.

But as recounted in Chapter 3, not that long ago the issue was highly controversial and new state laws were still being enacted to ban it. In the 2004 general election, Democrats decided to focus on the issue, hoping to push the Republican Party and its candidates into an unpopular stand. Republicans called the bet and raised it, putting the issue on the ballot with referenda in several states and campaigning against same-sex marriage as an issue of traditional family values. The referenda calling for a ban passed in a number of states and reverberated in many others.

In 2004, I knocked on the door of a mobile home just outside Rapid City, South Dakota. I was a field volunteer for the John Kerry–John Edwards presidential campaign and for South Dakota senator Tom Daschle's reelection effort. My area included several working-class neighborhoods on the eastern edge of the city. Our marching orders were to go door to door, talk with residents, ask about their general impressions of the campaigns, and try to find out which issue or issues seemed to resonate most with them.

This particular door was answered by a woman who was quite personable and willing to talk about all the campaigns. Her first observation was that there seemed to be an endless barrage of political television commercials running at all hours every day, referring to heavy advertising by both presidential campaigns, plus independent political action committee spots on both sides, in addition to a hotly contested US Senate race and a congressional campaign.

When I asked which issue or issues seemed to be the most important and would probably make the most difference in her voting decision, she did not hesitate: "gay marriage."

I was a little startled. Gay marriage issues were on the ballot in a number of states, including South Dakota, but

continues

Case Study: continued

the issue had not been debated or even widely mentioned. After my initial surprise, I managed to say, "Oh, really. Why is that?"

She said that no one in her family was gay, and she did not think she knew anyone who was gay, but it was just one more example of how morals in the United States were deteriorating. She felt the government had no business putting its stamp of approval on something that was "just not right," and she simply could not vote for anyone who could support such a thing. Clearly, the issue had become a symbol for a society moving away from traditional values.

A little more than ten years later, the notion of marriage equality is widely accepted, particularly among 18- to 35-year-old voters—even Republicans. According to Pew Research, in July 2015, 55 percent of Americans supported same sex marriage and 39 percent opposed it. And in June 2015, the US Supreme Court settled the matter. In *Obergfell* v. *Hodges*, the court held that the freedom to marry someone of the same sex was a right protected by the Constitution, and not up to individual states or local jurisdictions to prohibit or authorize.

Conclusion

Principle 4: Issues are vital tools in politics—to define yourself, divide the public, and provide ammunition against your opponent.

As I stated at the beginning of this chapter, issues grab people's attention. They give people something to rally around—either for or against. They are often made into cues or symbols and can be used or framed to generate strong reactions among the public. Governments exist to deal with and make decisions about issues. But in political communication, issues are just as important for what they tell the public about a candidate, an elected official, or a political agenda.

Notes

1. W. Lance Bennett, *News: The Politics of Illusion*, 9th ed. (Chicago: University of Chicago Press, 2012), 102.

2. John Zaller, *The Nature and Origins of Mass Opinion* (Cambridge, UK: Cambridge University Press, 1992), 41.

3. Pew Research Center, "Political Polarization in the American Public," June 12, 2014, http://www.people-press.org/2014/06/12/political-polarization-in-the-american-public/.

4. Ibid.

5. Ibid.

6. Bill Schneider, personal communication with author, October 2014.

7. William Kristol, "Defeating President Clinton's Health Care Proposal," memorandum, Project for a Republican Future, December 2, 1993, https://www.scribd.com/document/12926608/William-Kristol-s-1993-Memo-Defeating-President-Clinton-s-Health-Care-Proposal.

8. National Aeronautics and Space Administration, "Global Climate Change," https://climate.nasa.gov/evidence/.

9. M. Condon and K. Durkay, "States' Reactions to EPA Greenhouse Gas Emissions Standards," February 10, 2016, http://www.ncsl.org/research/energy/states-reactions-to-proposed-epa-greenhouse-gas-emissions-standards635333237.aspx.

10. University of Texas at Austin Energypoll, "3 out of 4 Believe Climate Change Is Occurring; Views of Key Energy Issues Are Shaped by Partisan Politics," September 2015, http://www.utenergypoll.com/wp-content/uploads/2014/04/October-2015-UT-Energy-Poll-Final2.pdf.

11. Ibid.

6

Political Research and Communication Planning

Principle 5: Without the most comprehensive and accurate information possible, the aim and content of a communicator's most costly and time-intensive activities would be based on guesswork. But even with the best information, effective political communication rarely occurs without careful planning.

Research provides eyes and ears for public affairs communicators. Without a lot of information about public attitudes and voting behavior, decisions would be grounded in speculation. But because most public affairs communication has a distinct purpose and an unforgiving deadline, and nearly always a price tag, removing as much guesswork as possible is essential. Today's political campaigns require major dollars. In the 2014 general election, the average US Senate campaign cost about $10.5 million; a House campaign about $1.6 million. Many of the 2016 presidential campaigns spent millions in the primaries, and predictions were that the general election candidates would go over $1 billion. Why in the world would anyone try to raise or spend that kind of money without as much information as possible to direct its use?

Government and advocacy communications also need to be targeted to audiences that either support or could potentially support the communicator's position on an issue or policy, and that communication tends to be deadline driven. Learning as much as possible about the audience's existing attitudes about an issue, policy area, or related subject increases the chances that a message can be developed that reaches the right people and persuades them to take an action.

The best information in the world is not worth much unless it is put to good use. Effective political communication rarely occurs without careful planning, and it is in their planning that communicators put research to work. The second part of this chapter describes the importance and qualities of communication planning.

Political Message Development

Here are a few of the questions political communicators try to answer before they start cranking out messages:

- What's the environment in which we are trying to communicate?
- Who are the different groups or audiences?
- What issues or values do they care about?
- What "language" do they speak? How do they communicate about government issues, if at all?
- How and where do they get their information?
- Have they ever heard of our candidate or organization or issue?
- What do they think of our candidate or organization or issue?
- Are people likely to listen to what we have to say?
- Are they likely to believe it?
- Are there opposing viewpoints on our issue?
- Are opposing candidates or people with opposing viewpoints trying to reach the same audience with their messages?
- Why are we trying to reach these audiences? How can they help us advance our cause?

• What are the most effective ways to reach them with our message: News media? Radio, television, or print advertising? Speeches and rallies? Direct mail, e-mail, or online social media? Skywriting?

• Do we need to use different media to reach different audiences? Which media for which audiences? What words, phrases, or images will be most effective in getting our messages across to our target audiences?

• Do we need different messages to appeal to different audiences?

• How will we know if our message is reaching the audience we want?

• How do we know if our communication is having the result we want?

Most political communication takes place in a highly partisan, highly competitive environment. Whether messages are aimed at citizens to generate support for or opposition to a political issue or at voters to generate support or opposition toward a candidate, the stakes are high and so is the cost. Effective political messages need to be on point and on target. Knowing as much as possible about the background and environment in which they are working can give communicators a solid starting place to make other decisions—about exactly what messages they should try to communicate and why, about what specifically the target audience needs to be persuaded to do, and about what kinds of creative messages will have the most impact. Most of the answers come from conducting either formal or informal research and then applying the results to develop a logical sequence of information.

Informal research can be as simple as knowing the political environment in which the communicator is working—talking to people; asking questions; and reading newspapers, websites, and blogs that focus on local events and issues. It can also involve the brief or broad use of formal research tools, such as short interviews, focus groups at political events, or online questionnaires.

In contrast, formal political research, particularly statistically representative inquiry, is based on systematic data gathering. It relies on objective tools and methods to probe and sample public opinion and help the communicator analyze and evaluate the political or issue environment. It provides information to establish or confirm salient issues and match those issues to different subsets of the public. The findings and analysis from this research should also help a campaign decide which issues have the highest priority. Communicators don't have time to talk about everything. What issues are the most important to their target audiences?

The research findings can also help determine whether certain candidates, public officials, or surrogate spokespersons have credibility on particular issues. Professional or public service experience in a particular area can give someone a lot more authenticity when speaking about certain issues. Lawyers can speak with authority on legal matters. Previous military service lends a measure of credibility on military budget or national defense issues.

Gathering the information necessary for effective communication may seem daunting and complicated, but it's not particle physics. It just requires a logical, step-by-step approach.

Targeting the Message

Just as important as crafting the right message is making sure it gets to the right audience with sufficient repetition and reinforcement to persuade the undecided and motivate the committed. A communicator can fire the most effective bullets ever made, but they are a waste of time and money if they miss the target.

Determining who the various audiences are or should be for a message is fundamental. Communicators need to know who already supports their candidate or issue, or is likely to give support based on age, gender, profession, income level, past voting behavior, political activities or interests, organization memberships, and other relevant criteria. It is also necessary to identify the people who oppose the candidate or issue, or are likely opponents based on the same criteria used to identify supporters. And it is necessary to identify those who are undecided—people who have not yet made up their minds and might be persuaded to give support. These undecided citizens are the major focus of political communication. In nearly all campaigns, they determine who wins and who loses.

Once supporters are known, communicators can begin to figure out the most effective ways to reach them with a message to fire them up and motivate them. It is also essential to know how to reach undecided people with persuasive messages that can win them over.

What message should be conveyed to opponents or likely opponents? None. No message is likely to change their minds. Why waste time and resources? It is much more important to concentrate on getting supporters motivated and convincing whatever undecided voters there are.

The people communicators need to reach with campaign or public issue messages not only come from all backgrounds and education levels but also have decidedly different amounts of interest. Veteran public opinion researcher Dave Petts of Normington, Petts & Associates in Washington, DC, describes three levels of political interest:

1. *Activists*. They're not only open to information, they actively seek it out. These are campaign and issue volunteers and contributors.

2. *Partisans*. They seek out information, but view it through a partisan lens.

3. *Persuadables*. They are the target in nearly all general election campaigns. They are not walking political encyclopedias. They tend to be very busy with their lives and more passive observers of politics. But they will listen, make up their minds during a campaign, and they will vote.[1]

So, one of the essential uses of public opinion research in communication is to help identify the target audience or audiences and how to reach them. Another essential function is to help determine exactly what to say to the audience or audiences. The goal is not to make up or change a public official's or candidate's position on an issue based on what it looks like people want to hear, but rather to help focus the message on those parts or elements of the candidate's or official's position that will be the most compelling—that are most likely to motivate supporters and persuade the undecided.

Tools of Political Research

As Petts explains, "Imagine you are able to talk to every voter, but you only have 20 seconds. What do you say? What is the most compelling information? Your experience or résumé? Your stand on a particular issue? Something about the opposition? Do you say something different to men and women; young people and older voters? Identifying the handful of messages that are most compelling to these persuadable voters is the fundamental purpose of research."[2] Two basic kinds of research are available to communicators: quantitative and qualitative.

Quantitative Research

The most commonly used tools of political research have not .changed much over the years. However, the sophisticated application of research and data collection now yields information not even imagined a few decades ago, and techniques to draw scientifically representative samples are light years ahead of where they used to be.

Political surveys have been around since at least 1824, when a local straw poll in Harrisburg, Pennsylvania, predicted Andrew Jackson's presidential victory over John Quincy Adams. Modern public opinion polling, using samples of 1,000 to 1,200 people to statistically represent a much larger base, began when Elmo Roper predicted the election of Franklin D. Roosevelt in 1936 and again in 1940 and 1944.

That same basic methodology is used today for campaign benchmark surveys. The benchmark is a quantitative research instrument, which means its results are statistically representative of a much larger base of people. It is designed and conducted to provide a valid and useful strategic blueprint for the campaign. Inevitably, things change in the course of a campaign: mistakes are made, opportunities arise, situations and circumstances occur that could not possibly have been foreseen. But the benchmark survey, usually conducted well before a campaign begins, is intended to provide a basic overall direction. In fact, it may help determine if a particular candidate or issue has or can realistically gain the support necessary to win.

The benchmark survey generally requires a lengthy telephone interview, sometimes twenty to twenty-five minutes. Drawing a scientifically representative sample of the electorate to poll is critical to the credibility and value of the process. For national surveys, sample sizes typically range from 1,000 to 1,500 interviews. For statewide surveys, the usual range is 600 to 800 interviews. For congressional districts, samples from 400 to 500 interviews are the norm.

Objective questions are asked to probe and measure the public's level of awareness of particular candidates or public issues, positive or negative perceptions about those candidates or issues, and the current standing of a race:

- If the election were held today, would you be more likely to vote for (Candidate A) or (Candidate B)?

- Would extensive experience in Washington, DC, make someone better qualified for the position of _____?

- Would the experience of owning and operating a successful business in the community for eighteen years make someone better qualified for the position of _____?

- If you knew one of the candidates had supported (Issue A), would you be more or less likely to support that candidate?

- How important do you think (Issue B) is to the community/ state/nation?

- What issues are you most concerned about in the coming election?

Responses to these kinds of questions yield crucial information about whom the campaign needs to speak to, what issues the campaign needs to talk about, and how it needs to talk about them. This provides the campaign with a critical starting point to develop effective political messages.

Projective questions test the appeal of messages the campaign might communicate over the course of the election. The goal is to test voter reaction to different pieces of information, both positive and negative, about the candidates. It is an attempt to project where the race will be once the campaign dialogue becomes fully engaged. Every good benchmark poll includes a combination of objective and projective questions. This indicates not only where the race begins, but where it is likely to go.

Case Study: "Dewey Defeats Truman"

That was one of the most famous newspaper headlines in US history. On November 4, 1948, the *Chicago Tribune* published its early edition proclaiming that New York governor Thomas Dewey had defeated incumbent president Harry Truman. But it seems the newspaper's early edition went to press before all the ballots were counted, and despite all public opinion polling predicting a Dewey victory, Truman wound up winning by 4.4 percent. The urgency of the newspaper's own deadlines contributed to the error, but so did complacent attitudes at national polling organizations like Gallup and the Roper Poll.

First and foremost, "We stopped polling a few weeks too soon," said George Gallup Jr., cochairman of the Gallup organization. After three presidential elections dominated by Franklin D. Roosevelt in 1936, 1940, and 1944, national pollsters were not looking for surprises. "We had been lulled into thinking that nothing much changes in the last few weeks of the campaign," Gallup said.[3]

As we will discuss later, Gallup's caution from the 1948 election still applies today. Just because something worked in the past does not mean it will apply today.

Apparently there were also deficiencies in some of the polling methodologies used at that time. *Penn Math*, a research-oriented website sponsored by the Department of

Mathematics at the University of Pennsylvania, analyzed the statistical model that early public opinion polls used to draw samples that were supposed to mathematically represent an entire state or even the country.

All major polls were using what was believed to be a more scientific method for choosing their samples called *quota sampling*. Quota sampling is nothing more than a systematic effort to force the sample to fit a certain national profile by using quotas: The sample should have so many women, so many men, so many blacks, so many whites, so many under 40, so many over 40, and so on. The numbers in each category are taken to represent the same proportions in the sample as are in the electorate at large. The basic idea of quota sampling is on the surface a good one: Force the sample to be a representative cross-section of the population by having each important characteristic of the population proportionally represented in the sample.

The following problem was identified in the University of Pennsylvania case study: "No matter how careful one might be, there is always the possibility that some criterion that would affect the way people vote might be missed and the sample could be deficient in this regard. . . . An even more serious flaw is the fact that ultimately the choice of who is in the sample is left to the human element. Recall that other than meeting the quotas, the interviewers were free to choose whom they interviewed."[4]

Today, polling is dogged by low response rates, with the people who are contacted often declining to be interviewed. Despite this problem, virtually every aspect of public opinion research is miles ahead of where it was in 1948, with nearly everything in the opinion polling process digitized and additional layers of pinpoint accuracy and knowledge provided by microtargeting. (Microtargeting is discussed in Chapter 9.)

Tracking polls and brushfire polls are other forms of quantitative research commonly used by political campaigns. They provide a snapshot of the progress of the campaign once the race is under way. Unlike benchmark surveys, brushfire and tracking polls are much briefer—often just a few questions.

A brushfire poll is usually done fairly early in a campaign to check progress. It's also used to test new issues or to see if a particular message might be effective. This is especially helpful in testing the waters for a potential attack on an opponent or seeing if an opponent's attack message might be working.

Tracking polls are generally conducted late in a campaign and over several days or evenings. They're intended to do just as the name implies: track how the race is going as election day draws closer. The most common question is, "If the election were held today, would you be more likely to vote for (Candidate A) or (Candidate B)?"

Case Study: Getting a Wrong Number in the 2016 Election

The integrity of public opinion research and the reliability of political polling in particular are of vital interest to political communicators because they are the "eyes and ears" of the communication process. When the accuracy and methodologies of political research are called into question, communicators have an urgent need to understand and evaluate the circumstances.

In the wake of the 2016 presidential election, one of the most commonly heard questions across the country was, "How did all the polls get it wrong?" Despite a few claims that it was a matter of partisan pollsters, the reasons that nearly every public opinion survey pointed toward a Hillary Clinton victory on November 8 have more to do with changing communications technology and changing attitudes toward public opinion polling than any political bias. The answers are not simple, and the American Association for Public Opinion Research has an ad hoc committee combing through the details to determine exactly what went wrong and open the door to corrective strategies.

In the meantime, several articles by public opinion scholars may shed light on what happened—and why. According to Fairleigh Dickinson University political science professor Dan Cassino, writing in the *Harvard Business Review*,

> The basic problem—and the reason pollsters have been nervous about just this sort of large-scale polling failure—comes from the low response rates that have plagued even the best polls since the widespread use of caller ID technology. Caller ID, more than any other single factor, means that fewer Americans pick up the phone when a pollster calls. That means it takes more calls for a poll to reach enough respondents to make a valid sample, but it also means that Americans are screening themselves before they pick up the phone.[5]

As long as people who refuse to pick up the phone for a pollster are a representative sample of the overall population—as long as their refusals are for random reasons—there's no problem, because people who *do* pick up the phone are also a representative sample. That just means the pollster has to make more phone calls to build an acceptable database.

The problem occurs when particular groups, such as evangelicals or conservatives, systematically exclude themselves from polls at higher rates than the overall public. Pollsters know that African Americans are less willing to participate in telephone polls than white Americans;

continues

Case Study: continued

that men are less likely than women. Therefore, statistical steps can be taken to ensure that the sample base remains representative. But if exclusion reflects characteristics that aren't commonly measured on polls or that can fluctuate, like church membership and political preferences, the problem is more complex.

In a November 9, 2016, *Pew Research Center* article, Andrew Mercer, Claudia Deane, and Kyley McGeeney explored this phenomenon of "nonresponse bias," which occurs when certain groups of people systematically do not respond to surveys despite equal outreach to all parts of the electorate.

> We know that some groups—including the less educated voters who were a key demographic for Trump on Election Day—are consistently hard for pollsters to reach. It is possible that the frustration and anti-institutional feelings that drove the Trump campaign may also have aligned with an unwillingness to respond to polls. The result would be a strongly pro-Trump segment of the population that simply did not show up in the polls in proportion to their actual share of the population.
>
> Some have also suggested that many of those who were polled simply were not honest about whom they intended to vote for. The idea of so-called "shy Trumpers" suggests that support for Trump was socially undesirable, and that his supporters were unwilling to admit their support to pollsters.[6]

A third possibility involves the way pollsters identify likely voters. "Pollsters develop models predicting who is going to vote and what the electorate will look like on Election Day. This is a notoriously difficult task, and small differences in assumptions can produce sizable differences in election predictions."[7] The writers suggest, for example, that a distinctly unenthusiastic 2016 Democratic electorate may have stayed home in droves and wreaked havoc with predictions.

Pollsters and political analysts need to identify what went wrong so they can prevent a recurrence and build models that account for them. But unless they find a way to fix the underlying issue of low response rates, it's not certain that they'll be able to. Without strong polling, the public and the markets won't know what's likely to happen and candidates won't know where to put resources to have the maximum effect.

As the Pew Report article concluded, "The role of polling in a democracy goes far beyond simply predicting the horse race."[8]

Qualitative Research

Qualitative research also plays an important role in helping political communicators gain information and understanding. Such studies are not meant to generate statistically representative data reflecting a much larger base of people, but rather to provide a deeper and more personal reaction to words, phrases, images, or advertising.

The most common tool is the focus group. Focus groups are open-ended discussions with as few as six participants, usually led by a trained facilitator with an agenda of particular questions and issues to probe. Focus group participants are usually selected from lists of various target audiences, contacted by a campaign, and asked to participate. The campaign is looking for reactions from particular target groups so they do not have to be drawn from a scientifically representative sample weighted to accurately reflect the entire electoral base.

Typically, focus groups discuss candidates in a particular race and are encouraged to share impressions and feelings about candidates or the campaign. They are asked about particular issues and, again, encouraged to share and interact about likes, dislikes, and impressions related to each issue. Frequently, the facilitator will suggest certain language that might be used to describe or discuss a particular issue, and then gauge how individuals in the group react. Sometimes, the group will be shown printed versions of verbiage or images and encouraged to respond.

Focus groups are often used to gauge reactions to proposed ads. Mock-ups, television scripts, images, characters, storyboards, or even rough-cut videos are presented for reaction and comment. The facilitator will probe for detail.

- What did you think of _____?
- Was that statement believable?
- How did the candidate come across to you in the spot?
- Was the language or imagery too strong?

In this kind of qualitative testing, the sessions are recorded and copious notes taken about participant reaction, about the language they use when discussing candidates or issues, or in their comments about ads and commercials. These notes and recordings can are then studied by the researchers for patterns or to substantiate impressions. Frequently, the group sessions are viewed from behind one-way windows by communicators so they can witness nonverbal reactions, such as facial expressions or body language, as well as comments; by staying out of sight, they can avoid exerting even subtle influences on participants just by their presence.

If a focus group turns thumbs down, many potential political print ads and campaign television spots undergo major alteration or are scrapped. And some of the language focus group participants use may find its way into subsequent communication, because campaign communicators have learned what people think and how they talk about issues.

Another form of qualitative research—a combination of qualitative and quantitative research—is Internet ad testing. Groups of 100 to 200 voters are selected to watch TV ads and provide their reactions. They are usually members of a prescreened panel who have agreed to participate in such studies. Typically, they fill out a survey prior to viewing the ad and are then asked additional questions after seeing the ad. Their feedback provides campaign decisionmakers with more reliable information about ad content than smaller focus groups do because the sample size is larger and voters are not swayed by the opinions of other participants in focus groups. Like all qualitative forms of research, it has drawbacks, but its use in statewide and national elections is increasing.

Using the Right Research the Right Way

Misusing research may be hazardous to your campaign. This warning should be required at the top of every piece of public opinion research. Research does not provide answers. Research provides information to use in creating answers. Taking raw data and proclaiming, "Aha!" can lead to public communication that would put strong coffee to sleep.

Case Study: The Patient Protection and Affordable Care Act or Obamacare?

In the 2009 public debate on the Patient Protection and Affordable Care Act, the White House and congressional Democrats looked at their research and determined that people supported the broad goals of health-care reform. Therefore, their messaging talked about "bending the cost curve," doing away with coverage limitations due to preexisting conditions, and making health-care more accessible for thirty-one million Americans who had not previously been able to afford it.

Republicans, on the other hand, used findings from their research as raw material in creating their messages. While

continues

Case Study: continued

Democrats were citing statistics and fiscal impacts, Republicans were busy warning about the government takeover of 16 percent of the economy and "death panels" of Washington bureaucrats deciding who would and would not get health care. Goodbye, Granny! The Democratic message sounded like a financial audit report, while Republicans were simply scaring the hell out of anyone who listened.

Republicans also framed the issue as *Obamacare*, even though President Obama and the White House had decided to leave it to Congress to develop the specific reform package. It was widely referred to as Obamacare even before the reform package really took shape. There were five significantly different versions of the legislation under active consideration in Congress, but it had already been branded by opponents. This name, picked up and used initially by the media in its news coverage, inexorably tied the issue to positive and negative perceptions of President Obama himself.

Guess which message a lot of people heard. Guess which message penetrated. Guess which messages were audience-tested to determine what words and phrases would have the most impact.

The Message Police

In many campaigns, the researcher's job is not over when the political message is devised, tested, and targeted to the right audience. The researcher, or pollster, then becomes the message police, ensuring that all communication stays "on message." (Recall from Chapter 2 that message discipline was a key tenet of the Republican Revolution.)

Why is staying on message important? A campaign can only communicate a handful of messages, meaning it has a limited number of shots at the voter's consciousness, so it makes sense to try to be sure every message counts. One of the ways to do that is to work key messages of the campaign into every communication, whether it is from the candidate or campaign spokesperson, or from surrogates who have been authorized to speak for the campaign.

Voter Identification

There's another form of collecting, organizing, and analyzing data used primarily in election campaigns. Rather than surveys and focus groups to identify patterns and trends or to probe for reactions to words or images, it involves capturing and using existing data about individuals, particularly individual voters. The goal is to allow a campaign to target organizational as well as communication resources as efficiently and accurately as possible.

Why? According to the 2010 Census, there are 316 million citizens in the United States. As of 2012, roughly 146 million citizens were registered to vote. About 31 percent identified themselves as Democrats, 27 percent as Republicans, and 40 percent as independents. (These numbers change from year to year, even from month to month, and the percentages vary widely among states and congressional districts.)

Here's the point: Most campaigns know that not everyone across the country or state or county or election district is going to vote for their candidate, so why waste more resources than necessary reaching out to people unlikely to vote their way? Why waste any more resources than necessary reaching out to people who most likely aren't going to vote at all? Why waste any more resources than necessary reaching people who identify themselves as members of your party if voter sign-in lists from previous elections show they don't actually show up on election day?

Mass media cannot be targeted to reach only Democrats or only Republicans or only undecided voters—that's why it's called mass media—but some targeting can be done by using viewer demographics: age, gender, marital status, household income, education, and so on. Assumptions can be made about which of these demographic groups tend to be the likely voters of a particular party, but they're assumptions. Waste is inevitable. The goal is to keep it to an absolute minimum.

Traditionally, an election campaign has needed to identify three large blocs of voters:

1. Base supporters, with a pattern of voting for that campaign's candidate or political party.

2. Opposing voters, with a voting pattern of support for the other side.

3. Undecided voters, not aligned with a particular candidate or either party, but likely to vote. They haven't made up their minds and seem to be open to persuasion.

The important blocs to a campaign are base supporters and the undecided. As the party identification numbers above show, base supporters seldom represent a majority of potential voters in most elections. So, to win, campaigns have to get their base voters to the polls *and* win over enough of the undecided voters to reach 50 percent plus one. Not very precise. Not very efficient. Campaigns wind up paying for a lot of people to see or hear their message who are not likely to vote for their candidate.

Organizationally, there are two main methods to reach out to targeted voters: individually by telephone and direct mail, or in geographic groups by election precinct. In many elections, especially local, election precincts have been the smallest workable political subdivisions in which to analyze voting behavior and set priorities for door-to-door candidate walks, canvassing, and other get-out-the-vote (GOTV) activities.

Major Changes in Voter Identification and Targeting

Over the past few elections, two factors have profoundly changed voter targeting nationally and in congressional districts. First, in today's highly partisan political environment, more people than ever are aligned with one party or the other or one candidate or the other. There have not been as many independent or undecided voters. And because the proportion of committed voters is higher—sometimes even a majority of the likely vote or very close to it—more campaign resources can and should be focused on getting committed voters to the polls on election day. In the presidential elections of 2004, 2008, and 2012, and in the 2010 midterm, the campaign that got the larger proportion of its base supporters out to vote won.

Case Study: 2004 Bush Campaign Base-Voter Strategy

In the 2004 presidential election, pollster Matthew Dowd was analyzing data for President George W. Bush's reelection campaign and noted that the undecided vote, usually about 20 percent of the electorate, had shrunk to only 7 percent. In other words, the vast majority of likely voters were aligned; they had already made up their minds.

Dowd ran the numbers and concluded that the Bush campaign could win a majority of the undecided vote and still lose the election. But more importantly, the campaign could win the election without carrying the undecided vote by focusing resources on maximizing the campaign's base turnout—their committed voters. This was an unprecedented change in voter targeting.

"Nobody had ever approached an election that I've looked at over the last 50 years, where base motivation was as important as swing, which is how we approached it," Dowd said. "We didn't say, 'Base motivation is what we're going to do, and that's all we're doing.' We said, 'Both are important, but we shouldn't be putting 80 percent of our resources into persuasion and 20 percent into base motivation,' which is basically what had been happening up until that point."[9]

continues

Case Study: continued

So, the Bush campaign's first priority changed from trying to persuade undecided people to vote to reelect President Bush to motivating people who had already decided to
vote for him to get to the polls and vote. That changed the
nature of the message being disseminated.

"Obviously that decision influenced everything that
we did," Dowd recounted. "It influenced how we targeted
mail, how we targeted phones, how we targeted media,
how we traveled, the travel that the president and the vice
president did to certain areas, how we did organization,
where we had staff. All of that was based off of that, and
ultimately, thank goodness, it was the right decision."[10]

The second major advance in the use of technology is in the
ability of campaigns to more accurately pinpoint likely voters by
geography and particular issues. Campaigns do so by data mining,
which in turn allows microtargeting. These techniques are discussed in detail in Chapter 9, but in general, both are based on
breathtaking advances in technology that have enabled the collection, organization, analysis, and use of vast amounts of data about
individuals.

The Future of Public Opinion Research: What's Ahead?

The techniques, sophistication, and accuracy of public opinion
research used in political communication have gone through a
major evolution since Harry Truman's 1948 reelection. Telephone
surveys largely replaced in-person surveys in the 1970s and
1980s. They were more cost-effective and highly accurate. Shared
service lines had disappeared, and more than 95 percent of all

households had telephones with a unique telephone number. Response rates of people willing to talk to an interviewer or complete surveys was around 60 percent, lower than in-person interviews but still high enough to be statistically representative of the larger electorate.

The Decline in Response Rates

Beginning in the 1990s and accelerating since, response rates have collapsed into single digits as fewer and fewer people are willing to take the time to participate in surveys. Many with caller ID are unwilling to take the polling call. Complicating the process even more, different demographic groups now have different response rates. For example, middle-aged and older voters in rural areas are considerably more likely to participate in a survey than younger voters in high-density urban areas. This can result in skewed samples, unrepresentative of the broader electorate. The Romney campaign in 2012 was shocked on election night to see exit polls showing an electorate as young as the one that propelled Barack Obama to victory in 2008. Romney's 2012 polling did not indicate younger voters would vote in the same numbers as they had four years earlier. It appears likely that the differences in response rates, something the Obama campaign carefully considered, played a role in the Romney campaign's surprise.

In the short run, distortions in sampling accuracy caused by low and differing response rates will continue to plague both academic researchers and campaign professionals. And according to researcher Dave Petts, "It is likely that Internet-based platforms will ultimately replace telephone surveys, just as telephone surveys largely replaced in-person interviews 40 years ago. We are moving quickly toward a day when access to the Internet will be as ubiquitous as telephones were in the 1970s. Public opinion research is being forced to evolve just as quickly."[11]

With the continuing decrease in response rates for surveys, many more telephone calls are required to generate a sample large enough to be statistically representative. The effect of this phenomenon is to drive up the cost of conducting telephone polls.

"Hyperfocusing" on Polls

In today's political environment, it is nearly impossible to read, hear, or watch news coverage of any election campaign that does not report where competing candidates stand in public opinion surveys. Years ago, campaigns would share poll results with the news media—if the results were favorable for that campaign, of course. But relative polling position was not always the first topic of a political news story. Now, particularly in larger campaigns, the media themselves have become major consumers of public opinion surveys. News stories focusing on the latest poll results are constant headline news items and cited in more and more campaign coverage. There is nothing inherently wrong or misleading about this practice. If the polls are conducted correctly and professionally, the results should be accurate within an acceptable margin of error. The problem is that few in the media understand or appreciate the limits of statistical accuracy in polling, and even fewer take the trouble to explain those limitations to their audiences. The danger is that this leaves many in the audience with the impression that such polling should be infallible, and that the polls or the pollsters must have been biased or incompetent if the final results do not match poll results exactly.

However, the larger problem is that constant poll results become the entire story of the campaign. The vast bulk of news coverage focuses on the "horse race" aspect in place of more in-depth scrutiny or substantive comparisons about candidates and issues.

Communication Planning

Before he became the thirty-fourth president of the United States, Dwight D. Eisenhower wore the five stars of a General of the Army. In World War II, he commanded the D-Day landings on the beaches of Normandy, the invasion of Europe on June 6, 1944. It was the largest, most complex, and one of the most successful military operations in the history of the world. It took months and months, thousands of people, and unbelievable logistics and details to plan. In later years, recalling everything that went into the amazing accomplishment, Eisenhower summed it all up with, "Plans are nothing. Planning is everything."

The Planning Process

In political communication, if you do not have a precise idea of where you are trying to go, you are most likely going nowhere. Whether the intent is to communicate about a candidate or an issue or to convey messages to or from a congressional committee or other decisionmaking body, to particular blocs of voters, or to the public at large, it is important to remember that communication is a process, not an event. As with any logical process, there is a series of steps to follow:

1. Communicators need to consider exactly what they need to say to exactly whom and exactly how and when they need to reach them.
2. They should figure out exactly how much their communication effort is going to cost and where the money will come from.
3. They need to determine how they will know if they are reaching the people they need to reach and how they will assess if their message is having the desired effect.

Communicators who do not answer these questions before they start creating messages are committing first-degree communication malpractice. In all probability, their communication campaign will be a dud, and few people will notice—except of course the candidate or organization for which they are trying to communicate.

In political campaigns, like every other kind of marketing, effective communicators try to take careful aim in everything they do. Shooting from the hip may result in powder burns where they are least wanted. Unforeseeable circumstances, crises, or opportunities always arise during the course of a campaign, so the best course is to plan for everything that can be planned for—and remain prepared.

In marketing and public relations, several nine-step and ten-step strategic planning processes are commonly used and taught.

There are also abbreviated planning models, such as ROPE (Research–Objectives–Program–Evaluation) and RACE (Research–Action–Communication–Evaluation). But a political campaign requires a more detailed planning model because campaigns are about details—about considering as many possibilities, angles, and contingencies as the communicators can imagine. Most planning processes, no matter what they are called, have the same basic steps. For purposes of elections, I have attempted to synthesize the essentials of political communication planning into a model.

Helfert's Easy, Logical Planning Model for Elections, or HELP ME!

   I. Conduct situation analysis.
      A. Who are we? Who is our candidate? Why is our candidate running? (Include history, qualifications, and relevant current or previous offices.)
      B. What is the political environment? What are the characteristics of the state, district, city, or ward? (Include population demographics, political party profile, and voting history.)
      C. Are there overwhelming or obvious attitudes or behavior trends?
   II. Conduct research. (Campaign research is discussed in detail earlier in this chapter.)
      A. Even smaller campaigns do informal research. Frequently, it is borrowed from or shared with other campaigns.
      B. Different types of research are used for different purposes at different times in a campaign:
        1. Polling, such as a baseline public opinion survey, is quantitative, statistically projectable, and representative. The ultimate goal of any benchmark survey is to provide the campaign with a strategic blueprint that will last for the duration of the campaign and measure the saliency of issues and attitudes.

2. Focus groups are qualitative and not statistically projectable or representative.

3. Tracking polls are very small sample telephone polls, usually conducted over several successive evenings to track movement (e.g., how independents are breaking).

III. Use the research. (Identify the audience we must reach to win.)
- A. What groups are for us?
- B. What groups are persuadable (undecided)?
- C. What do they care about?
- D. What do we need to tell them to win them over?
- E. What will motivate them to actually vote?
- F. Is that enough to reach 50 percent plus one?

IV. Set campaign objectives. (How are we going to win?)
- A. Can we reach the voting groups or blocs we need?
- B. How can we tell them what we need in order to win them over and get them to vote?
- C. How much money will it require and how are we going to obtain it?

V. Develop campaign strategies.
- A. Have a media plan.
- B. Decide on travel and events.
- C. Find surrogates. (Who else can speak for us that people will listen to?)
- D. Line up endorsements. (What individuals and groups will be credible and help sway our audience?)

VI. Develop tactics to implement strategies. (What specific steps will be taken to make the strategies happen?)

VII. Establish a campaign timeline—not just for the overall campaign but for each step, including fundraising. (Will we have the money to buys ads, do direct mail, and so on? Will we have it when we need it?) This will usually be back-timed from election day, and back-timed from each event.

VIII. Develop an overall campaign budget—including a detailed communication budget.

IX. Conduct the campaign.

X. Monitor the progress of the campaign. Measure and
   evaluate as it proceeds.
   A. Use measurements such as tracking polls, media polls,
      and news coverage.
   B. Make changes as needed or as opportunities appear.
   C. Did we win? (Or, did we come close? Did we win phase
      one and set the stage for phase two? Or, did we lose?
      Why? Where do we go from here? Do we try again?)

Media Planning

Any organized effort intending to use media to communicate a
message needs and deserves a detailed plan. The plan should spell
out how media will be used, how it will be coordinated, how it
will be timed, and how it will be paid for.

Deciding how the campaign will use media, and which media at
what time, is critical. This includes decisions about the following:

Paid advertising
  • Television spots (mass or targeted audience)
  • Radio spots
  • Print ads
  • Web ads/pop ups
  • Signage/bumper stickers
  • Lapel stickers
  • Robo calls

Generated (free) media; news coverage; earned media
  (reaching voters through the media)
  • News releases
  • News conferences
  • Interviews/Statements
  • Speeches
  • Debates
  • Editorial boards

Direct voter communication (individually targeted)

- Speeches
- Rallies
- Door-to-door canvassing
- Phone banks
- New media
- Website
- E-mail
- YouTube
- Myspace
- Facebook
- Twitter
- Flickr

Third-party communication

- Endorsements or attacks (527 political organizations)
- Surrogates
- Social networking

Paid media, the campaign's advertising, is not cheap. Even free media is not totally free. Someone has to write news releases, fact sheets, and the other necessary tools; coordinate news conferences; and be available to talk with the news media—and such people usually want to be paid something for their efforts.

A media timeline should coordinate how the ad campaign will work. What day of which week is the television advertising going to start? How about radio? Web ads? Direct mail? Will the various media be coordinated so they support one another? If a particular ad or mail piece is going to be used on a particular date, when does it need to be written, designed, produced or printed, and ready to go?

Even an issue advocacy campaign relying on organization members or volunteers will need to be coordinated. What are the key dates to conduct activities? When is the committee hearing on the legislation you are interested in? When does the legislation go to the floor for a vote? When is the regulatory committee holding its hearing on your issue?

Along with decisions about which media to use and how, and when to use them most effectively, are decisions about what budgets will be required. Even the most basic elements of campaign communication—signs, lapel stickers, and bumper stickers, which are fundamental to generate visibility or name identification—are not inexpensive to design, print, and distribute. The money must be raised and available when needed.

If an issue advocacy campaign is planning to bring people to the capitol or city hall for a rally or to conduct office visits with elected officials, how are people getting there? Rallies usually involve sound systems and probably flyers. They are not terribly expensive, but there is a cost.

In some low-budget campaigns, costs may determine which media are used and which activities are realistic. In nearly every case, there are up-front costs associated with production and coordination requirements. Considering and making decisions about what, how, how much, and when are essential.

Conclusion

> Principle 5: Without the most comprehensive and accurate information possible, the aim and content of a communicator's most costly and time-intensive activities would be based on complete guesswork. But even with the best information, effective political communication rarely occurs without careful planning.

This chapter opens with the words, "Research provides eyes and ears for public affairs communicators." This is true for election campaigns, policy communication from governments, and advocacy communication to governments. All three are aimed at generating public support or opposition toward a candidate or an issue. The more the communicator knows about relevant public opinions and attitudes, the more effective the communication can be. Without such information, essential decisions about what to say to whom are guesswork.

Once research has provided information to help the communicator develop the most effective messages, identify who would be most responsive to those messages, and ascertain the most effective means to reach those people with the appropriate messages, all that knowledge must be organized into a communications plan. The plan needs to detail what is being said to whom, through what medium, when it needs to be said, and what that communication will cost.

Notes

1. Dave Petts, synthesized from his classroom comments.

2. Ibid.

3. George Gallup Jr., quoted in Will Lester, "'Dewey Defeats Truman' Disaster Haunts Pollsters," *Los Angeles Times*, November 1, 1998, http://articles.latimes.com/1998/nov/01/news/mn-38174.

4. *Penn Math*, Department of Mathematics, University of Pennsylvania, "Case Study 2: The 1948 Presidential Election," https://www .math.upenn.edu/~deturck/m170/wk4/lecture/case2.html.

5. Dan Cassino, "Why Pollsters Were Completely and Utterly Wrong," *Harvard Business Review*, November 9, 2016, https://hbr.org /2016/11/why-pollsters-were-completely-and-utterly-wrong.

6. Andrew Mercer, Claudia Deane, and Kyley McGeeney, "Why 2016 Election Polls Missed Their Mark," Pew Research Center, November 9, 2016, http://www.pewresearch.org/fact-tank/2016/11/09/why-2016-election -polls-missed-their-mark/.

7. Ibid.

8. Ibid.

9. Matthew Dowd, PBS *Frontline* interview, "2004: The Base Strategy," April 12, 2005.

10. Ibid.

11. Dave Petts, from his classroom comments.

7

Political Speeches

Principle 6: The spoken word has always been a primary channel for political communication. It still is.

For most of the past 2,500 years, leaders and would-be leaders have relied on the spoken word to communicate with the public. Their ability to influence an audience has been based on a shared meaning of words and phrases. That common understanding enabled the evolution of nations and societies and the development of the institutions that held them together.

In the long march toward American democracy, from Magna Carta in 1215 to the US Constitution in 1789, a shared meaning of words and phrases defined the terms and conditions under which our forebears agreed to live. That common understanding remains central to our ability to function as a society and make our political system work. Our government, our laws, and our processes of selecting leaders rest on our common understanding and acceptance of the meaning of words and phrases: on political rhetoric and communication.

The Purpose and Practice of US Political Speeches

From the nation's beginnings, as now, political speeches have had two main functions: to persuade the audience either that a certain public policy is the best or worst solution to a problem, or that a certain candidate, political party, or agenda is preferable to the alternatives. In both cases, the speech usually attempts to get the audience to take a prescribed action that supports or opposes a policy, party, agenda, or candidate.

Even with all the contemporary channels of communication, public speaking remains an essential part of a public official's or candidate's ability to communicate with the public. In today's communication environment, the hallmark of effective political rhetoric is simplicity, directness, and—the speaker hopes—a pithy, memorable phrase or two. It doesn't always happen.

US Political Oratory at Its Best

Political communication has occasionally soared, comforted, and consoled, sometimes putting momentous events into context:

> that from these honored dead we take increased devotion to that cause for which they gave the last full measure of devotion— that we here highly resolve that these dead shall not have died in vain—that this nation, under God, shall have a new birth of freedom—and that government of the people, by the people, for the people, shall not perish from the earth.[1]

In the Gettysburg Address, in two or three minutes—272 words—Abraham Lincoln not only dedicated a plot of ground in Pennsylvania as a cemetery, he gave lasting definition to the purpose of a bloody war in which Americans were killing Americans in a struggle for the ultimate soul of the nation.

In the depths of the Great Depression, with widespread business closures, millions of Americans out of work, and a national sense of hopelessness, Franklin Delano Roosevelt delivered a political message to the 1932 Democratic National Convention calling for a fundamental change in the role of government, and offering the public a ray of hope and optimism, something in very short supply for most Americans at that time. "I pledge you, I pledge myself, to a new deal for the American people."[2]

In his inaugural speech a few months later, Roosevelt began a series of pep talks to the American public, trying to rouse people from years of despair: "This great nation will endure as it has endured, will revive and will prosper. So, first of all, let me assert my firm belief that the only thing we have to fear is fear itself—nameless, unreasoning, unjustified terror which paralyzes needed efforts to convert retreat into advance."[3]

In 1961, young, charismatic John F. Kennedy sought to evoke a sense of security and idealism and to challenge a generation to serve their country and the world: "And so, my fellow Americans: ask not what your country can do for you—ask what you can do for your country. My fellow citizens of the world: ask not what America will do for you, but what together we can do for the freedom of man."[4]

One of the most electrifying advocacy speeches ever delivered took place on the steps of the Lincoln Memorial on a hot August day just two and half years later. A young Atlanta, Georgia, preacher and civil rights activist—Martin Luther King Jr.—was speaking to a rally of 250,000 people and to a national audience, trying to reconnect the conscience of the public with the constitutional promise of equality for all Americans. And he was trying to spur a hesitant Kennedy administration and reluctant Congress to take action:

> I have a dream that one day this nation will rise up and live out the true meaning of its creed: "We hold these truths to be self-evident, that all men are created equal."
> I have a dream that one day on the red hills of Georgia, the sons of former slaves and the sons of former slave owners will be able to sit down together at the table of brotherhood.[5]

There have been discussions ever since about whether King plagiarized parts of his speech from Archibald Carey's address to the 1952 Republican National Convention. Carey, a lawyer, judge, pastor of an African Methodist Episcopal church in Chicago, civil rights leader, and confidant of King's, told the convention:

> We, Negro Americans, sing with all loyal Americans: "My country 'tis of thee, Sweet land of liberty, Of thee I sing. Land where my fathers died, Land of the Pilgrims' pride, From every mountainside, Let freedom ring!" That's exactly what we mean—from every mountain side, let freedom ring. . . . may the Republican Party, under God, from every mountainside, Let freedom ring![6]

Whatever the origin, King's dreams helped spur the process. Less than a year later, the slain President Kennedy's successor, Lyndon B. Johnson, signed into law the Civil Rights Act of 1964, landmark legislation that outlawed discrimination based on race, color, religion, sex, or national origin. Johnson summed up the compelling need for and intent of the bill:

> We believe that all men are created equal. Yet many are denied equal treatment. We believe that all men have certain unalienable rights. Yet many Americans do not enjoy those rights. We believe that all men are entitled to the blessings of liberty. Yet millions are being deprived of those blessings—not because of their own failures, but because of the color of their skin. The reasons are deeply imbedded in history and tradition and the nature of man. We can understand—without rancor or hatred—how this all happened. But it cannot continue. Our Constitution, the foundation of our Republic, forbids it. The principles of our freedom forbid it. Morality forbids it. And the law I will sign tonight forbids it.[7]

Seven months after that, in his State of the Union speech, President Johnson pushed for passage of the Voting Rights Act of 1965. Johnson used a powerful tool of persuasion: he told a story. He put a human face on a political issue.

> My first job after college was as a teacher in Cotulla, Texas, in a small Mexican-American school. Few of them could speak English, and I couldn't speak much Spanish. My students were

poor and they often came to class without breakfast, hungry. They knew even in their youth the pain of prejudice. They never seemed to know why people disliked them. But they knew it was so, because I saw it in their eyes. I often walked home late in the afternoon, after the classes were finished, wishing there was more that I could do. But all I knew was to teach them the little that I knew, hoping that it might help them against the hardships that lay ahead. Somehow you never forget what poverty and hatred can do when you see its scars on the hopeful face of a young child.

A speech given and adapted many times, along with the ability to deliver it well, took Ronald Reagan from B-movie actor to national spokesman for a conservative, business-friendly political philosophy to governor of California to president of the United States and ultimately to an enduring political symbol.

You and I have the courage to say to our enemies, "There is a price we will not pay." "There is a point beyond which they must not advance." And this—this is the meaning in the phrase of Barry Goldwater's "peace through strength." Winston Churchill said, "The destiny of man is not measured by material computations. When great forces are on the move in the world, we learn we're spirits—not animals."

Reagan added, "There's something going on in time and space, and beyond time and space, which, whether we like it or not, spells duty." And then, borrowing a phrase from Franklin Roosevelt, he concluded, "You and I have a rendezvous with destiny."[8]

Reagan had delivered the speech to business organizations around the country for several years to supplement his income from a fading Hollywood acting career. Then, in the 1964 presidential campaign, after a highly visible switch from the Democratic to Republican Party, he was asked to give a speech supporting Senator Barry Goldwater's candidacy against President Lyndon Johnson. He delivered a slightly retooled version of his basic speech, now called "A Time for Choosing," to rave reviews at a high-dollar Hollywood Republican fundraiser. It was so well received, it wound up being nationally televised, and his national political career was under way. Despite its recycled nature, many scholars consider "A Time for Choosing" to be among the best speeches Reagan ever made.

In 1987, President Reagan stood at Berlin's Brandenburg Gate urging an end to four decades of Cold War pitting the United States and Western Europe against the Soviet Union, which included much of Eastern Europe. Reagan spoke at the Berlin Wall, separating the East and West sectors of the city, and rhetorically addressed Soviet leader Mikhail Gorbachev directly:

> There is one sign the Soviets can make that would be unmistakable, that would advance dramatically the cause of freedom and peace. General Secretary Gorbachev, if you seek peace, if you seek prosperity for the Soviet Union and Eastern Europe, if you seek liberalization: Come here to this gate! Mr. Gorbachev, open this gate. Mr. Gorbachev, tear down this wall![9]

Barack Obama, a state senator few people had heard of, put himself squarely on the national stage with his keynote address to the 2004 Democratic convention: "I stand here today, grateful for the diversity of my heritage, aware that my parents' dreams live on in my two precious daughters. I stand here knowing that my story is part of the larger American story, that I owe a debt to all of those who came before me, and that in no other country on Earth is my story even possible."[10]

Obama firmly established the theme for his own presidential campaign four years later:

> It's the hope of slaves sitting around a fire singing freedom songs. The hope of immigrants setting out for distant shores. The hope of a young naval lieutenant bravely patrolling the Mekong Delta. The hope of a mill worker's son who dares to defy the odds. The hope of a skinny kid with a funny name who believes that America has a place for him, too. Hope! Hope in the face of difficulty! Hope in the face of uncertainty! The audacity of hope! In the end, that is God's greatest gift to us, the bedrock of this nation. A belief in things not seen. A belief that there are better days ahead.

Make no mistake: each of the iconic speeches quoted here was a political message. Each message was clad in carefully chosen words to convey a vision, a set of beliefs, a new direction; but each was a political message nonetheless. Few examples are more dramatic or memorable.

American Political Oratory at Its Worst

As high as political communication can soar, it can also plunge back to earth with a resounding crash or a dull thud. George Washington has always been and will remain one of the most admired figures in US history. He was a bold, imaginative leader with a strong sense of personal honor and public responsibility. Though quite intelligent, Washington did not have the benefit of formal schooling in England or in the colonies at Harvard University or the College of William and Mary, like many of his colleagues. Despite being very well read, throughout his life he remained self-conscious, even embarrassed, about his lack of formal education. He schooled himself in grammar and vocabulary, and learned to express his thoughts in a very formal and correct manner. But a great public speaker? Not so much. In fact, his second inaugural address delivered in Philadelphia in 1793, is generally ranked among the worst presidential speeches ever. Perhaps mercifully, it was also the shortest:

> I am again called upon by the voice of my country to execute the functions of its Chief Magistrate. When the occasion proper for it shall arrive, I shall endeavor to express the high sense I entertain of this distinguished honor, and of the confidence which has been reposed in me by the people of united America. Previous to the execution of any official act of the President the Constitution requires an oath of office. This oath I am now about to take, and in your presence: That if it shall be found during my administration of the Government I have in any instance violated willingly or knowingly the injunctions thereof, I may (besides incurring constitutional punishment) be subject to the upbraidings of all who are now witnesses of the present solemn ceremony.

Taking the prize for the worst inaugural address in history—and
the longest, at 8,445 words—was William Henry Harrison in 1841.
By all accounts, his speech was free of style or rhetorical flourish.
It may also have been fatal. The sixty-eight-year-old President Harrison spoke for an hour and 45 minutes in a cold rain storm without
a hat or coat. Thirty-two days later, he died of pneumonia.

Sometimes it is not the rhetoric that crashes, but the timing.
The message can be spot on in conveying what the speaker
intended at the moment, even while being be one he or she
would later love to take back. "Major combat operations in Iraq
have ended," President George W. Bush announced to the nation
on May 1, 2003, in a speech from the flight deck of an aircraft
carrier off the coast of San Diego, California. "In the battle of
Iraq, the United States and our allies have prevailed. Because of
you," he said, addressing the assembled naval personnel, "our
nation is more secure. Because of you, the tyrant has fallen and
Iraq is free."

To add impact to the event, rather than arriving in the customary presidential helicopter, Bush landed in the copilot's seat of
a navy jet, emerging in a flight suit, helmet under his arm. After
changing, he spoke from a podium in front of a huge banner proclaiming "Mission Accomplished." The powerful visual backdrop
and triumphal words, however, did not create the historic image
the administration intended. Instead, the speech and banner
became symbols of an unpopular war that would drag on for eight
more years. In his final press conference as president, Bush con-
ceded, "Clearly, putting 'Mission Accomplished' on an aircraft
carrier was a mistake," he said. "It sent the wrong message. We
were trying to say something differently but, nevertheless, it conveyed a different message."[11]

Occasionally, a political message is conveyed in a careless
off-the-cuff public statement that comes to define a political
leader or candidate. In 2004, Democratic presidential nominee
John Kerry told a group that in the Senate, he had initially voted
to fund President Bush's combat operations in Iraq before changing his position: "I actually voted in favor of the $87 billion
before I voted against it."[12] The Bush campaign, already trying to

frame Kerry as a "flip-flopper," was handed a huge gift and used Kerry's quote against him with devastating impact.

If a political message reaches the wrong audience, it can have a thermonuclear effect. As mentioned in Chapter 3, Republican presidential candidate Mitt Romney was working hard to convince the nation in 2012 that he was not the out-of-touch plutocrat that Democrats were trying to paint. Then, in a speech to a small, private gathering of well-off financial backers, he said:

> There are 47 percent of the people who will vote for the president (Barack Obama) no matter what. . . . who are dependent upon government, who believe that they are victims, who believe the government has a responsibility to care for them, who believe that they are entitled to health care, to food, to housing, to you-name-it. . . . These are people who pay no income tax. My job is not to worry about those people. I'll never convince them they should take personal responsibility and care for their lives.[13]

Unfortunately for Romney, his comments were captured on a miniature video camera and leaked to the news media, going viral on YouTube within days. His own words conveyed a political message that was the exact opposite of the one he was trying to put forth publicly.

Sometimes a single slip can sink your ship. In the heat of a debate during the 2012 Republican presidential primary, Texas governor Rick Perry announced that as president he would immediately abolish three federal agencies, but he could only recall two of them. "Oops," he said when the name of the third just wouldn't come to him, and he may always be remembered for it.

These examples of political speeches and political messaging, good and bad, all occurred at events of great importance or in political campaigns for the highest office in the nation. But such political communication takes place every day at every level of governance, from the voting precinct to city hall, the county courthouse, the state capitol, and Washington, DC. At every level, the penalty for missing the mark can be devastating, or at the very minimum a missed opportunity. (Or in the case of Perry, a later opportunity to lead the federal agency he couldn't remember but wanted to abolish.) Done correctly, a spoken message can play a role in an election victory or the adoption of an important government policy. And every once in a while, truly effective political communication captures great ideas in words and phrases that live on long after the event or the speaker.

Riding the Same Train in Opposite Directions

In the heat of a political campaign, the speeches of opposing candidates are not always worlds apart. In *The Political Speechwriter's Companion*, Bob Lehrman writes about the opposing candidates in the 2008 presidential race:

> They spoke seven days apart: first the skinny black senator from Illinois, winner over Democratic rivals who hadn't even heard of him five years earlier; then the white-haired senator from Arizona who had been in the public eye for almost four decades. And what Barack Obama proposed at an outdoor stadium in Denver and John McCain at a convention hall in St. Paul differed in tone, delivery, and ideas both about what was wrong with the country and how to fix it.
>
> But in other ways, their speeches were quite similar. Both speakers used the theme of change. Both addressed not just the people in front of them but all Americans. Both speakers used the same basic structure. Both used a technique that politicians sometimes call litany. Both used rhetorical techniques like antithesis. Both used stories to inspire. In short, McCain and Obama demonstrated that even when politicians find little common ground on issues, they share beliefs in one area: rhetoric.[14]

Practice May Not Make Perfect, but It Sure Makes It Better

One of the most obvious marks of a good speech is the delivery. A great delivery can elevate a mediocre speech, and a poor delivery can take the air out of a great one. A speaker may convey a message that is powerful. It may be gentle, or matter-of-fact, or humorous. But to be effective, it has to sound as if the speaker is talking to us rather than reading. That ability comes in part from experience and getting comfortable with public speaking. More than anything else, it comes from knowing the particular speech and practicing it.

The greatest stage and film actors rehearse, rehearse, and rehearse. They typically think through and practice the delivery of every line and word until they have it just right. Yet trying to get some politicians to run through a speech a time or two before they actually deliver it can be a daunting challenge. I cannot tell you how many times I've been told, "I don't have time. Just make sure it's in large print," or, "This isn't my first speech, you know. I don't need rehearsals." Sometimes they don't want to take the time, and sometimes they simply believe they're so polished and experienced, they just don't need to rehearse.

Occasionally—but only occasionally—speeches from the floor of the US House or Senate are memorable, even majestic. More commonly, speakers either stumble through a speech or simply read the words before them, as if they were seeing the text for the first time—because, in fact, many of the speakers *are* seeing the words for the first time; or maybe the second, if they happened to look it over on their way to the floor.

Typical is a floor speech I wrote for a member of Congress on an issue that was really important in his district. I suggested several times that we sit down and run through it or, alternatively, that he close himself in his office and read it out loud a couple of times. He refused: "I don't have time. And besides, I've done this a few times. Just give me the final version in 16-point type."

I watched his speech on the C-SPAN monitor. I never saw anything but the top of his head because he never took his eyes off the text. As he read, his delivery was a bit short of dramatic. I got a video clip of his speech and played it for him. I asked him if he wanted the video sent to the television stations back home. After that, he was much more willing to rehearse.

Case Study: Bill Clinton's Delivery

It's unlikely that any of President Bill Clinton's oratory will be included among the most momentous or unforgettable ever delivered, but even his most bitter enemies would acknowledge that he's one of the most gifted public speakers in US political history. His 2012 address to the Democratic National Convention was, according to many observers, the highlight of the entire event, and there were some outstanding speakers, including First Lady Michelle Obama and former Michigan governor Jennifer Granholm.

It's hard to believe that twenty-four years earlier, at the 1988 Democratic Convention, Clinton's thirty-three-minute introduction of candidate Michael Dukakis was so long and tedious that he was actually booed. In fact, his biggest applause line was, "In conclusion." He became the butt of jokes and even appeared on the *Tonight Show* to join in poking fun at himself. Only four years later, he was the Democratic nominee. And in his acceptance, he referred to the earlier speech: "I ran for president this year for one reason and one reason only. I wanted to come back to this convention and finish that speech I started four years ago!"[15]

As a communication director in the Clinton administration, I had a number of opportunities to study his speaking style before small and large groups of all kinds. It was clear that he always seemed to speak *with* the audience rather than *to* them. And whether he was in a small room or a huge auditorium, he had the gift of making every person feel like he was speaking directly with them.

Author and public-speaking consultant Sam Harrison writes that Bill Clinton uses three simple speaking techniques:

1. He knows when to stop and go. Clinton uses hard-stop pacing to add emphasis to lines: "We're going to keep President Obama on. the. job." and "President Obama started with a much. worse. economy." He squeezes every word for maximum impact. And Clinton has no fear of dead air, using frequent pauses to garner attention and gain drama: "Listen to me now. [pause] No president, [pause] not me, [pause] not any of my predecessors, [pause] no one could have fully repaired all the damage."

2. His gestures sync with his words. Clinton's best visual aids are his hands. His arm movements are open and wide, relaying an image of accessibility and authenticity. To guide the audience's emotion and attention, he often extends his hands with palms facing up or out: "Let me ask you something [palms up] . . ." or "Folks, this is serious [palms out]. " He'll also overlap hands in front of chest to reinforce intimate statements such as, "This is personal to me."

3. It's how he says it, as much as what he says. Clinton uses facial expressions to put his words on display. He offers a small, knowing smile when saying, "and that brings me to health care." He raises his chin in defiance saying, "let's take a look at what's actually happened so far." Clinton bites his bottom lip with frustration after stating, "and they refused to compromise. . . ." And he squints his eyes with determination when delivering lines like, "democracy does not have to be a blood sport."[16]

Every elected official and candidate would love to connect with an audience as well as Bill Clinton. While very few are in that league, it's a worthwhile target to shoot for, and not just to be more admired or to get more speaking invitations. The ability to speak effectively makes a big difference in a politician's ability to influence the public and public policy.

The Art of Speechwriting

Effective speeches are not just well-crafted essays read out loud. They are written for the ear rather than the eye, to be heard rather than read. That usually means shorter, simpler, and more direct sentences. In *Speechwriting in Perspective: A Brief Guide to Effective and Persuasive Communication*, Thomas H. Neale and Dana Ely of the Congressional Research Service state that "written sentences up to 30 words long are easily understood by average readers." But any spoken sentence longer than 8 to 16 words is "considered difficult for listeners to follow by ear, and according to some cognitive researchers, may be too long for the average listener to absorb and analyze quickly."[17]

Given such limitations, a frequent challenge is to explain complex thoughts and processes clearly and, in very good speeches, memorably. To do this, speechwriters and orators often utilize a number of rhetorical techniques.

The Speechwriting Process

Monroe's motivated sequence is a technique to organize persuasive speeches to inspire the audience to take action. It was developed by Alan Houston Monroe at Purdue University and published in his book, *Monroe's Principles of Speech*.

- *Attention:* Get the attention of your audience using a detailed story, shocking example, dramatic statistic, quotations, and so on.

- *Need:* Explain the problem; show how the problem connects to your audience. Establish that the audience's action is necessary to solve the problem.

- *Satisfaction:* Let the audience know there is a solution. How will the audience's action solve the problem?

- *Visualization:* Tell the audience what will happen if the solution is implemented, or what will happen if it does not take place.

• *Action:* Tell the audience what they can do personally to solve the problem. Call on them to act.[18]

Writers have long used a variety of rhetorical devices to make speeches more interesting, more memorable, and of particular importance today, more quotable. In *The Political Speechwriter's Companion*, mentioned earlier in this chapter, Bob Lehrman explains and illustrates some of these mechanisms:

• *Parallelism:* At least two clauses or sentences with the same structure. "That these dead shall not have died in vain; that this nation, under God, shall have a new birth of Freedom." (Abraham Lincoln, 1863)

• *Antithesis:* Parallel structures to present contrast. "That those who have been left out, we will try to bring in. Those left behind, we will help catch up." (Richard Nixon, 1969)

• *Simile and metaphor:* Comparison of two unlike things. "For a working person to vote for Ronald Reagan is like a chicken voting for Col. Sanders." (Walter Mondale, 1984)

• *Understatement:* Statement that minimizes the significance of what the speaker says. "I gave the Taliban leaders a choice: turn over the terrorists or face your ruin. They chose unwisely." (George W. Bush, 2001)

• *Hyperbole:* Exaggeration—often for comic effect. "If my opponent's campaign were a TV show, it would be named 'Let's Make a Deal.' You'd get to trade your prosperity for the surprise behind the curtain." (Ronald Reagan, 1984)

• *Rhetorical question:* Question to involve the audience. "Can we forge against these enemies a grand and global alliance, North and South, East and West, that can assure a more fruitful life for all mankind? Will you join in that historic effort?" (John F. Kennedy, 1961)

• *Apostrophe:* Addressing someone not present; shows courage— standing up to the enemy. "Come here to this gate! Mr. Gorbachev, open this gate. Mr. Gorbachev, tear down this wall!" (Ronald Reagan, 1987)

• *Repetition:*

1. Anaphora: Repetition at the beginning of successive sentences or clauses. "We shall fight on the beaches. We shall fight in the fields and in the streets. We shall fight in the hills. We shall never surrender." (Winston Churchill, 1940)

2. Epistrophe: Repetition at the end of clauses or sentences. "There is not a black America and a white America and Latino America and Asian America—there's the United States of America." (Barack Obama, 2004)

3. Climax: Repetition in which clauses or sentences are arranged in increasing order or importance. "And now I ask you ladies and gentlemen, brothers and sisters, for the good of all of us, for the love of this great nation, for the family of America, for the love of God; please make this nation remember how futures are built." (Mario Cuomo, 1984)

• *Alliteration:* Repetition of words beginning with the same sound. "In the United States today we have more than our share of the nattering nabobs of negativism." (Spiro Agnew, 1970)[19]

Speechwriters have become essential in helping public officials and candidates deliver messages to various audiences. It might be to earn votes, raise money, build name recognition and credibility, or generate grassroots support. The speechwriter's job is to make sure the speaker's message comes across professionally and powerfully.

For most speechwriters, especially those on staff, there are a lot of other responsibilities before the drafting process begins. The job usually starts with meeting with the speaker to develop speech ideas and figure out details to match the speech to the event. The writer needs to know about the audience, including number, age, gender, and any unique characteristics: Are they military veterans? Realtors? Ranchers? Environmentalists? Bankers?

West Wing Writers is a private sector speechwriting and communications firm started in 2001 by a group of former White House speechwriters. They work with top level CEOs, philanthropists, entertainers, and athletes. The firm's mantra for its clients is, "You only give a speech that only you can give. If anyone can give it, what's the point?"

If it's a stump speech, the writer needs to be sure that key issues and positions are stated correctly, clearly, and in a way that inspires the audience and generates applause. A policy speech to a business audience might call for a more serious tone. The writer would help gather facts, examples, illustrations, or whatever else is needed to convey the appropriate substance and organization that leads to the desired point or points in the desired tone. In fact, the writer often turns into a researcher, digging out details and background information (votes, statements, budgets, dates, etc.) to support the speech's content.

Whether on staff or independent, the speechwriter has to fact-check items that require absolute accuracy beyond the initial research. For higher-level officials or candidates, this usually means running speech drafts through a gauntlet of advisors or senior staff, and sometimes policy experts, to double-check statements or facts and data. Coordination between the speechwriter and policy, communication, and organizing staffs can be frustrating because there is sometimes a feeling on the part of everyone concerned that they need to "touch" the speech by inserting their choice of words or phrases. In the end, such coordination is crucial.

After helping to develop the ideas in the speech, drafting it, and reviewing it with staff and the official or candidate, the speechwriter has to make any final edits, turn out the final version of the speech, and then make any last-minute changes.

Yet even with all these creative and administrative responsibilities, the absolute essence of speechwriting, and the biggest challenge in writing a speech for someone else to deliver, is finding the speaker's voice. The words the writer puts in the speaker's mouth have to sound genuine. Few things render a speech as inauthentic as much as a speaker who generally talks like a cast member on *Duck Dynasty* suddenly sounding like a professor of classical literature, or someone who normally speaks in a more formal style trying to come across like one of the boys at a tailgate party. The speechwriter has to use words and phrases that sound natural and authentic coming out of the speaker's mouth. That means being familiar with the speaker's vocabulary, use of idiomatic expressions, regional accent, and the speaker's normal rhythm and cadence. When the words just don't fit, the result can be devastating.

Case Study: Mr. Speaker Does Dickens

The Speaker of the Texas House of Representatives in 1977 was a successful cotton farmer from the plains of west Texas. He was a proud graduate of Texas A&M University. He was intelligent, forthright, and a gentleman, unfailingly courteous and thoughtful. As Speaker, he was the second most powerful official in the legislature after the lieutenant governor, who presides over the Senate. He was many things, but none of them was a great orator.

The Speaker of the Texas House is elected by all 150 members. On opening day of each legislative session, after an address by the governor, the first order of business is to elect the Speaker. This is followed by a lot of pomp and circumstance, a call to order, and the freshly elected presiding officer's maiden speech.

The new Speaker's speechwriter had turned out an exquisite piece of work for the occasion. It quoted Charles Dickens's *A Tale of Two Cities*, it referred to several Greek philosophers, and I think there were some quotes from John Locke in there. It was beautiful!

There was just one problem. The Speaker was, as I mentioned, from the high plains of West Texas. And though he was an educated man, there are a lot of mouths out of which certain words just do not roll. So when he observed that, "It wuz the best of tams. It wuz the wust of tams," a few in the packed House gallery could be heard tittering. When he began to wax eloquently about the great thinkers of the "Eye-talian Rena-zants," some in the audience began to snort audibly. I was standing on one side of the House floor and happened to look to the back of the chamber near a door into the speaker's office. The speechwriter stood in the doorway listening, and tears were running down her cheeks.

The Speechwriter's Role

Speechwriters have been putting words in the mouths of public officials and candidates for office for many years. It is safe to say that most public officials, from state senators, US representatives and senators, to statewide officials and the mayors of large cities, either have someone on their staff who writes or helps them write speeches, or they consult with outside professional speechwriters when needed. High-level appointed officials, such as cabinet secretaries and other government agency heads, will generally have speechwriters or people on their communication or press staff who write for them in addition to other duties. It is hardly a secret that the White House has a team of speechwriters turning out speeches almost constantly for the president and vice president.

There are at least a few people who think this is flat wrong, that public officials should either write their own speeches or give their speechwriter public acknowledgment—sort of like movie credits— at the end of each presentation. Author and former English professor David McGrath wrote in the *Washington Post* that a politician's use of words written by someone else without attribution is dishonest. He wonders why "selling term papers to students to use as their own is still illegal, but selling speeches to politicians to use as their own remains a legitimate enterprise." That speechwriters give their permission for the speakers to pretend the words and thoughts are their own, McGrath says, does not make it okay.[20] Some speechwriters have likened their profession to screenwriting, penning dialogue to be spoken by others. But in the entertainment world, audiences buy seats to witness this fiction. They know the actors don't write their own material, and authors are acknowledged in screen credits or theater programs. When was the last time you saw or heard a writer credited at the end of a speech by a presidential candidate or member of Congress?

Others are less concerned about acknowledging speechwriters than about where speechwriters go wrong. Ross K. Baker teaches political science at Rutgers University, and for a number of years he wrote speeches for several US senators. Echoing, somewhat, the case of the Texas speaker, he offers this slant on the "speechwriter problem":

Many of them are much too good for the people for whom they work, or they think that their bosses are better than they actually are. They put the most thoughtful phrases into the mouths of people who have never taken five minutes to reflect on anything. Where restrained and serviceable words might do, they want the speaker to utter deathless lines. They end up, many times, debasing the language and causing pedestrian politicians to think of themselves as philosopher-kings.[21]

The involvement of the speaker in the speechwriting process varies even at the highest level. Adam Frankel, one of President Obama's senior speechwriters from the presidential campaign through three years in the White House, told me that Obama is a talented and very active speechwriting partner and that he composes a good portion of every major speech he gives. Bill Clinton was famous for working closely with speechwriters and making changes almost until the moment the speech was delivered. By every account I can find, Ronald Reagan wrote and rewrote "A Time for Choosing" himself, but for speeches in general relied on a staff of speechwriters in the White House because of the never-ending demand.

The simple fact is many public officials and candidates give so many different kinds of speeches today that they need speechwriters to help out. In a typical day, they may be asked to give a speech on a particular issue, make a statement at a news conference, chair a legislative committee meeting on another issue, attend a candidate forum, speak at a fundraiser, be interviewed by reporters, and participate in a talk show. And at every stop, they are expected to exhibit a command of details and sound as though they know what they are talking about. So, speechwriters will most likely remain an important part of the political communication process.

Conclusion

Principle 6: The spoken word has always been a primary channel for political communication. It still is.

Speeches have always been the most powerful and enduring expressions of political messages. Even with all the changes in communication technology, it seems highly unlikely that a candidate for office or a public official will be remembered for his or her tweets or Facebook posts. But an outstanding speech becomes part of our history.

Notes

1. Abraham Lincoln, "Gettysburg Address," November 19, 1863, http://www.abrahamlincolnonline.org/lincoln/speeches/gettysburg.htm.

2. Franklin D. Roosevelt, "Address Accepting the Presidential Nomination at the Democratic National Convention in Chicago," July 2, 1932, http://www.presidency.ucsb.edu/ws/?pid=75174.

3. Franklin D. Roosevelt, "Inaugural Address," March 4, 1933, https://books.google.com/books?id=bHpQCczJrwkC&pg=PA98&lpg=PA98&q=%E2%80%9C.

4. John F. Kennedy, "Inaugural Address," January 20, 1961, https://www.theguardian.com/theguardian/2007/apr/22/greatspeeches.

5. Martin Luther King Jr., "I Have a Dream," August 28, 1963, https://www.archives.gov/files/press/exhibits/dream-speech.pdf.

6. Archibald Carey, "Address to the Republican National Convention," July 8, 1952, https://books.google.com/books?id=S8p8Q82NPk8C&pg =PA146&lpg=PA146&dq.

7. Lyndon B. Johnson, "Radio and Television Remarks Upon Signing the Civil Rights Bill," July 2, 1964, http://www.edb.utexas.edu/faculty/salinas/students/student_sites/Spring2007/steven_woodall/LBJcomments.pdf.

8. Ronald Reagan, "A Time for Choosing," October 27, 1964, http://ourpresidents.tumblr.com/post/11989521985/you-and-i-have-a-rendezvous-with-destiny-in.

9. Ronald Reagan, "Tear Down This Wall," June 12, 1987, http://www.historyplace.com/speeches/reagan-tear-down.htm.

10. Barack Obama, "Keynote Address at the Democratic National Convention," July 27, 2004, http://www.pbs.org/newshour/bb/politics-july-dec04-obama-keynote-dnc/.

11. George W. Bush, "Mission Accomplished," May 1, 2003, https://www.usnews.com/news/blogs/press-past/2013/05/01/the-other-symbol-of-george-w-bushs-legacy.

12. John Kerry, presidential campaign speech, March 16, 2004, http://www.cnn.com/2004/ALLPOLITICS/09/30/kerry.comment/.

13. Mitt Romney, fundraising speech, September 18, 2012, http://www.nytimes.com/2012/09/19/us/politics/mitt-romneys-speech-from-mother-jones-video.html.

14. Bob Lehrman, *The Political Speechwriter's Companion* (Washington, DC: CQ Press, 2010), 1.

15. Bill Clinton, "Address Accepting the Presidential Nomination at the Democratic National Convention in New York City," July 16, 1992, http://www.presidency.ucsb.edu/ws/?pid=25958.

16. Sam Harrison, "3 Techniques Bill Clinton Uses to Wow an Audience," September 6, 2012, http://www.fastcompany.com/3001087/3-techniques-bill-clinton-uses-wow-audience.

17. Thomas H. Neale and Dana Ely, *Speechwriting in Perspective: A Brief Guide to Effective and Persuasive Communication* (Washington, DC: Congressional Research Service, 2007).

18. Alan Houston Monroe, *Monroe's Principles of Speech* (Chicago: Scott, Foresman & Company, 1951).

19. Lehrman, *The Political Speechwriter's Companion*.

20. David McGrath, "In the Words of My Speechwriter . . ." *Washington Post*, September 4, 2008.

21. Ross K. Baker, personal communication with the author.

8

Political Advertising
and Television

Principle 7: Despite the digital media revolution and profound changes in media and media audiences, paid advertising by election campaigns and interest groups will continue to be an essential tool to reach target audiences with political messages.

Advertising is commonly used in all three venues of political communication: election campaigns, government policy communication, and issue advocacy. The most pervasive use is in election campaigns. The digital revolution has dramatically changed the focus and priorities of political campaign communication. Not only are there many new and effective conduits to reach target audiences, but for most campaigns, it is not a choice of which communication channels to use, but a matter of using most or all of them to reach desired audiences. E-mail, YouTube, Facebook, mobile devices, Twitter, Pinterest, and Tumblr are all considered essential.

As we will explore in depth in Chapter 9, communicating political messages online changes not only the targeting but also the form and content of messages compared to those conveyed through traditional print and broadcast media. This happens for two primary reasons:

1. Online messages can be targeted to much more defined groups than mass media; therefore, effective communicators shape the content of their message to suit these narrower groups.
2. Most online communication, particularly in social media, is intended to be two-way rather than the one-way messaging of mass media. Mass media is about getting a single message out to the largest possible audience. Social media is about conversations.

Make no mistake: social media communication that conveys persuasive messages to highly targeted audiences is political advertising, just as surely as the most expensively produced television spot aimed at a mass television audience.

Online advertising is growing rapidly. According to *2015–2016 Political Advertising Outlook* from the market research firm Borrell and Associates, campaign spending in digital media in 2016 would top $1 billion—a 576 percent increase over the 2012 election.[1] But television continued to attract the largest audiences of potential voters. That means, at least for the next few years, political campaigns and public affairs communicators needing to reach the public with their messages will have to invest in both digital media and television. Kantar Media's Campaign Media Analysis Group predicted that $4.4 billion from political campaigns and super PACs would go into television ads in the 2016 presidential race. And there is a very good reason for this.

TV Remains the Best Way to Reach Most Voting Adults

Mass media advertising, particularly on television, continues to be the dominant medium for political campaigns. Some media observers predicted a dramatic decline in political spending on television advertising and a massive redirection to online media in 2016, and they turned out to be prophetic. But most political media analysts would insist that the sudden change in 2016 had more to do with the candidacy of Donald Trump than a sudden shift in the public's media habits. When most of the predictions for significant increases in campaign expenditures for television advertising were made, Trump had not yet emerged as a serious, much less leading, Republican candidate for the presidency. Conventional wisdom at the time expected the general election to boil down to Democrat Hillary Clinton and Republican Jeb Bush, and that expenditures for television advertising would skyrocket. What few observers foresaw was the effectiveness of Trump's use of social media—particularly Twitter and Facebook—along with campaign rallies as a primary means of communicating his message to the public. Of course, Trump's campaign was helped by the $5.2 billion in "earned media," or free news coverage he received over the 2016 campaign, approximately $2 billion more than Clinton. (This phenomenon is further discussed in Chapter 9.)

Analysis continues into whether the effectiveness of Trump's reliance on social media has ushered in a new dynamic in political communication, or whether it was more a reflection of his media celebrity and penchant for explosive comments and personal insults.

According to the Nielsen Company's *Total Audience Report* for the first quarter of 2016, which measures media usage across platforms and devices, television continues to be the most used medium when viewers of live programming and "time-shifted," or recorded, content are measured (see Figure 8.1).[2]

Television Advertising: Lights! Camera! Politics!

Television has only been a powerful campaign tool since 1952, when Dwight Eisenhower and Adlai Stevenson used the brand new medium to reach millions of voters and potential voters in a new way. Those first TV messages were primitive by today's standards. The initial spots for both sides featured simple cartoon images and sing-along soundtracks.

Eisenhower, the most admired living American according to a national poll at that time, had commanded the Allies in their

Figure 8.1　Number of US Adult Users per Month (in millions)

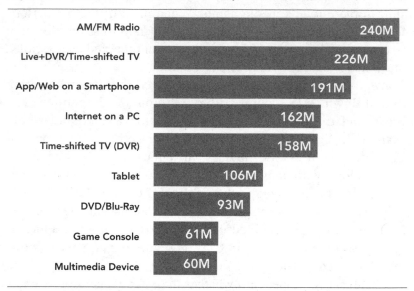

AM/FM Radio	240M
Live+DVR/Time-shifted TV	226M
App/Web on a Smartphone	191M
Internet on a PC	162M
Time-shifted TV (DVR)	158M
Tablet	106M
DVD/Blu-Ray	93M
Game Console	61M
Multimedia Device	60M

Source: "Nielsen Total Audience Report, Q1 2016," June 27, 2016, http://www.nielsen.com/us/en/insights/reports/2016/the-total-audience-report-q1-2016.html.

World War II victory in Europe. He won the 1952 election and defeated Stevenson again in 1956. Stevenson, former governor of Illinois and a leading political intellectual, did not exactly embrace the new medium. He said in 1956, "The idea that you can merchandise candidates for high office like breakfast cereal is the ultimate indignity to the democratic process." Rather than relying on catchy TV spots, he opted for substantive issue messages—mini-speeches—which aired later in the evening, unfortunately after many people had gone to bed.

Television advertising has been the most powerful mechanism for a political campaign to reach out to the public ever since, and the ability of a campaign and a candidate to use it well has remained essential. As Roger Ailes, former network television producer and media consultant to Richard Nixon in 1968, said, "Television is no gimmick, and nobody will ever be elected to major office again without presenting themselves well on it."[3]

In 2012, there were more television ads than ever before. According to communication professors John C. Tedesco and Scott W. Dunn in *The 2012 Presidential Campaign: A Communication Perspective*, television dominated spending in large campaigns— especially presidential races: "The 2012 presidential campaign shattered records for spending on advertising, especially by third party groups unaffiliated with the candidates or their political parties. And for the first time, the two major party campaigns and their supporters spent more than $1 billion on television advertising, with more than $580 million and $470 million spent to support Obama and Romney, respectively."[4]

More than half of those totals, about $640 million, came from super PACs. In *Citizens United* v. *Federal Election Commission*, the US Supreme Court decided that political contributions and spending were a form of free speech and that corporations, like individuals, had a right to that free speech. That decision led to the creation of dozens of super PACS, some funded by large groups, others by just a few donors. The court's ruling ended requirements that donors be identified. Following that, some of the country's largest corporations dumped hundreds of millions of dollars into super PACS that made huge expenditures in media, much of it to attack President Obama. However, the Obama campaign had a few super PAC allies of its own that pumped millions into attacks on Mitt Romney.

Apart from super PACs, the campaign organizations themselves used a combination of attack spots and positive appeals to try to convince undecided voters and reassure committed supporters that their candidate had the character, judgment, and experience to deserve election, while the opponent did not.

Even with all the new ways to reach voters, no medium appeals to emotion more overtly or with more impact than television advertising. Whether viewed on a flat screen or mobile device, television has more potential for strong appeal than any other medium because it focuses the audience's visual and audio senses on messages arriving one by one. That viewer focus makes it a powerful and effective vehicle for political appeals to emotion.

Radio: Alive and Well

Radio may be the most overlooked medium in today's political and public affairs advertising, at least by political observers and commentators. But it is not overlooked by political communicators. Although satellite media and music downloads have captured a lot of the audience that used to tune in to radio broadcasts for entertainment, radio is still alive and well. According to the Davis Group (a media-buying service based in Austin, Texas), 53 percent of the radio audience aged twenty-five to fifty-four listens via broadcast and "pure plays," online sources such as Spotify and Pandora. Of these radio listeners, 23 percent get their tunes only via live streaming on their digital devices. So, the radio audience has not diminished; a lot of them are just tuning in online.[5] According to the Nielsen Company's 2015 report, radio still reaches 92 percent of people eighteen and older. The average person eighteen and older spends 447 minutes per day watching television, but they also spend 162 minutes a day listening to radio—nearly four times the daily minutes spent listening to audio on their computers, five times the listening time on smart phones, and more than three times the listening time on tablets.[6]

The nature of the medium has dramatically changed. Top 40 and rock stations no longer dominate the airwaves. Country music seems to attract the largest number of music listeners, and in many markets, news-talk stations lead in ratings. But overall, the numbers indicate that many people still drive around with their car radios on.

Radio and Television Advertising Costs

Radio advertising time usually costs much less than television time. Of course, radio does not have the impact of television. Unlike when watching TV, most people listen to radio while they are doing something else, and they are not using both their visual and audio senses. Still, as we have seen, a lot of people listen to radio.

Here are some very approximate figures to illustrate the difference between television and radio ad rates, and the difference in costs among a few markets. Rates are based on audience size, measured by ratings surveys of every television program and, for radio, by ratings that measure the audience in quarter-hour segments. These ratings surveys are conducted quarterly by companies such as Nielsen (rates shown here are from first quarter 2017). The costs for both media depend on the time of day or specific program in which an advertiser wants to run a commercial. Markets like New York and Los Angeles, with significantly larger broadcast audiences, logically cost more than smaller markets. The rates shown in Table 8.1 represent local stations in the various markets, not the three major networks or cable TV outlets.[7] Network advertising is national, and rates can be as much as a thousand times the local rates. And rates for local cable TV outlets, such as CNN or Fox News, would actually be a bit lower than the local network stations.

The most desirable times for political advertising are in and around newscasts and news-oriented programming, like *60 Minutes* and *20/20*. Research tells political ad buyers that people who pay attention to the news are more likely to be voters than people who focus on sports or reality shows. People who watch CNN, Fox News, or MSNBC are more likely to be voters than people who watch cable networks HSN (Home Shopping Network) or MTV (Music Television).

Table 8.1 Local Advertising Rates for Television and Radio, 2017

Market	TV (early morning local news)	TV (early evening local news)	Radio AM Drive (6–10 AM)	Radio PM Drive (4–7 PM)
New York, New York	$1,200–$2,500	$6,500–$12,350	$600–$1,500	$300–$1,450
Los Angeles, California	$1,200–$2,500	$5,600–$7,750	$325–$1,525	$325–$1,280
Orlando, Florida	$1,000–$1,200	$1,200–$2,825	$215–$425	$260–$400
Cincinnati, Ohio	$500–$600	$500–$850	$200–$475	$200–$470

Source: Rate estimates furnished by The Davis Group, Media Planning and Placement, Austin, Texas, June 26, 2017.

It is important to remember that these rates will get a political message run only once. That's it. And because, as pointed out in Chapter 2, one of the foundations for persuasive communication is repetition, seeing or hearing an ad one time will not get the job done. People need to hear a message more than once for it to break through the clutter of all the other messages out there and have any chance of persuading. Political advertisers know their message must be seen or heard multiple times to be remembered at all by the audience, and heard even more frequently to really sink in. How many ads of any kind do you remember seeing or hearing just once? So, political advertisers usually budget to have their ads run several times per day on most of the stations in a market for at least several weeks. Ever wonder why political campaigns cost so much?

Radio's lower costs make it attractive to smaller, local campaigns that do not have large media budgets. In fact, for many smaller campaigns, radio is the major advertising medium.

Radio offers several important advantages though, even for campaigns with multimillion dollar media budgets. Radio is much more "targetable" than television. Television programs tend to have a larger, broader audience. Radio audiences tend to be narrower and well-defined by station preference. A campaign can target a fairly specific group of voters by buying time on the particular station they tend to listen to. This allows election or issue campaigns to target specific messages to specific audiences. Consider how many various formats are available on our radio dials according to News Generation[8]:

- 80s Hits
- Active Rock
- Adult Contemporary
- Adult Hits
- Adult Standards/Middle of the Road
- Adult Urban Contemporary
- Album-Oriented Rock
- All News

- All Sports
- Alternative
- Children's Radio
- Christian Adult Contemporary
- Classic Country
- Classical
- Comedy
- Country
- Easy Listening
- Educational
- Gospel
- Hot Adult Contemporary
- Jazz
- Mainstream Rock
- Modern Adult Contemporary
- New Country
- News Talk Information
- Nostalgia
- Oldies
- Pop Contemporary Hit
- Religious
- Rhythmic
- Soft Adult Contemporary
- Southern Gospel
- Spanish
- Talk-Personality
- Urban Contemporary
- Variety
- World Ethnic

Radio can often be more geographically targeted, as well. A lot of voters live in rural areas or communities—even small- or medium-sized cities—that do not have their own television stations, but are covered by large-market broadcast outlets. For example, many heavily populated areas of New York State and New Jersey are part of the New York City television market. Many people in New Hampshire watch Boston television. Yet many smaller communities have their own radio stations, which tend to be dominant with local audiences.

Because radio is far less expensive, it is a valuable tool with which to repeat and reinforce television messages. A barrage of radio spots can strengthen a candidate's name recognition or the awareness of an issue campaign's message.

The Importance of Emotion in Political Messages

The role of emotion and emotional appeals in politics has been controversial since the earliest days of the republic. Thomas Jefferson and James Madison both wrote that decisions based on reason rather than passion were far preferable. Yet in one of the Federalist Papers, essays individually authored by Madison, Alexander Hamilton, and John Jay to promote adoption of the Constitution, Madison acknowledged that, as much as the use of reason and logic led to better outcomes, emotions were a necessary part of the public's acceptance of this new form of government.

In the more than two centuries since, many political scientists, journalists, and pundits have taken the view that emotions have no proper place in political and policy communication. "Just give the public information," they've insisted. "People are perfectly capable of considering the facts and making a decision." These political observers have taken strong issue with the overt use of emotion in political appeals, suggesting that doing so debases the entire process.

Traditionally, political science scholars have argued that emotions can obscure clear decision-making, and that unemotional reason is always vastly preferable in weighing the positive and negative aspects of choices about candidates or issues. The best decisions, we have been told, are made in the cold, clear light of logic. There are notable examples to illustrate the pitfalls of public actions motivated more by emotion than by careful reason.

However, a growing body of communication research suggests valid reasons for the use of emotional messages. Recent studies in neuroscience and physiology suggest that emotion may be a necessary part of the decisionmaking process itself—that making a sound, logical decision may be unlikely without elements of emotion. A concept called *affective intelligence* suggests that emotion plays an important part in people's political decisionmaking by prompting them to focus their reasoning powers to make judgments on certain questions. Affective intelligence theorizes that emotion can act as a sort of mental surveillance system to activate the reasoning processes and allow new information to be considered.

One of political communication's leading scholars, George Marcus of Williams College, recounts in *The Sentimental Citizen: Emotion in Democratic Politics* that "emotions play a critical role in prompting people to pay attention to politics in an efficient and rational way. Confronted with a constant need to make political judgments—not only during election periods, but also during the ebb and flow of ordinary national events—people need to find a way to make sense of their world without having to think hard and long about it." According to Marcus, "Emotion plays an essential role in a person's ability to make a rational decision. Contrary to classical notions of cool, emotionless decision making, affect is the force that organizes and drives how we make sense of new information."[9]

Ted Brader, faculty associate at the Center for Political Studies at the University of Michigan, has conducted extensive research into the effect of specific emotions on political decisionmaking. He reached the following conclusions:

- Appeals to enthusiasm motivate viewers to get involved and act on existing loyalties.

- Rather than leading to disengagement or withdrawal, appeals to fear and anxiety heighten a person's attention to political information.

- Positive emotions, such as hope, pride, or security, tend to motivate people to make decisions more aligned with previous attitudes, such as patriotism or partisan loyalty.

- Appeals to fear provoke viewers to seek out new information and reconsider their choices.[10]

Other research supports the idea that fear often leads people to consider new information, even motivating them to consider changing existing beliefs or opinions, and that anger is more likely to generate resistance to new information, especially if it is inconsistent with what someone already thinks. In other words, making someone afraid may push them to look around and consider other possibilities. But if they are angry, they are less open to new information and more likely to rely on partisanship or attitudes they have already accepted.

What does all this mean to political communicators? It tells them that including appeals to emotion in messages can lend more impact and help break through the clutter so their messages are received and considered by the audience. And it means that if a message's emotional appeal is well-conceived and well-executed, the message is more likely to have the desired effect. It also means that appeals to different emotions can have different effects.

The emotion may be positive: love, happiness, security, hope, or pride. Or it may be a negative emotion: anger, resentment, envy, or— most frequently in political messages—fear. It might be fear for your life, your safety, or your financial security. It might be fear for your family's well-being or their future. It might be fear that something is being taken away from you or given to someone else who doesn't deserve it. In all cases, research indicates pretty clearly that political messages that effectively appeal to emotions have more impact on the public than those that are more informational.

I would argue that in addition to being effective, emotional appeals in political advertising are absolutely appropriate. Politics is prompted by emotions and feelings, given focus by emotions and feelings, and resolved by an emotional act. The act of voting on a punch card, a voting machine, or a paper ballot is an emotional activity.

Don't you walk out of the polling place feeling pleased with yourself for doing your civic duty? Isn't the process of deciding whom you're going to vote for an emotional reaction to how the candidates or issues or parties and their agendas make you feel? Don't you support the candidate you feel is more honest, or capable, or qualified? Don't you tend to identify with the party or political figure that makes you feel more secure about the nation's future or your financial future, or makes you feel that the country is watching out for those who need a little help, or makes you feel it's important for government to play the smallest possible role in our lives?

As much as our founders preferred that important policy decisions be made on the basis of reason rather than emotion, they understood that emotion powered the process, that emotion set the mood and created a context for the use of reason. So it is in political campaigns. Emotion attracts people to the process. Emotion leads people to participate. Emotion makes people feel like they have a stake in the outcome. Without it, politics and political campaigns are cold, sterile, and incredibly boring affairs. Public interest and public participation drop off significantly.

Every political ad is an appeal to emotion. Even the blandest positive spot introducing or recounting a candidate's record is aimed at making you comfortable with that candidate or making you feel confident.

Conveying Emotion in Political Spots

The political messages people are most likely to remember even years later were usually carried in television spots, and they were almost certainly messages with strong emotional appeals. It should come as no great surprise that the most memorable spots, according to communication research, were intended to scare the hell out of people.

One of the most effective appeals to fear occurred on September 7, 1964, as millions of Americans watching the NBC Monday

Night Movie viewed what became the best-known political television ad in history. It was the "Daisy" spot, produced and paid for by President Lyndon Johnson's reelection campaign. It began with a little girl in a meadow counting out loud as she picked the petals on a daisy. When she reached "nine," an ominous male voice overrode her voice in the slow countdown cadence of a missile launch. The girl's face looked toward the sky, the picture froze, and the camera zoomed in on one of her pupils until blackness completely filled the screen. When the countdown reached zero, the black screen became a bright flash accompanied by a thunderous sound, followed by a billowing mushroom cloud. As the atomic fireball expanded and rose, Johnson's voice was heard, "These are the stakes. To make a world in which all of God's children can live, or to go into the dark. We must either love each other, or we must die." An announcer then intoned, "Vote for President Johnson on November 3rd. The stakes are too high for you to stay home."

The spot instantly embodied fears that Republican candidate Barry Goldwater's aggressive brand of conservatism would result in international confrontation. Amazingly, it officially aired only once but became such a focus for the news media that it was shown over and over in newscasts and on political talk shows.

As briefly referenced in Chapter 5, in 1988, Vice President George H. W. Bush's presidential campaign ran a spot criticizing his opponent, former Massachusetts governor Michael Dukakis, for being soft on crime, as represented by a weekend prison furlough program initiated by Dukakis's predecessor. The appeal to fear was more subtle than a mushroom cloud, yet still powerful. The ad focused visually on an African American in a line of men in prison uniforms going through a revolving door. Meanwhile, the narrator pointed out that some of the furloughed prisoners had committed crimes during their furloughs, including kidnapping and rape. The appeal was to fear, and the message was clear: if you vote for our opponent, men like this will be out on the streets preying on innocent people. The ad, which became known as the Willie Horton spot, was widely criticized both for racial overtones and for deceptively suggesting Dukakis was to blame for allowing imprisoned criminals to commit additional crimes.

Appeals to positive emotions can be memorable as well. In 1984, President Ronald Reagan's reelection campaign began with a spot known as "Morning in America." It was a series of shots of small-town America and suburban life over soft, swelling music. In gentle tones, the announcer described the restoration of economic and foreign policy strength under Reagan and asked, "Why would we ever want to return to where we were four short years ago?" The now-iconic spot used a montage of patriotic, idyllic images—American flags, young children, and people going to work—with a narration that was soft and understated. It was entirely positive and aimed at instilling pride in our country and confidence in the administration of President Reagan.

In 2008, after years of war in the Middle East and economic struggle at home, Barack Obama ran a campaign appealing to hope. "Yes we can!" became the slogan for his campaign and a recurring theme in the campaign's communication. Not confined to broadcast media, the advertising included a four-minute, twenty-five-second web video that overlaid and intercut music, celebrities, and an Obama speech, all repeating the "Yes we can" theme. Following a Wall Street collapse, two wars, and a huge budget deficit under President George W. Bush, messages from the Obama campaign in speeches, television ads, direct mail, and online repeated and supported the idea that the election was about hope and a change in direction for the country.

On-the-Job Training

When I first wrote and produced a political television spot, there weren't many people in the business, and they didn't teach political media production in the University of Texas Journalism School. A good friend decided to run for a seat on the Austin City Council and asked me to help put together his media. I wasn't aware of any correspondence courses I could take on the spur of the moment, so I used my meager skills from writing and producing television news stories. And I knew rule number 1: Tell a story.

At the time, I thought the resulting TV spots were pretty hot stuff. Today, they'd be laughably primitive in technique and technology. But I did remember to tell a story.

Over the next twenty years, I learned rule number 2: Even a touch of emotion can make a message effective. It does not have to evoke white-hot anger, induce people to quake in terror, or make children cry. Sometimes, just a bit of human connection can make a policy message much more interesting to the public and more effective. Weaving emotional threads into a spot, either positive or negative, can give the message a lot more impact. It can help it stand out from all the other political commercials on the air and, sometimes, even get people talking. It might be a heartbreaking scene of an elderly couple watching their household belongings being moved into a van as the announcer explains how they couldn't afford to stay in their home because the incumbent had voted for so many utility rate or tax hikes. Or it could be as simply sentimental as showing a candidate walking down the street holding hands with his wife.

Case Study: "It's What John Would Have Wanted"

A longtime, highly respected Texas state senator died suddenly on a Friday, a month and a half before the November general election. He'd been running without serious opposition. The State Democratic Executive Committee met in emergency session over the weekend to choose a nominee to take his spot on the ballot and selected a young state representative from within the district. However, our Republican governor had other ideas. His appointed secretary of state, the state's chief election officer, found that the late senator had died one day too close to election day to allow the ballot to be changed. Therefore, the senator would be on the ballot forty-four days after his death. And only if he won would there be a special election to fill the vacant seat. Then and only then could voters choose between live candidates. So, we had to put together a campaign to get a deceased senator reelected.

It got better. A well-known doctor had been running a long-shot campaign against the senator, and the Republican Party of Texas decided to back him to the hilt. We didn't have the money or time to explain that according to Texas election law, voters had to elect the dead senator to bring about a special election in which they'd have a real chance to elect their state senator, so we went in another direction. We produced radio spots with the late senator's widow talking about how proud her husband had been to serve the people of the senate district, and that "John would have wanted you to have a choice." It became a simple matter of fairness. That message was reflected in direct mail and print ads in the district's small-town newspapers.

Even though we were outspent by a ton, the deceased senator won nearly two-to-one. And thirty days later, the new Democratic candidate, riding a weird sort of momentum against the same opponent, won handily.

There is another dimension to the use of emotion: humor can be very effective in political messages. Done well, it can devastate the opposition. If you can get people laughing at something an opposing candidate or elected official said or did, sometimes the opponent never recovers. However, caveats apply:

- It has to be really funny or it will be a spectacular dud and could make the advertiser look bad.

- Great care must be taken to avoid anything that can be construed as offensive.

- There will be very few opportunities for the effective use of humor in political messaging. Communicators should not try too hard.

Visual and Audio Imagery

Ted Brader writes in *Campaigning for Hearts and Minds*, "Campaign ads use symbolic images and evocative music to trigger an emotional response in viewers."[11] He explored the use of emotional visual and audio cues in campaigns in an extensive research program, which determined that the use of particular visual images or music in political television spots created emotional moods that translated into measurable responses to the ad.

Emotional elements can be integrated into radio and television spots through music (gentle, uplifting, or ominous); through sound effects; through the tone of an announcer's voice (alarmed, soft and warm, or a little snarky); even by using a man or a woman's voice. In a television spot, emotional appeals can be introduced through the choice of background colors or, occasionally, the use of black and white images; through camera angles and lighting; through still photos and screen freezes; and through the use of on-screen type to lend credibility and authority to data, voting records, and quotes. All these elements can add emotional impact to a political spot.

Radio used to be called "theater of the mind" because listeners often visualize what they're hearing. When sound effects, different kinds of music, and different announcer voices are used, radio can create powerful moods. It might be positive: pride or hope for the future. It could be negative: anger or fear. Produced well, a single radio ad can convey more than one mood to the audience. It might begin with an announcer sounding like the "voice of doom," describing a threat or negative situation. The announcer might be backed by music or sound effects that convey a sense of unease. Then the ad can switch to a very positive mood, perhaps with the candidate's voice talking about a solution to the problem or threat, and probably washed in more uplifting music.

Brader concludes, "We should not be surprised that politicians rely heavily on emotionally laden advertising."[12] Indeed. If something works and works effectively, how in the world could anyone expect it not to be used—especially in an activity as intense, competitive, and consuming as a political campaign?

Print Media: Reinforce the Message, Reinforce the Look

Smart public communicators, given a limited number of opportunities to attract and hold their audience's attention, make sure the different media they employ work together. They want every piece to support every other piece and reinforce the overall message. In effective campaigns, the connection to the audience—which is critical for candidates, but just as important in issue communication—is reflected in all the visual elements: television spots, newspaper and online ads, and all printed material, such as mailers and brochures. As much as possible, they share a "look," such as the color scheme, the typeface of the campaign logo, or the use of a slogan.

Visual elements in print will be marked by crisp, uncluttered graphics and design and, of paramount importance, images—usually photographs. The look of the images should fit with the narrative message and the desired feel of the campaign. That's why it is so common to see photos of politicians—incumbent or challenger—usually in black and white, with loosened tie and sleeves rolled up, talking to people. Occasionally even listening! Shots with families are also very common, and probably one at a microphone or some other official-looking venue with the candidate or public official standing and speaking. Campaign literature also commonly features the politician either with the "look of eagles" (gazing off in the distance and thinking great thoughts) or as a "straight shooter" (looking directly into the camera—right into voters' eyes—and being honest with them).

Graphics are an often-overlooked but important element. Effective campaign communicators are attentive to choices of color, typeface, and the overall look of a campaign logo. They adapt their logo for everything visual, from signs and bumper stickers to printed materials and the graphics in television spots.

I started working in political media in a time when campaign graphics were pretty much an afterthought ("I guess we'll need signs"). Then candidates rushed to be the first one in the race to establish red, white, and blue as their colors, even though that choice sacrificed visibility for "patriotism." Very little thought was given to readability.

My business and creative partner for nine years, an amazingly talented graphic designer named Bob Korba, taught me about a hierarchy in the visibility of colors and color combinations. White type on a dark green background is most visible because of the contrast of white letters against a dark passive background. (White letters on black actually starts to blur a little.) That's why most highway signs are white on dark green. Next is white on dark blue, then white on black, and on through the color spectrum. The worst possible choice, yet commonly used, are white letters on a bright red background. The color wavelengths of white and red are short and very close in the light spectrum, so they tend to blur together.

Also important is the typeface, or font. Many "contemporary" sans serif fonts, such as Helvetica, Calibri, or Arial, are used because of their clean look. We are familiar with them because one of them is the default typeface on most computers. Then there are serif typefaces, like Times New Roman, Garamond, and Caledonia. Serifs are those horizontal lines at the top and bottom of some letters that look like feet. They are considered more traditional. If you read a newspaper or magazine, you are probably reading the text in one of the serif typefaces—with good reason. They are easier to read. The serifs give each letter more character and let it stand out from the letters next to it and from the white paper background.

Although most people might not think about color selection and typography when they view an ad, if political communicators ignore these considerations, they're missing an opportunity. If a campaign logo isn't bold, clean, and easy to read, what's the point? If the look isn't repeated on every visual piece a candidate, official, or organization puts out, that candidate, official, or organization is missing an opportunity to reinforce its visual message and identity.

The look is even more essential in television and videos. The images, impression, and the words need to be carefully thought through to ensure they do not convey unintended or incorrect messages.

Visual images reinforce the idea that the candidate is one of us, shares our values, and cares about the same things we do. They are part of telling a story.

The Power of Negative Ads

No other form of political communication is so blatantly and carefully designed to appeal to emotion as a negative—or attack—television spot. And no other form of political communication is so effective at generating an emotional reaction. As much as candidates love to disavow their use, negative ads are an important part of nearly every successful competitive campaign for one simple reason: they work.

In *Political Campaign Communication: Principles and Practices*, communication professors Judith Trent, Robert Friedenberg, and Robert Denton lay out three functions for attack ads:

1. If the candidate uses them early enough in the campaign and they are aired frequently, they can set the rhetorical agenda for the opponent, who will, in some fashion, have to respond.

2. The attack ads may well cause a defensive posture—even in a challenger—and therefore reduce the time, thought, and money that can be allocated to presenting a positive image.

3. Employment of attack ads can function to divert public attention away from those issues that might threaten the incumbent or prove embarrassing for the challenger.[13]

In past elections, political commentators shook their heads at the mere mention of negative ads. They said it demeaned the process and that only candidates who have nothing to offer would stoop to attack their opponent. Further, pundits claimed that negative political ads turn off the public and lower voter participation.

Wrong, wrong, and wrong. A great deal of recent research indicates that negative ads can actually focus voter and news media attention on issues, voting records, and performance, rather than on irrelevant imagery. Until such ads hit the public's "overload" point, studies find they can increase voter turnout. However, that depends on the nature of the negative ad. An ad that is sleazy—filled with innuendo, out-of-context quotations, or outright lies—can cause a backlash against the campaign. If both sides spend all their time maliciously disparaging each other, voters might be completely turned off and stay away from the polls in droves.

There are two broad types of negative ads: *contrast ads* and *attack spots*. Contrast or comparison spots, even those with particular votes, quotes, or graphics on screen, are intended to generate positive feelings toward one candidate and negative feelings toward the other. Research finds that these spots tend to convey more actual information to the public than any other type of ad because they usually focus on specific issues.

In a famous example, Republican Ronald Reagan's 1984 presidential campaign contrasted his record on taxes with Democratic opponent Walter Mondale's. A side-by-side list appeared on-screen, while an announcer said:

> Here's the difference between the two ways of dealing with the nation's economy. With Reaganomics, you cut taxes. With Mondale-nomics, you raise taxes. Reaganomics: You cut deficits through growth and less government. Mondale-nomics: You raise taxes. With Reaganomics, you create incentives that move us all forward. With Mondale-nomics, you raise taxes. They both work. The difference is Reaganomics works for you. Mondale-nomics works against you.[14]

Full-on attack spots are designed to motivate more than inform—to make you either angry at the opponent or fearful about the future if he or she is elected. Attack spots can be absolutely legitimate if they are honest. They can call into question a candidate's record, previous statements, or perhaps which interests are contributing to the candidate's campaign.

In the 2007 campaign for governor, the Louisiana Democratic Party ran a series of television spots against front-runner and eventual winner Bobby Jindal. Several ads distorted Jindal's record in Congress, accusing him of proposals that had come from others, misstating the effect of pieces of legislation, and in one spot, completely misquoting a statement he had made. According to the nonpartisan FactCheck.org at the University of Pennsylvania's Annenberg Public Policy Center, "The Louisiana Democratic Party [was] serving up a hard-to-stomach mix of exaggeration, mischaracterization and falsehood."[15]

The Nature of Negative Ads

Attack ads descend from the kind of bitter and very personal messages that have a long tradition in US politics. In 1800, the words in a message may have been carefully crafted, but rather than appealing to the best in the American people, they appealed to the worst. Vice President Thomas Jefferson ran for president against his former friend and colleague, incumbent President John Adams. Jefferson hired an early political media consultant to prepare broadsides—the colonial version of political advertising—who wrote that Adams was a "bald, crippled and toothless man who wants to start a war with France," and a "hideous hermaphroditical character, with neither the force and firmness of a man nor the gentleness and sensibility of a woman."[16]

Not at all shy about responding in kind, Adams called Jefferson a "mean-spirited, low-lived fellow; the son of a half-breed Indian squaw, sired by a Virginia mulatto father," and warned that "murder, robbery, rape, adultery and incest would be openly taught and practiced" should Jefferson win.[17]

Until recently, campaigns generally would prefer to begin their presence on television with positive image spots conveying a gentle message, either to introduce a challenger to the public or to convey an elected official's record and accomplishments. Attacks would tend to come along later, sometimes in response to events or to poll numbers. Nothing motivates a candidate to attack like being behind in the polls. Then, if things are rocking along pretty well, a campaign would tend to finish on an upbeat note. But again, this would depend on public opinion polls. It can be difficult to drop the attack mode and go back to smiles and waves if you're losing.

The explosion of third-party involvement, including the purchase of advertising time and production of ads on behalf of particular candidates, has changed this model. Frequently, candidates can now let independent organizations run attack ads while they stay at arm's length from the unpleasantness and run spots of their own with warm, fuzzy images.

This practice should raise serious concerns. Following the US Supreme Court's *Citizens United* decision, mentioned earlier in this chapter, business corporations are considered people and can spend as much money as they wish to influence campaigns in which they have a financial stake.

Working through independent "527" committees, they can and do spend millions, much of it on television advertising.[18] And the committees don't have to reveal where the money came from, so the public has no way of knowing who's trying to buy what.

Case Study: Swift Boat Veterans for Truth

One of the most famous and apparently effective examples of attack advertising is still controversial more than a decade later. During the 2004 presidential campaign, an independent group calling itself Swift Boat Veterans for Truth began an ad campaign accusing Democratic candidate Senator John Kerry of Massachusetts of misrepresenting his combat record as commander of a US Navy swift boat in Vietnam in 1968 to 1969. Kerry had been highly decorated, winning the Silver Star, the Bronze Star, and three Purple Hearts, which were awarded for being wounded in action.

The Swift Boat Veterans accused Kerry of lying about his service and the circumstances of his combat decorations. Members of the group claimed in statements and interviews that Kerry's account of events in Vietnam was untrue. However, it turned out that few, if any, of the Swift Boat Veterans had actually served with Kerry at the time of his combat operations or were even with his unit.

In 2005, the Internal Revenue Service released information indicating that more than half of the group's financial backing came from three sources, all prominent Texas donors of President George W. Bush, Kerry's election opponent. Yet even though an exhaustive investigation by the navy's inspector general debunked the accusations and confirmed Kerry's decorations, the charges and ensuing furor became front-page news in the middle of a hotly contested election—and ultimately may have cost Kerry the White House.

Since then, the term *swiftboating* has come to describe a campaign that attacks opponents by dishonestly questioning their credibility and even their patriotism. Swiftboating has become synonymous with political smear.

The other larger concern is that today there is little accountability and no apparent shame in flat-out lying in political advertising. There have been assumptions and some research results over the years indicating that voters will "punish" campaigns for running attack ads. However, in a recent article, political science professors Conor Dowling and Amber Wichowsky found less chance for backfire if the attacks are sponsored by third-party groups.[19] Their research determined that when campaigns let a political party or outside group do their dirty work, voters simply do not connect candidates to the ads. They also found that "in some circumstances, a group-sponsored attack ad produces less polarization than one sponsored by a party."[20] This helps explain why the Swift Boat Veterans attack ads produced no significant consequences for the George W. Bush campaign.

The real damage to our system, then, is inflicted not by appeals to our emotions, but by political messages that are untrue or that twist or distort the truth, the facts, or the actual record. Yale Law School professor emeritus Peter H. Schuck suggested several remedies in a *Washington Post* piece:

- Local media should do what some national media do: objectively assess competing claims for accuracy and publish those assessments prominently.

- Foundations—perhaps even the political parties themselves—should fund nonpartisan organizations with reputations for objectivity to do the same.

- Congress should require, subject to the constraints of the First Amendment's protections of individual and organizational privacy, noncandidate producers of all election ads to identify themselves and their largest donors.[21]

Can Negative Be Positive?

Some eminent political scholars find negative advertising to be a destructive force—that "attack advertising actually suppresses voter turnout." In *Going Negative: How Political Advertisements Shrink & Polarize the Electorate*, Stephen Ansolabahere of Massachusetts Institute of Technology and Shanto Iyengar of the University of California–Los Angeles write that attack ads can and are being used strategically to suppress voter turnout, and claim further that such ads "may pose a serious antidemocratic threat."[22] They believe that candidates who might benefit from low voter turnout pay for negative advertising to discourage participation. "The real concern for Twenty-First Century democracy is not manipulation of naive voters by sophisticated 'image-makers,' but the shrinking of the electorate by political strategists who are fully aware of the consequences of their actions."[23]

Some scholars find attack ads can improve the electoral process. In his book *In Defense of Negativity: Attack Ads in Presidential Campaigns*, Vanderbilt professor John Geer asserts that "negativity can advance and improve the prospects for democracy. . . . While it is true that free press is an essential part of any regime that purports to be democratic, that is only part of the story. We also need the criticisms from competing candidates to ensure that we more fully vet the respective plans and qualification of these politicians."[24]

Geer suggests that there are "payoffs" for democratic life from the ability of candidates to go negative:.

1. The threat of criticism provides politicians incentive to adopt sound policies and to be the type of individuals who will attract votes.

2. Criticism can increase the quality of information available to voters as they make a choice in elections. To make good decisions, they need to know the past record of candidates and what they propose to do in the future.[25]

Negativity (and the threat of it) makes accountability possible. Without accountability, democracy falters. If an incumbent does a poor job in office, it is unlikely that person will be (publicly) self-critical. Of course, challengers are likely to raise more problems than may actually exist. The elected officials not only need to set the record straight but must point out potential weaknesses of the opposition.

Conclusion

Principle 7: Despite the digital media revolution and profound changes in media and media audiences, paid advertising by election campaigns and interest groups will continue to be an essential tool to reach target audiences with political messages.

Despite the digital revolution, despite the ever-increasing cost of television advertising, despite any public concern over the huge amounts of campaign contributions from virtually anonymous sources, and despite the lack of any sort of "truth filter" on the political ads we see, paid advertising by election campaigns and interest groups will continue to be an essential tool to reach target audiences with political messages. In 2012, there were more television spots than ever before, but the 2016 campaign actually saw a decrease in expenditures. Along with broadcast advertising, the amount spent online is reaching new heights each year. Given all the research into the effect and effectiveness of emotional appeals in political campaign messaging, it is highly likely that we will continue to see and hear many political ads that try to make us afraid, angry, sad, proud, or hopeful.

Notes

1. Borrell and Associates, "2015–2016 Political Advertising Outlook," August 17, 2015, https://www.borrellassociates.com/industry -papers/papers/2015-to-2016-political-advertising-outlook-august-15 -detail.

2. "The Nielsen Total Audience Report: Q4 2016," April 3, 2017, http://www.nielsen.com/us/en/insights/reports/2017/the-nielsen-total -audience-report-q4-2016.html.

3. Roger Ailes, Nixon-Agnew campaign media consultant, newspaper interview (1968).

4. John C. Tedesco and Scott W. Dunn, *The 2012 Presidential Campaign: A Communication Perspective* (Lanham, MD: Rowman and Littlefield, 2014), 78.

5. Conversation with Monica Davis, owner, Davis Group, Austin, Texas, 2015.

6. Nielsen Company, "Total Audience Report: Q4 2015" March 24, 2016, http://www.nielsen.com/us/en/insights/reports/2016/the-total -audience-report-q4-2015.html.

7. Ibid.

8. "Guide to Radio Station Formats," May 2015, http://www.news generation.com/broadcast-resources/guide-to-radio-station-formats/.

9. George Marcus, *The Sentimental Citizen: Emotion in Democratic Politics* (State College: Pennsylvania State University Press, 2002), 18.

10. Ted Brader, *Campaigning for Hearts and Minds* (Chicago: University of Chicago Press, 2006), chap. 6.

11. Ibid., 13.

12. Ibid.

13. Judith Trent, Robert Friedenberg, and Robert Denton, *Political Campaign Communication: Principles and Practices* (Lanham, MD: Rowman and Littlefield, 2011), 152.

14. "The Living Room Candidate," 2008, http://www.livingroom candidate.org/files/pdf/LESSON_01.pdf.

15. FactCheck.org, August 29, 2007, http://www.factcheck.org/2007 /08/overspiced-louisiana-gumbo/.

16. "Founding Fathers' Dirty Campaign," CNN, August 22, 2008, http://www.cnn.com/2008/LIVING/wayoflife/08/22/mf.campaign.slurs .slogans/.

17. Ibid.

18. These are tax-exempt organizations organized under Section 527 of the US Internal Revenue Code. Robert Yoon, "Your Guide to Political Committees on the 2016 Presidential Campaign Trail," CNN, January 28, 2015, http://www.cnn.com/2015/01/28/politics/2016-election -political-committee-explainer/index.html.

19. Conor Dowling and Amber Wichowsky, "Attacks Without Consequence? Candidates, Parties, Groups, and the Changing Face of Negative Advertising," *American Journal of Political Science* (March 2014).

20. Ibid.

21. Peter H. Schuck, "Why Government Fails So Often, and How It Can Do Better," *Washington Post*, August 26, 2014.

22. Stephen Ansolabahere and Shanto Iyengar, *Going Negative: How Political Advertisements Shrink and Polarize the Electorate* (New York: Free Press, 1997).

23. Ibid.

24. John Geer, *In Defense of Negativity: Attack Ads in Presidential Campaigns* (Chicago: University of Chicago Press, 2006), 10, 11.

25. Ibid., 13.

9

Political Communication in the Internet Age

Principle 8: The Internet and the digital revolution have changed a lot of things, but not quite everything.

Few advances in technology have had such a profound impact on so many people in so short a time as the Internet. How, when, and where people communicate has advanced with amazing rapidity in the past few decades, and digital communication continues to bring enormous change in the way we relate to each other, the way we access information, the way we learn, and the way government and politics are conducted. While a few of us are still trying to figure out how to use digital devices competently, there is now a generation that cannot imagine a world without the Internet and social media. For people of my Baby Boomer generation, it's hard to believe that the Internet is now considered a "middle-aged" technology.

Research within the US Department of Defense led to the transmission of the first internet message in 1969. In 1991, Tim Berners Lee, a software engineer at a Swiss particle physics laboratory, invented an information system that allowed documents

187

to be connected to other documents by hypertext links and enabled searches by moving from one document to another. He called it the World Wide Web (www). In the years since, our society has been transformed from receiving most news and information from printed publications and the television to receiving information via wireless media on laptops, electronic tablets, and smartphones. Today, more and more people get most or all of their information from websites and blogs, rather than from network television or radio.

Politicians Log On

It did not take long for political campaigns to discover the Internet and use it to communicate with the public. The 1992 Bill Clinton presidential campaign was the first, according to political communication scholars John Hendricks and Lynda Lee Kid in *Techno Politics in Presidential Campaigning: New Voice, New Technologies and New Voters*. At the time, however, websites were barely interactive, if at all, and served primarily as sites to post text, including speeches, candidate bio information, issue positions, and arguments. The Internet was essentially a one-way information-sharing medium. Campaigns continued to rely on more traditional channels of communication for voter outreach, such as television, direct mail, and telephone banks.

By 1996, according to the Pew Research Center, about 20 percent of Americans were going online at home, at work, or at school: "Nearly three-fourths of this group, about 21 million Americans (12% of the voting age population) obtained political or policy news from online sources this year, and of them, about 7 million (4%) used the Internet and/or commercial services for information about the Presidential election."[1] The Pew Research Center's postelection survey found that 3 percent of voters identified Internet sites as their principal sources for election news, and about 10 percent of voters got at least some information online.

At that time, the Internet was still not really interactive. However, the 1996 Clinton reelection campaign pioneered an important use of the Internet's e-mail function: fundraising. Although the return was small by today's standards, a new tool was established.

In 2000, presidential primary candidates Republican Senator John McCain and Democratic Senator Bill Bradley both used the Internet as an effective fundraising tool and to recruit campaign volunteers. By then, about 50 percent of Americans were online, and the Internet was an essential source of political news and information as more and more news outlets moved online, including broadcast and cable television networks. This began a downward spiral that continues today in the number of people who regularly read newspapers and magazines or receive most of their news and information from television news outlets.

Campaigning Online

The Internet, even in its earlier, less-interactive stages, brought major advances in the ability of political campaigns to identify various target audiences and communicate more directly with them.

In the 2004 campaign, Democratic presidential primary candidate Governor Howard Dean took advantage of the Internet's expanded interactivity in different ways. Besides prodigious online fundraising, Dean used Meetup.com to reach out to thousands of motivated volunteers and to provide supporters with a medium to locate and communicate with others in their area. Through its web site, the Dean campaign generated more than 100,000 handwritten letters from supporters in other states to voters in the key Iowa and New Hampshire constituencies.

Online Fundraising

In addition to using the Internet to recruit volunteers and organize, Howard Dean's 2004 presidential primary campaign was equally adept in using the new technology to raise money. This ability to raise both money and effort from genuine grassroots supporters instead of large corporate interests profoundly changed US politics. For the first time, candidates and campaigns had a realistic method with which to raise necessary funds without relying so heavily on major donors or special interests. The ability to reach thousands of small contributors via e-mail proved effective and workable.

"By early December 2003, more than 530,000 Americans had registered as active supporters, and millions of dollars had flowed into the Dean coffers, independent of the Democratic party's own fundraising apparatus," wrote Sean Dodson and Ben Hammersley in *The Guardian*.[2] On one occasion, Vice President Dick Cheney organized a $2,000-per-plate lunch event for President George W. Bush. Dean went online and challenged supporters to join him "for lunch" on their computers. The website included an image of Dean eating a turkey sandwich. He outraised the Bush-Cheney event. "Although he had close to 10 times the war chest of the other candidates for the Democratic nomination, yet was spending far less than his network-free opponents, Dean's effective use of the Internet was not just about the money," Dodsen and Hammersley concluded. It was also about the ability to reach out and encourage supporters to help in other ways.[3]

In the 2008 presidential campaign, Senator Barack Obama had raised $25 million in the first quarter of 2007, $6.9 million of it in online contributions under $200. This was more than 20 percent of the total all candidates raised in that period. His opponent Senator John McCain raised less than half that.

The 2012 Obama reelection campaign and the Democratic National Committee completely rewrote the book on grassroots political fundraising, raising $1.1 billion from 4.5 million contributors, nearly 3 million of whom had not contributed in 2008. About $690 million of that was raised online. The campaign reported an average contribution of $65.89.

The campaign website itself is often a major money generator for political campaigns. Most home pages will prominently feature some sort of "Contribute" button, allowing supporters to make a contribution by credit card on the spot. But e-mail has become one of the most frequently used and effective vehicles for political fundraising by campaigns, party organizations, and advocacy organizations. If you have ever donated to a candidate or political party, sent a check to a nonprofit advocacy organization, signed a petition, attended a political event, or signed into a political website, you probably furnished your e-mail and in return have probably received endless appeals for donations. The messages may appear to be impromptu. They aren't.

Small armies of fundraising specialists, many specializing in online and e-mail appeals, work for the Republican and Democratic National Committees, their Senate and House reelection committees, and numerous other partisan support organizations, not to mention all the campaigns seeking direct contributions. Many of those organizations will exhort you to send $3, $4, or $5 right now. You have to beat a deadline and your contribution will be matched or even doubled if you act quickly! These messages are called rush letters. And they work. The wording in most of these fundraising pitches is no more off-the-cuff than the fact that your name and e-mail address are on their list. Every message is pretested. The response to each appeal is carefully measured and compared to other messages, down to the subject line designed to get you to open the e-mail. The 2012 Obama campaign used the phrase "I will be outspent" in one e-mail subject box. It raised $2.6 million. Another that was headed "Some scary numbers" raised $1.9 million.

Online Advertising

Internet advertising has become a potent means of reaching target audiences and individuals with political messages. According to Epolitics.com:

> Options for online advertising by political campaigns have expanded exponentially, including the ability to target ads with great precision. Some advertising vendors can match voter databases with commercial advertising networks to hit, say, only past Democratic primary voters in a given Congressional district who are female between the ages of 25 and 40. Even Google Ads can actually be targeted on several levels, not just by topic ("keyword") but also (for instance) geographically or by time of day.[4]

Online advertising can be remarkably effective at volunteer recruitment, so much so that many online organizers argue that recruiting ads should start running as soon as a candidate announces so that no potential support is wasted. Campaigns can also use digital ads to persuade voters, spread messaging, and, as election day closes in, drive voter turnout.

How does a campaign pay for ads? Sometimes online advertising is like television or radio, where the advertiser pays by the number of impressions, or people who see the ad (typically measured in cost per thousand). With Google and Twitter ads, though, the advertiser usually pays per viewer click. These are the most commonly used Internet advertising vehicles:

- Online display ads
- Google search ads
- Facebook ads
- Twitter ads
- Video ads
- Blog ads

From Block Walking to Data Mining

For decades, the largest and most sophisticated political campaign's "ground game" was constructed on a foundation of local election precincts. Voting tabulations from individual precincts in past elections yielded a basis for decision-making for future elections. Based on actual voting, campaigns tried to predict which precincts would be most likely to support or oppose candidates of a particular political party or certain types of issues. Precincts were usually sorted by the campaigns into several categories. Specific terms vary, but these convey the categories:

- *Get-Out-The-Vote (GOTV)*. These are precincts with a voting history deemed favorable and reliable. They required a focus on motivation and mobilization on election day.
- *Swing*. These precincts could go either way, but had enough potential votes to make a carefully targeted effort at persuasion and mobilization worthwhile.

- *Cut-Margin.* Precincts in this category had mostly opposition voters, but enough favorable voters to make a highly targeted persuasion and motivation effort worth the trouble.
- *Enemy Boxes.* These are precincts dominated by the opposition's voters. Campaigns tip-toed around them and hoped they all slept through election day.

Successful national and statewide campaigns were usually those that could put together the most effective ground game, relying on local organizations to help identify and motivate local voters, precinct by precinct.

The essential nature of campaigns' ground game has not changed. Few candidates have been successful without an effective organizational effort. The most brilliant, beautifully produced political messages need to be actuated by coordinated efforts to reinforce the messages and translate them into action—getting people to go to the polls and vote. However, technology has created some highly effective tools that now allow a campaign's organizational efforts and messaging to be targeted at individual voters instead of election precincts. These technological advances have given political organizations a profoundly increased ability to collect, organize, and utilize data.

Data Mining

Data mining has been an important tool in business for more than twenty years. In *Retail Is Detail: A Retailer's Playbook for Beating Walmart,* authors Bill Scott and James Hawkins describe its use:

> By and large, retailers are inundated with volumes of unusable data. Data mining is the automated extraction of hidden, predictive information from data bases. Generally, data mining is the process of analyzing data from different perspectives and summarizing it into useful information. It allows users to scrutinize data from many different dimensions or angles, categorize it, and summarize the relationships identified. Technically, data mining is the process of finding correlations or patterns among dozens of fields in large relational databases.[5]

Data mining is now used extensively by campaigns and political organizations to identify and mobilize supporters across the country. What data is there to mine? Think about all the public records that exist about you: tax records, party affiliation, political contributions, home and secondary addresses, business information, and professional licensing records, among others. Put that data together with your voting history, and a campaign can make pretty accurate assumptions about your political proclivities and what issues might pique your interest. Now imagine how precisely that information enables specific messages based on your habits and interests to be targeted to you via direct mail and e-mail. A campaign can pinpoint media and reach out to individual voter households, even in precincts with few of its voters.

The campaign can supply volunteers with detailed target lists of people in their area to call or visit, along with which issues would most likely be of interest. Rather than trying to battle market by market throughout swing states—those that could go either way—campaigns can amass files of individual voter profiles and information, allowing likely voters to be pinpointed within larger areas that do not support that campaign.

Case Study: Bush Campaign Data Mining Strikes Gold

The 2004 Bush-Cheney reelection campaign did not take a back seat to anyone in adapting technology to communication. They brought in the marketing research and "knowledge management" firm TargetPoint Consulting to conduct surveys, overlay the results on thousands of existing data points, and use the results to identify more distinct groups within the larger target audience.

Reporter Chris Cillizza described the results in a 2007 *Washington Post* story: "Bush campaign manager Ken Mehlman said, 'In 2000, we very broadly talked to people on broad issues. In 2004, instead of talking about what we thought was most important, we talked about what the voters thought was most important.'"[6]

Cillizza's analysis found that data mining helped turn the tide in two critical states:

> In Ohio, the key battleground of the 2004 campaign . . . Black voters—who had traditionally not been drawn to the GOP—wanted to hear candidates talk about education and health care. As a result, they received a series of contacts—direct mail and phone calls, primarily— emphasizing Bush's accomplishments on just those two issues. It was a much different message from the president's broader attempt to cast the election as a choice between staying the course in Iraq and the anti-terrorism effort or switching teams in midstream.

It worked. Nationwide, Bush won 11 percent of the black vote, a two-point increase from 2000; in Ohio, he won 16 percent, an improvement of 7 percentage points. Bush won Ohio by 118,601 votes, or approximately 2 percent of the more than 5.6 million votes cast for the two major-party nominees.

In New Mexico, data mining identified a segment of 19,000 lower- and middle-class, middle-aged Hispanic women whose children attended public schools. They were strongly resistant to Republican candidates—just one in five said they would back a GOP candidate—but about half said they would back Bush. Why? Because 80 percent of the group strongly supported his No Child Left Behind education initiative.

"The Bush campaign made a targeted strike with a message focused on his push for testing and standards in public schools. It focused particularly on the 6,000 women in the group who were all but certain to vote. Again, the goal was not to win Hispanics or even Hispanic women but rather to minimize the Bush campaign's losses in this particular demographic."

Bush won New Mexico by 0.79 percent, winning 49.84 percent of the vote to John Kerry's 49.05 percent. Bush carried New Mexico by 5,988 votes. It was the only state he lost in 2000 and then won in 2004.

Microtargeting

Since the 2004 election, digital technology has evolved quickly, enabling the collection and manipulation of vastly more data. Data mining evolved into microtargeting, giving campaigns and other organizations a greater ability to target political messages to particular groups of likely voters—even individuals—rather than relying on mass messaging. Being able to direct a message to an identifiable group with common characteristics or interests, or to individual voters, makes a campaign's communication process more effective because messages can be very specific. It also saves money because campaigns are not paying to send messages to all possible voters via mass media.

How does it work? Campaigns and other political organizations can purchase extensive consumer information about individuals or small groups of like-minded people gathered, maintained, and continually updated by commercial data brokers. What information? How often do you make purchases with credit cards? Do you use a CVS Pharmacy, Rite Aid, or Rexall card for discounts at the drug store? How about your car registration? Do you own a home or rent? Are you married? Divorced? Do you contribute to charities? Do you have a college degree? Got kids in college? What magazines do you subscribe to? How about browser cookies from some of the Internet sites you visit? What information about you does your Facebook page or LinkedIn profile contain? And so on.

"All of this information can then be combined with the available IDs to build demographic profiles of different types of voters," explains Strategic Telemetry president Ken Strasma on his Winning Campaigns website.[7]

Even if a campaign does not have individual identities, demographic profiles can be applied to groups of voters with particular characteristics by using a number of statistical techniques. Using statistical modeling processes, individual voters can be put into groups to be targeted with messages that should be especially effective with them. Political organizations have given these groups informal names: Downscale Union Independents, Tax and Terrorism Moderates, Older Suburban Newshounds, Flag and Family Republicans, Young Cultural Liberals, Terrorism and Health-Care

Democrats, Education-Focused Democrats, and Christian Conservative Environmentalists, to name a few.

Case Study: 2012 Obama Campaign Data Collection Operation

In the 2012 presidential election, the Obama reelection campaign didn't just rewrite the book on collecting and using voter data. They wrote a completely new book.

The campaign put together the most massive database in political history, merging information from dozens of sources into one comprehensive system. This megafile allowed the campaign to organize turnout data on millions of voters. They could then cross-tabulate the data with information from pollsters, fundraisers, consumer databases, and, significantly, with files of social media and mobile contacts with voters in critical swing states like Ohio, Michigan, Pennsylvania, and Virginia. Incredibly specific messages could be targeted with devastating accuracy using the most-effective media channels.

Time magazine's Michael Scherer described the operation in a November 19, 2012, article: "From the beginning, campaign manager Jim Messina had promised a totally different, metric-driven kind of campaign in which politics was the goal but political instincts might not be the means. 'We are going to measure every single thing in this campaign,' he said after taking the job. He hired an analytics department five times as large as that of the 2008 operation."[8]

The data compilation was so complete that the campaign was able to make media-buying decisions, such as targeting television spots to the desired audience, without using the Nielsen ratings on audience size and demography

continues

Case Study: continued

for every television program. "We were able to put our target voters through some really complicated modeling, to say, O.K., if Miami-Dade women under 35 are the targets, [here is] how to reach them," said one official. As a result, the campaign bought ads to air during unconventional programming, like *Sons of Anarchy*, *The Walking Dead*, and *Don't Trust the B—in Apt. 23*, skirting the traditional route of buying ads next to local news programming. How much more efficient at ad buying was the Obama campaign of 2012 than the 2008 one? "On TV, we were able to buy 14% more efficiently . . . to make sure we were talking to our persuadable voters," the same official said.[9]

The Obama database collected much more specific information on its voters than Republicans gathered, including data on Facebook and other social media use. "Online, the get-out-the-vote effort continued with a first-ever attempt at using Facebook on a mass scale to replicate the door-knocking efforts of field organizers," Scherer reported. "In the final weeks of the campaign, people who had downloaded an app were sent messages with pictures of their friends in swing states. They were told to click a button to automatically urge those targeted voters to take certain actions, such as registering to vote, voting early or getting to the polls. The campaign found that roughly 1 in 5 people contacted by a Facebook pal acted on the request, in large part because the message came from someone they knew."[10]

The megafile also accommodated an amazingly effective fundraising effort. Not only were an unprecedented number of people contacted, but the campaign continuously tested fundraising pitches to determine which was the most effective with which group of supporters. They raised more than $1 billion. "That data-driven decisionmaking played a huge role in creating a second term for the 44th President and will be one of the more closely studied elements of the 2012 cycle," Scherer wrote. "It's another sign that the role of the campaign pros in Washington who make decisions on hunches and experience is rapidly dwindling, being replaced by the work of quants [quantitative analysts] and computer coders who can crack massive data sets for insight."[11]

None of this would have been possible without the next-generation digital tools of the Internet—Web 2.0. "Were it not for the Internet, Barack Obama would not be president. Were it not for the Internet, Barack Obama would not have been the nominee," *Huffington Post* editor in chief Arianna Huffington told a panel discussion on the intersection of politics and the Internet shortly after the 2008 election.[12]

Social Media

Social media is truly democratized communication. Based more on starting conversations than disseminating messages, it offers, at the least, two-way interaction. Because it enables user-generated content, traditional top-down communication is much more difficult and "message discipline" nearly impossible. Today, effective government or policy communicators have to manage the communication process in both traditional media and Internet and social media, which allows them to reach out to desired audiences without the filter of the news media.

In 1999, electronic design consultant Darcy DiNucci coined the term "Web 2.0" to describe, not the World Wide Web itself, but the next generation of web sites. The Internet had not changed so much as the technology of the sites on it. They now empowered interactive social networking sites, blogs, and video sharing, and in just a few years led to today's social media platforms, with user-generated content creating a place for conversations and user communities.

What Sites Are Out There?

There are now at least fifty active social media sites, but four of them continue to be most widely used in various types of political communication:

- Facebook is by far the most heavily used social media platform, claiming 1.35 billion active users per month and 864 million per day. The average user spends 21 minutes on Facebook per day. Facebook is also comprehensive. Users can post images and videos, send detailed messages, and publicly interact.

- Twitter is used primarily for short messages, originally limited to 140 characters. It is ideal for event updates, blog post pushes, and breaking news. Campaigns also use Twitter to interact with specific individuals and targeted groups.

- YouTube is a video site with wide reach that continues to grow. Political communicators are learning that a staggering number of searches are done on YouTube, which makes it essential for them to stake out their issue's name to bring users to their videos.

- Flickr is used to publish activity photos. It hosts more than 4 billion images and attracts more than 30 million visitors per month.

Other social media platforms can be highly effective for different kinds of political messages and target audiences. LinkedIn is very useful for policy organizations with a business orientation. In its 2014 Social Media Update, Pew Research Center found that 50 percent of Internet users with college educations used LinkedIn. Myspace can still be a viable and effective network for the right audience, and there are dozens of other networks with niche focuses ranging from veterans to volunteers.[13]

Who Is Using Social Media?

Although social media began as a platform used primarily by young people, its use has expanded dramatically. In its 2014 research, Pew found that 81 percent of US adults were using the Internet, and more than half the adults 65 and older who went online were using Facebook. That's 31 percent of all seniors. It's not just that more adults are going online. More online adults are expanding their use of social media sites; 52 percent were using two or more sites—a 10 percent increase in one year. Here are a few more surprising statistics:

- The fastest growing demographic on Twitter is the 55–64 year age bracket, up 79 percent since 2012.

- The 45–54 age bracket is the fastest growing demographic on Facebook and Google Plus.

- YouTube reaches more US adults aged 18–34 than any cable television network.[14]

Every bit as important to political communicators as changes in who uses social media are changes in how it is being used. Research from the Pew Center; the Nielsen Company, long the most credible source for public media viewing habits; and other media research reveals broad and significant trends in media usage.

- News audiences for traditional media—print and broadcast— have been shrinking for several years.

- Television news itself is now viewed less on TV screens and more on smartphones. Data from the American Press Institute finds that Millennials now get 74 percent of their news online.[15]

- Many newspaper and television reporters tweet, blog, and use Facebook to convey breaking news between print editions or newscasts.

- Jim Downie, digital opinion editor at the *Washington Post,* has told my classes that 50 percent of the *Post*'s online readers access the newspaper through Facebook. Downie said fully 60 percent of that online access is from mobile devices.[16]

- More and more traditional news sources, print and broadcast, are expanding their online presence.

- A growing number of serious online-only news organizations are in operation, such as BuzzFeed and Vox, with expanding staffs of serious reporters.

- More online news consumers share news, images, and video with others, which I would argue reflects a deeper and more active interest in events and politics than simply perusing the latest headlines.

- Many social media news consumers still access news from traditional sources as well. This is very important. It means that a significant number of people get their news from both social media and traditional print and broadcast sources, whether on websites or in print.

Mobile Apps: Good News and Bad News

Mobile applications, software applications designed to run on mobile devices such as smartphones and tablets, offer political communicators opportunities to zero in on particular demographic groups of voters and potential voters, specifically Millennials. Research indicates that Americans consume more than 5.5 hours of digital media every day, 65 percent of it on mobile devices.[17] That's a 30 percent increase from 2012. Clearly, this is an audience that cannot be overlooked in effective political messaging.

The increasing use of mobile apps to access music and sports programming—as well as computer games (such as Pokémon Go)—also presents political communicators with significant obstacles. According to broadcast industry marketing manager Paula Minardi's 2016 Internet Trends Report published in *AdExchanger Politics*,

More voting audiences, especially millennials, are blocking ads, skipping them or simply opting for ad-free content experiences—

just because they can. Whether trying to raise funds, gain awareness or motivate supporters to get out the vote, candidates will be affected.

There are now around 45 million monthly active ad-blocking users in the US—and growing. Ad-blocking rates vary by region, ranging from around 8% of ads in Washington, DC, to more than 16% in Oregon. Some traditional swing states hover near the top end of the range, with Nevada and New Hampshire topping 14%, while Florida is just under 13%. Since US ad-blocking rates have grown nearly 50% in the last year alone, those numbers will likely climb even higher in 2016 as more voters become familiar with ad-blocking software, especially on mobile devices.[18]

Ad avoidance will remain a key challenge for political campaigns. In order to get their political messages out, communicators will need to solve the challenge of reaching a key demographic group that is rapidly expanding its use of mobile apps.

How do all these changes affect political communicators and their audiences? Overall, candidates and elected officials can now convey messages to audiences almost instantly, with pinpoint accuracy, and without the filter of the news media. They use Facebook, YouTube, Twitter, Snapchat, and other digital platforms to augment traditional public communication. Social media allows a quick reaction to breaking news and events or to public statements by an opponent, which increases the chances of getting that reaction included in the news coverage of the event or original statement.

The 2016 Presidential Campaign

Political pathologists will be stirring through the ashes of the 2016 presidential election for many years trying to understand everything that happened. Without a doubt, a major factor in the election of President Donald J. Trump was an amazingly effective use of social media.

In June 2015, Donald Trump wasn't really a serious contender for president. The Republican Party had sixteen more-seasoned political figures—some more experienced, some better financed, some more credentialed or with more impressive political pedigrees, but all much more plausible candidates for national office than a real estate tycoon from Manhattan whose celebrity status arose from a "reality" TV show.

In 2015, his Republican opponents wrote him off as loud but transitory noise. Then they sneered. Then they took umbrage. Then they tried to compete. But they waited too long. By the time they took him seriously, the constant news coverage, much of it as a result of his relentless use of social media, had moved him to the top tier and, ultimately, to become the Republican nominee for president of the United States. In the general election campaign against Democratic nominee, former first lady, US senator, and secretary of state Hillary Clinton, he was given little chance.

Case Study: @realDonaldTrump

Many factors led to Donald Trump's surprising election victory, but one of the major reasons was his highly effective use of social media—particularly Facebook and Twitter. His messages rarely contained any details of his positions or thoughts on government policy or issues, but more often were filled with angry reactions and playground style name-calling of opponents and others who questioned or disagreed with him. He routinely referred to Senator Ted Cruz as "Lyin Ted," Senator Marco Rubio as "Little Marco," Senator Lindsey Graham as "dumb" and "really sad," Senator Elizabeth Warren as "Pocahontas," former Florida governor Jeb Bush as "low energy," and his Democratic opponent, former US secretary of state Hillary Clinton, as "Crooked Hillary."[19] Yet importantly, what the media occasionally referred to as his "Twitter rants" apparently had great appeal among his strongly antiestablishment electoral base.

Overall, Donald Trump's tweets served two important communication functions. First, they reached his growing number of followers with many variations of a powerful message: "Drain the swamp in Washington, DC." The message was absolutely unfiltered by the news media. According to the *Wall Street Journal*, on election day, Trump had 15,570,255 Twitter followers; Hillary Clinton had 11,196,739. On one day, October 19, Trump tweeted his followers 87 times, and he averaged 11 tweets per day throughout the campaign.[20]

Second, social media played a major role in driving Trump's coverage in the mainstream media. Cable television news had quickly become hooked on Donald Trump. His penchant for grandiose, astonishing, often explosive statements made him "great copy." His tweets, rally speeches, and even major "policy" speeches contained little, if any, depth or detail. Yet they were "breaking news," covered live and usually in their entirety by CNN, Fox News, and MSNBC, then featured prominently in broadcast network news programs. After that coverage, they were endlessly analyzed by pundits.

Combining his heavy use of Twitter with almost daily campaign rallies—generally boisterous and with huge audiences—Trump was rewarded with extensive, nearly daily news coverage. According to media analytics firm mediaQuant, Trump received nearly $4.6 billion in free air time from June 2015 to September 2016, nearly double Hillary Clinton's $2.4 billion. In fact, Trump received about $400 million in free air time in May 2016 alone, about what Senator John McCain spent in his entire 2008 presidential race.

In her November 14, 2016 post, "A Media Post-Mortem on the 2016 Presidential Election," Mary Harris wrote, "Trump closes the 2016 Presidential Election with $5.2 billion in earned media. Even for our mediaQuant analysts who monitor over 4,000 brands, topics, celebrities and

continues

Case Study: continued

---

storylines every day, that number is almost surreal in sheer magnitude. Clinton's final earned media total also broke all election records at $3.2 billion, well ahead of Obama's 2008 and 2012 earned media totals."[21]

Other social media platforms were also used extensively by both campaigns. *USA Today* wrote that Trump had 22.7 million likes and followers on Facebook, Twitter, and Instagram combined, compared to Clinton's combined 15 million. But on YouTube, Clinton had 16.4 million views compared to Trump's 8.1 million.[22]

Important questions are being asked by political communicators and communication scholars. Will Donald Trump's 2016 presidential campaign become the model for political communication in the future? Have traditional media simply been overshadowed and outperformed, even for national campaigns? Or was Donald Trump's breathtaking success in using social media to create and drive his media outreach a reflection of his celebrity and his penchant for saying things that seem completely outrageous.

Online Communication: Still Only Part of a Winning Campaign Strategy

The Internet and social media have revolutionized political communication. But they have not completely replaced more traditional means of disseminating messages and reaching out to supporters and contributors. To maximize returns, smart campaigners combine online fundraising with traditional methods, such as direct mail and events. Communication through a campaign website, e-mail, and social media have to be a huge part of an overall communication effort. But even though social media users and audiences continue to expand into older age groups, social media outlets overall tend to reach a younger, more affluent, more educated audience. Overreliance on new media can miss large blocks of potential or likely supporters or activists. Traditional media platforms may play a smaller role today in how people communicate with each other and get their information, but they are far from obsolete.

Newspapers, network and local television, and radio still reach millions and millions of people every day. They still offer credible, effective vehicles to quickly reach a broad audience with a single message.

Online Policy Communication

As I pointed out in earlier chapters, political messages don't just fade away after election day. Officials and government agencies use many of the same media to reach out to constituents and interested members of the public about public policy issues. Why? People who hold political office inherently want constituents to feel that they are well represented. That compels officials to be sure voters are aware of their positions on issues. In today's communication environment, this means putting their spin on how they voted or how they feel about those issues so constituents don't just see it in the news.

In Congress, many members post videos on YouTube to be sure folks back home don't miss their news conferences, statements, or speeches. And a lot of senators and representatives maintain busy Facebook sites and send out tweets, especially about controversial issues or votes. "When you go down to the House floor and you make a speech to the C-SPAN audience, you reach three to four million. But take that video, put it on your YouTube site or put it in Twitter, put it on Facebook and then you're getting that multiplier effect," one representative told the Congressional Management Foundation (CMF), a nonprofit, nonpartisan organization that encourages, assists, and provides training to get Congress to communicate more actively with the public.[23]

Every member of the US House and Senate has an active website filled with information about the member and issues he or she is involved in. Every news release, every speech, every floor statement is quickly posted. Every legislative committee has a website with detailed information about issues, usually with transcripts and video of committee hearings. Most of the individual congressional sites are increasingly interactive, not just so constituents can sign up for e-mail newsletters or request a Capitol tour, but to solicit questions and comments about particular issues. More and more state legislators and local officials around the country are building individual websites as well, but even among those that exist, interactivity is far from uniform.

The CMF has been around since 1977, focused on helping Congress and congressional offices communicate more openly and effectively. In a series of reports, CMF surveyed 260 congressional staffers to explore the use of the Internet and social media in two-way communication between congressional offices and congressional constituents. The conclusion: "The behavior of Congress and citizens has been altered. Americans who previously had not participated in public policy debate are now engaged: congressional staffers have new and instant means for assessing public opinion on emerging policies and issues; and legislators are opening new windows into both the legislative process and their own personalities."[24]

Based on the survey, although legislative staffers see attendance at state or district events (such as town hall meetings) and direct personal communication as most important in helping them understand constituent views and opinions, 64 percent think Facebook is also an important tool, 42 percent say Twitter is important, and 34 percent believe YouTube is important.

One House chief of staff observed, "There are two different goals for communication—responding to those who are already engaged, and getting your message to those who aren't paying attention. Those goals aren't often met with the same techniques, but offices need to develop strategies for each."

On an interesting demographic note, the CMF survey found very different attitudes toward social media between congressional offices that quickly embraced the new technologies and those that came to the party a little later. Also—to no great surprise—attitudes differed markedly between younger staffers who were very familiar and comfortable with social media, and older, often senior, staff members who grew up before the digital revolution. In each case, the attitudinal difference was the same: younger staffers and offices that were quick to harness the technology believed more strongly that social media enabled congressional offices to reach people not previously being reached and enabled more meaningful interaction with constituents. They were also more comfortable with controlling their message on social media.

Online Issue Advocacy

Advocacy and other organizations with a particular issue focus use the same communication tools to reach two distinct audiences: their constituents in the public and government decisionmakers. They need to rally and organize constituents to the issue or cause to build and maintain a sufficient critical mass so they can be the voice for a large group of people, which gives them credibility with decisionmakers. And they need to reach decisionmakers with a message that makes a convincing case for their issue, which gives them credibility with their constituent group. If the advocacy organization is focused on a reasonable issue, if it actually represents a credible constituency (size matters), if it has facts and figures to make a good case for its position, and if it knows how to communicate that information to decisionmakers, then it can be a very effective force.

Organizations are not the only users of social media on the advocacy side. According to Catherine Ho of the *Washington Post,* "Many K Street leaders view so-called media and digital advocacy, not traditional lobbying, as the fastest-growing segments of the influence industry."[25]

Ho reported that an October 2016 survey conducted by opinion research firm Prime Group found that 38 percent of responding Washington lobbyists, association executives, and think tank leaders said they expect organizations to increase their use of social media to influence policymakers, and 21 percent expect organizations to increase their digital capabilities.

But remember the warning from earlier about political campaign communication: online communication is a large part of a winning strategy, but not all. As with campaign and policy communication from elected officials and government agencies, social media is an important part of the advocacy process but not the entire process. Congressional legislative staffers indicate that they are likely to pay attention and consider substantive information and data from easy-to-navigate websites or Facebook pages, but they also value well-written printed materials in the mail or delivered in personal visits, including targeted visits by organization supporters from the boss's state or district, particularly if they are local leaders.

And depending on the issue, their bosses may be motivated to actively support it through the use of old-fashioned means, like speaking about the issue at news conferences featuring other elected officials, at rallies or "summits," or by allowing the advocacy organization to include its name in news releases.

As with media strategies in election campaigns, the smart, effective, and timely use of online media in advocacy communication is increasingly important. But like election communication, total reliance on online media would ignore sizable and important audiences.

Conclusion

> **Principle 8:** The Internet and the digital revolution have changed a lot of things, but not quite everything.

Political communicators occasionally get so caught up in how modern technology allows them to target a message with speed and precision that they forget their essential purpose. They lose focus on the principle outlined in Chapter 2: Political communication has one purpose: to persuade people to agree with the communicator in order to win an election or to win support for a position on a public policy issue. To be effective, no matter what the medium is, communicators have to keep in mind that their paramount responsibility is the development of persuasive messages in words and phrases that connect with the individuals or groups in the target audience and make a convincing case for agreement with the communicator.

Notes

1. Pew Research Center, "2016 Election," http://www.pewresearch .org/topics/2016-election/.

2. Sean Dodson and Ben Hammersley, "The Web's Candidate for President," *The Guardian,* December 18, 2003, https://www.theguardian .com/media/2003/dec/18/newmedia.uselections2004.

3. Ibid.

4. "Digital Politics in 2016: Evolution or Revolution?" http://www .epolitics.com/2016/11/07/digital-politics-2016-evolution-revolution/.

5. Bill Scott and James Hawkins, *Retail Is Detail: A Retailer's Playbook for Beating Walmart* (New Hebron, MS: NewHebron Publishing, 2011), 58.

6. Chris Cillizza, "Romney's Data Cruncher," http://www.washington post.com, July 5, 2007.

7. Ken Strasma, "Micro-Targeting: New Wave Political Campaigning," Winning Campaigns Learn from the Experts Articles, http://www .winningcampaigns.org/Winning-Campaigns-Archive-Articles/Micro -Targeting-New-Wave-Political-Campaigning.html.

8. Michael Scherer, "Inside the Secret World of the Data Crunchers Who Helped Obama Win," *Time,* November 19, 2012, http://swampland .time.com/2012/11/07/inside-the-secret-world-of-quants-and-data -crunchers-who-helped-obama-win/.

9. Ibid.

10. Ibid.

11. Ibid.

12. Arianna Huffington, Panel discussion at the 2008 Web 2.0 Summit, November 5–7, 2008, Palace Hotel, San Francisco, CA.

13. Pew Research Center, *Social Media Update 2014* (Washington, DC: Pew Research Center, 2015).

14. Ibid.

15. American Press Institute, http://www.mediainsight.org/PDFs /Millennials/Millennials%20Report%20FINAL.pdf, 3.

16. Jim Downie, personal communication, Johns Hopkins University, October 2015.

17. Greg Sterling, "All Digital Growth Now Coming from Mobile Usage—comScore," Marketing Land, April 3, 2016.

18. Paula Minardi, "2016 Internet Trends Report," *AdExchanger Politics*.

19. Jasmine C. Lee and Kevin Quealy, "The 332 People, Places and Things Donald Trump Has Insulted on Twitter: A Complete List," *New York Times,* October 23, 2016, updated June 2, 2017, http://www.nytimes .com/interactive/2016/01/28/upshot/donald-trump-twitter-insults.html ?_r=0.

20. Jon Keegan, "Clinton vs. Trump: Live Twitter Stats," graphic on graphics.wsj.com, July 19, 2016 (updated November 20, 2016).

21. Mary Harris, "A Media Post-Mortem on the 2016 Presidential Election," mediaQuant blog, November 14, 2016, http://www.mediaquant .net/author/mary-senatori.

22. Jefferson Graham, "Trump vs. Clinton: How the Rivals Rank on Twitter, Facebook, More," *USA Today,* August 4, 2016, https://www .usatoday.com/story/tech/news/2016/08/04/trump-clinton-social-media -twitter-facobook-youtube-snapchat/87974630/.

23. Congressional Management Foundation, Washington, DC, http:// www.congressfoundation.org/projects/communicating-with-congress /social-congress-2015.

24. Ibid.

25. Catherine Ho, "K Street Says Social Media Are Growing Faster Than Traditional Lobbying as Way to Influence Washington," *Washington Post,* November 3, 2016.

10

Communicating Through the News Media

Principle 9: One of the most effective ways to reach a lot of people with the same message at the same time is still through the news media.

Organizations of all kinds, including political campaigns, policy advocacy organizations, and the government, have a story to tell. Savvy public affairs communicators have learned that if they do not tell their story and tell it well, somebody else will, and they may not like the result. Certainly, if a political campaign does not continuously and aggressively tell its story, an opponent will be glad to.

Media coverage of a political campaign or government policy issue—assuming it is positive coverage and not an exposé of mistakes, misstatements, or scandal—not only allows the subject to reach the media's readers, listeners, or viewers, but also lends a degree of credibility simply by its appearance. Like it or not, many people still think that if a news item weren't real, it would not be in the newspaper or on television. So, for campaigns and in government, a great deal of time and effort is devoted to trying to get the news media's attention and enlisting their help in getting a story told to the public.

As Chapter 9 describes, websites, e-mail, blogs, and an ever-changing menu of online social media provide many opportunities to reach the public without media filters. Social and technological changes have made a big difference in the ways politicians and government go about communicating with the public. Yet frequently, mass media news coverage of an issue or policy is the only practical way to reach the broad public or even a more targeted audience. And for many smaller local political campaigns not awash in money for extensive advertising or direct contact programs, it can be the only way to get a message or information out to voters.

The Power Relationship Between Politicians and the News Media

It is axiomatic that those with political power—those who hold elected or major appointed office, for example—have a greater ability to attract news media coverage than those without political power. The news media are inherently more interested in what those with power do or say. This gives the politically powerful much more access to the news media, more credibility, and more opportunity to use the news media to get their message out to the public.

This relationship has the following outcomes:

- It creates a symbiotic relationship between those with political power and the news media. They need each other to function effectively, and to a degree, they have to rely on each other.
- It creates a frequently shifting and occasionally delicate power balance between the two.
- It creates a permanent challenge for those who do not have political power, whether they are candidates trying to win power or individuals or organizations trying to influence the decisions of those in power. They do not command news attention as easily as those with power, so they must use strategies to attract it.

In *Making Sense of Media and Politics*, Hebrew University of Jerusalem political science and communication professor Gadi Wolfsfeld lays out five principles concerning politics and the news media.

1. "Political power can usually be translated into power over the news media." Not only do those who have political power have more ability to attract news coverage, they have more ability to determine what is covered and how it is covered. Consider that there are newsrooms full of reporters at the White House, the departments of state and defense, and just outside both houses of Congress, not to mention governors' offices and city halls, just waiting for someone to do or say something.

2. "When authorities lose control over the political environment, they also lose control over the news." As discussed in Chapter 5, the George W. Bush administration largely shaped the national dialogue following 9/11. The White House was able to move public opinion to support the US invasion of Afghanistan in October 2001 and Iraq in March 2003. But by late 2004, with support for the Iraq war fading, the administration's ability to control the conversation was fading along with it. Then in August 2005, the administration's relief efforts in the wake of Hurricane Katrina led to nagging questions about competence. The Bush administration never regained the ability to control the dialogue or the news.

3. "There is no such thing as objective journalism (nor can there be)." It's not a matter of political bias, despite what partisans on both sides claim. It's the fact that journalists have to choose to report on just a few items among a ridiculously large number of world events. Even in the digital age, the news media has to make decisions about what people need to know and what can be ignored.

4. "The media are dedicated more than anything else to telling a good story, and this can often have a major impact on the political process." This speaks to the idea that journalists seem to be increasingly concerned with grabbing our attention rather than providing us with intelligent coverage. As a result, we see an emphasis on sensational news coverage rather than substantive reporting on issues.

5. "The most important effects of the news media on citizens tend to be unintentional and unnoticed." The primary motivation of most news professionals is to produce good stories that get attention. Any effects that occur because of those stories should be seen as unintentional byproducts. Wolfsfeld says that the most important influences of the media are also unnoticed because people are not usually aware that they are being influenced, such as in media decisions about what *not* to cover.[1]

Communicating Political Messages to the Media

Sometimes the media will initiate a story about an issue or action the campaign or organization wants the public to know about, but often the campaign or organization must initiate the process. This section covers the main tools for getting a message out via the media.

Press Releases

The most frequently used tool for expressing political ideas and thoughts is a press release. Press releases are usually written like news stories to get a reporter or editor's attention. "Look! Here is a newsworthy event or statement!" The idea is to convince the media that the event or statement described in the release deserves news coverage or inclusion in a story in their publication, website, or broadcast. Experienced government communicators also know that in many smaller news markets, press releases may be run in a publication exactly as they are received, so they keep in mind that they may actually be writing the story the public will read.

These releases are transmitted to the news media, usually to reporters or editors who are covering a particular elected official, election campaign, or issue. They are commonly issued to:

- announce legislation or new policy,
- make issue or position statements,
- respond to opposition statements or actions,
- announce third-party endorsements,
- announce issue-oriented events,

• announce campaign fundraising goals or amounts, and

• offer commentary on events or public opinion polling.

A news release may be accompanied by a fact sheet or back-grounder, which provides additional background detail, such as data, financial details, legislative history, or an individual or organization's "bio" information.

Press Conferences

The most visible tool for communicating a message through the news media is the press conference, which is used by campaigns, elected officials, government agencies, and advocacy organizations. Many of the political messages we receive are delivered through prepared statements or responses to reporter questions at news conferences. We have all seen candidates announce their plans to seek office at a news conference, or make or respond to accusations about situations that have arisen during a campaign. Press conferences are used to announce candidate endorsements. Or they may be called to address specific issues in a campaign.

Simply put, their purpose is to provide a stage for what are hoped to be "newsworthy" announcements or statements. In the case of a candidate, the campaign notifies the appropriate news media—those who are covering that particular campaign or beat, which might be city hall, the state capitol, or Congress. The candidate generally begins with a prepared statement and then answers questions from the media. Sometimes the prepared statement is only a pretext for the news conference, and the real news comes in responses to questions.

Government officials routinely use press conferences to get messages out. The most familiar are probably presidential press conferences. The president begins with a statement about a particular issue or action, then answers questions from White House reporters about that issue and anything else they want to ask about. The same general process is used by other public officials across the spectrum, but it is often not as structured.

One of the challenges for the officials or communication staffers is to maintain control of the message: to make sure what they want conveyed to the public is conveyed exactly the way they want, and that all news stories read, heard, and seen by the public contain that message. This involves message discipline (discussed in Chapter 3), which means, "This is what we're saying, this is how we're saying it, and we're not saying anything else." The goal is to prevent misstatements, misinterpretation, or straying off the intended message.

There are several ways to control the message in a news conference:

- Use a prepared text, or talking points, to make certain that facts and figures are stated accurately or to frame issues using certain words and phrases like "the Republican majority's obstruction," "the president's unconstitutional overreach," or "job-killing policies."

- In White House press conferences, the president gets to call on reporters rather than just letting anyone ask a question. The White House press staff usually knows in advance which reporters are likely to ask what questions, so the selection of people to call on can become very strategic. A few other officials are accorded the privilege of selecting questioners, such as congressional leaders, cabinet officials, governors, and mayors.

- Don't answer a question. This can be done either by ignoring it, refusing to acknowledge the reporter, or replying with some long soliloquy that says nothing about the question and provides nothing to build a story on but doesn't let the reporter indicate that the official refused to respond.

- At any campaign or government official's news conference, there will be someone handing out copies of a prepared statement. Reporters, even those who have captured the proceedings on a video or audio recording, will quote from or refer to the written statement when they put their stories together, so it is one more iteration of the message.

News conferences can be organized on fairly short notice. When an official or organization is reacting to an action, decision, or rapidly changing situation, the ability to respond quickly can be the difference between having their response be a part of the initial news story or included in follow-up coverage the next day—if at all.

News conferences are critical communication tools for many advocacy organizations because they are essentially free. But even then, the cost and availability of a location for a news conference can be a major obstacle. When locations are not made available in government buildings, advocacy news conferences are frequently held on the steps of the capitol or city hall.

More often than not, a lot of thought goes into the location or backdrop for the speaker because most news conferences are produced with a television audience in mind. Depending on the topic, you might see the US-Mexican border, a national park, a polluted river, or the US or state capitol dome behind the speaker. For indoor conferences, backdrops covered with an organization's name or logo have become common. At the very least, you will see the official seal of the government agency or American flags in the background, or perhaps a group of people who are the subject of the news conference standing behind the speaker.

An advantage of holding a news conference at a topical location is that it offers television cameras a nearly irresistible opportunity for "cut-away shots" to use over an announcer's introduction to the story or over part of the speaker's statement. Communication research finds that visual images, even when the audience is focused on what the speaker is saying, add impact and memorability to the message.

The Importance of Media Relations in Political Communication

Successful press or media relations require more than endlessly cranking out press releases or calling press conferences. Working effectively with the media is based on relationships. Ideally, those relationships are symbiotic and professional. Both parties realize that they benefit from interacting with each other. The communicator appreciates the reporter's objectivity. The reporter understands the communicator's goal of generating positive news coverage. There is mutual self-interest: the reporter needs a source and resource for news stories, tips, reactions and comment, referrals and direction, background clarification, and off-the-record information; the public affairs communicator has a potential outlet for stories, a reporter who might investigate or develop a tip and is committed to telling the public what's going on.

The communicator-reporter relationship works best when there is a degree of mutual respect. Reporters can be a bit derisive about communication professionals, referring to them as hacks or flacks and suggesting that they will say absolutely anything to generate good coverage for their boss or organization. Conversely, some communicators look down on reporters, expecting them to believe anything they are told. Evidently, the process works best when the counterparts treat each other with a degree of professional respect.

One of the most important things for political communicators to keep in mind when they reach out to the public through the news media is that their first audience *is* the news media. If they are trying to get a reporter to write about or cover a story, or an editor to assign a reporter to cover whatever they are promoting, they have to get the journalist's attention in a way that makes the journalist want to read and learn more—in a way that says there's a story to be had. Reporters and editors have to see that the story they're being asked to tell connects to their readers and viewers. How does it affect them—their lives, their families, their incomes, their financial security? How does it affect the things they believe in, the values they hold? If that connection is not made, why would people bother to read or watch the story? When the communicator has a legitimate story to tell—not just fluff or hype—the news media can help them tell that story.

Case Study: Mediating Minnesota

The director of the Federal Mediation and Conciliation Service (FMCS), an independent government agency, was asked if federal mediators could use their dispute-resolution skills to help settle a long-standing environmental dispute in Minnesota. The issues involved the intensity of use in the

Boundary Waters Canoe Area Wilderness and Voyageurs National Park, both along the Canadian border. How many visitors at a time? Motorboats on lakes? Which lakes? Motorized boat portage between lakes? These and other issues had raged in and out of the courts for eighty years.

FMCS was a small, independent federal agency created in 1947 as part of the Taft-Hartley Act. It existed primarily to help labor unions and management reach agreement on collective bargaining contracts and avoid strikes, lockouts, and other work stoppages. Over the years, federal mediators' skills had proved highly effective. They had also helped promote agreement in other workplace and regulatory controversies. Federal mediators had even been used to help resolve some border issues in Bosnia-Herzegovina.

After some research into the dispute, FMCS determined that the quarrelling parties had not really spoken to each other in years except through press releases. Mediators designed a process that would bring together representatives of all viewpoints with an interest in the controversy, from lodge owners and outfitters who used the wilderness areas to a range of conservation groups. There were a lot of people that disagreed about a lot of things, and FMCS wanted to get them to a bargaining table with mediators who could help steer the discussion toward resolution. Then, one of the US senators from Minnesota started making public statements about FMCS, accusing the federal government of forcing its way into a local matter.

FMCS quickly decided that it needed to tell its story. The agency needed to introduce the people of Minnesota to the mediation process and to FMCS and explain the completely voluntary process that mediators hoped might end the long-running dispute. They needed the assistance of the news media, so they held press conferences in Minneapolis–St. Paul and Duluth and met with reporters and editors in every town possible.

continues

Case Study: continued

With high visibility in the news media, FMCS was able to turn public opinion around quickly and win many, many converts to its brand of conflict resolution. Within a week or so, informal polling by the newspapers found that FMCS was more popular and trusted than most politicians.

As a side note, mediation appears to have worked. After about a year and a half of monthly negotiating sessions, committees representing all the disputing businesses and organizations had reached agreement on fifteen out of sixteen issues that had been at the root of the dispute for decades, and they figured out how to settle the sixteenth on their own.

Opinion in the News Media

For major political figures, government agencies, and advocacy organizations, media relations efforts do not end with the publication or airing of a news story. Winning support from, influencing, or gaining access to the editorial or opinion pages of a newspaper or magazine can be a very productive effort.

Editorial Endorsements and Editorial Boards

Another important media function—primarily for print media, but for more and more online publications as well—occurs not at the city desk or in the newsroom, but in management offices. It is the media outlet's decision to give a candidate or an issue its editorial endorsement, and the inherent visibility and credibility it provides is huge. Many times, a key media endorsement has been pivotal in launching, sustaining, or strengthening a campaign, or letting the air out of one.

Some political observers minimize the effects of endorsements, arguing that they are usually predictable: conservative publications are going to endorse conservative candidates and issues; more liberal publications are going to endorse liberal candidates. But that's not always what happens. In 2012, the *Des Moines Register* endorsed Mitt Romney over President Barack Obama, the first time since Richard Nixon's 1972 reelection the paper had backed a Republican. As it turned out, the *Des Moines Register* joined a long list of publications that had endorsed Obama in 2008, but switched their support in 2012, including, for example, the *New York Daily News, Los Angeles Daily News*, and the *Fort Worth Star-Telegram*. However, a number of news publications endorsed Obama for the first time in 2012, like the *San Antonio Express-News* and the *San Francisco Examiner*.

Is an editorial endorsement likely to be the difference in most elections? Certainly not in a presidential campaign or, perhaps, in a US senatorial or congressional race. But it can be life or death for down-ballot candidates. Even in the major races in which candidates are well-known, follow-up research over the years indicates that endorsements can be especially important in helping undecided voters make their voting decision.

Typically, editorial support is the result of a meeting between an official's or advocacy organization's staff and a publication's editorial board, a face-to-face session with top management, appropriate reporters, editors, or columnists to discuss a candidacy, to get information about a single issue, or sometimes—particularly with elected officials—to talk about a range of issues on a regular basis.

Editorials are the voice of a newspaper and the only place where opinions are openly stated, as opposed to "unbiased" news stories. They are the first thing people look to when they turn to the editorial pages. An editorial endorsing a particular position or piece of legislation has been known to change even the most committed policymaker's mind and can do much to influence public opinion. Editorial support for an issue often leads to significant coverage of the issue in the news pages. Such support is highly likely to be the buzz among political observers and opinion leaders and can also provide an important endorsement to cite in subsequent communications.

Another very important benefit of communicating with a publication's editorial board is the possibility of influencing news coverage. This is not to suggest that winning over the editorial board automatically translates into news stories favoring a particular candidate or issue. But bringing important facts, background, or context to the attention of reporters and editors can lead to more complete coverage, or simply to an increase in news coverage.

Op-Eds

Another effective and persuasive tool sometimes available to public affairs communicators is the op-ed, an opinion article with analysis or comment on an issue from someone with particular credentials, experience, or authority. The author's credentials establish his or her credibility on the issue and are important considerations in the ability of an op-ed to persuade convincingly. In fact, newspapers usually run a brief summary of the author's academic or professional credentials at the end of the piece to assure readers that the author's opinion is worthy of serious consideration. Credentials might also signal a predisposition on an issue.

In the case of newspapers, because op-eds are published in the opinion section of the paper, research indicates that their readers tend to be a bit better educated, more thoughtful, more inquisitive, and more interested in competing ideas than typical newspaper readers. However, in more targeted publications, there tends not to be as much difference between opinion readers and general ones.

Op-eds are usually timely—tied to current or pending actions, controversies, debates, or issues—or they immediately follow and comment on other articles or public statements. To have influence, they try to offer a viewpoint on something people care about at that moment.

Public affairs communicators have learned that op-eds have to present cogent, well-reasoned, well-organized, and compelling arguments, and they have to be well-written. Because they appear on the same page as the work of professional columnists, they will be consciously or unconsciously compared in quality to the work of professionals. An additional benefit is that such opinion pieces are often shared—passed around on the Web or circulated in social media like Facebook. Once in a while, op-eds can be used to "correct"— to argue or at least comment on controversial pronouncements made by public officials or even by high-visibility writers.

Case Study: George Will Takes on Native Hawaiians

In 2007, national columnist George Will wrote a piece absolutely torching the Native Hawaiian Government Reorganization Act, rather benign legislation that allowed the transfer of the administration of cultural resources in Hawaii to a Native Hawaiian government long recognized by the United States. Although hardly a major issue in most of the country, the bill was a big deal in the State of Hawaii. The legislation had passed the US House and was awaiting a vote in the Senate. Will's column, "Social Engineers in Paradise," appeared in the *Washington Post*. In it, he equated the recognition of a Native Hawaiian government to the rise of Nazism and called it "a mockery of the Pledge of Allegiance." He likened a panel that would determine who was actually a Native Hawaiian to Hermann Goering, Hitler's second-in-command in Nazi Germany.

The bill's sponsors, Senator Daniel Akaka and Representative Neil Abercrombie, were concerned that Will's column, appearing just days before the Senate vote, could sink it. Their offices were on the phone to the editor of the *Washington Post* immediately demanding a retraction of the Will column. Ultimately, the *Washington Times* offered the two legislators an opportunity to respond in an op-ed, which ran under the title, "George Will Column Misstates the Past and Present."

This case wasn't just a matter of opposing views or opinions on an issue. The op-ed attempted to refute the George Will column with a great deal of credibility, using facts and historical data to argue point by point that Will's claims were baseless.

Opportunities to refute a published piece with an op-ed do not happen very often. The responders have to catch the

continues

Case Study: continued

"offending" article immediately and make a strong case that it is substantively inaccurate and that, left unrefuted, it could lead to unfair or unjustified actions. In this case, it probably did not hurt that the responders were members of Congress and sponsors of the legislation in question.

(The Senate and House sponsors of the legislation circulated the op-ed to members of both houses and the bill passed.)

Online Opinion

The digital information revolution has changed how political communicators go about their business (see Chapter 9). Political campaigns, government officials, and outside interest and advocacy organizations have had to learn how to use digital media in all its forms to get their messages out to intended audiences. Yet some basic tenets of effective communication remain unchanged.

What's different about communicating opinion online:

- Timeliness—communicators must respond more quickly, often the same day if they are reacting to an event or a statement, or the subject will be old news and everyone will have moved on.

- An opinion piece must be part of a conversation. It has to include links and acknowledge or address other writers.

- The audience must be included in the conversation.

- The medium and the audience are more about immediacy than long, carefully organized recitations. Arguments do not need to be absolutely definitive or completely polished.

- Other than major media outlets' websites or blogs, there are few online opinion outlets that come with a pedigree. The communicator has to check them out for credibility, integrity, and audience. Are they honest? Do they have an agenda? Does anyone pay attention to them? To whom do they link? Who links to them? How credible is a particular site or blogger?

What's the same:

- The strongest positions are grounded in facts and often based on original reporting.
- Effective communicators have to be intellectually honest and try to anticipate and preempt the best counterarguments.
- Writing should be clear, concise, and vivid.
- The subject should be of interest to the readers.

News Media's Changing Role in Political Communication

Members of the news media have been full partners in communicating political messages to the public as long as there have been political messages. Before the advent of today's many avenues for mass communication, newspapers were virtually the only link between politicians and the public, other than public speeches or the occasional broadside or flyer.

Journalism Through the Mid-Twentieth Century

For generations, what most people knew about major events, actions, and decisions was reported and described by print journalists. The partnership continued with the advent of radio and into the television age. When Dwight Eisenhower's presidential campaign produced the first political television commercial in 1952, politicians began to communicate directly to large swaths of the public (see Chapter 8). Even then, most communication about issues was still through the news media. Reporters and editors decided what to convey to the public and how to convey it. Broadcast news reporters were still journalists, and journalists were still the main conduit for information from the government and political campaigns to the public.

The public has relied on journalists to use their access, knowledge, and experience in covering politicians and the operations of government to describe what was going on and, frequently, to interpret it and explain its meaning. For the most part, the public interest has been well served. At one time, though, the news media had unspoken agreements with public officials and each other that certain aspects of our leaders' lives would not be reported. No one actively lied about the fact that Franklin Roosevelt could not walk without braces and canes. Nobody lied about the dalliances of John Kennedy or Lyndon Johnson. Capitol Hill reporters did not lie about the ethical questions or raging alcoholism that plagued some of the nation's most senior congressional leaders. But neither did they tell the truth about them.

Evolution in Media News

Through the mid-twentieth century, nearly every political message to the public was filtered through the news media, usually in press conferences, interviews, statements in the media, or press releases. For decades, these were the sources of everything most people knew about the workings of their government. All that began to change with the advent of cable television news, and change accelerated with the technological and communication revolution that followed (see Chapter 9). Now, fewer and fewer Americans rely on traditional news coverage, especially in newspapers, for their information. More and more of those who do read newspapers or watch television news do so online.

We have also seen a change in the basic nature of news gathering and reportage. In *News: The Politics of Illusion*, W. Lance Bennett, professor of communication and professor of political science at the University of Washington, asserts that a change to media ownership by large corporations rather than news organizations has led to a stronger emphasis on profit than on journalistic excellence or objectivity.

"If it bleeds, it leads" was the cynical axiom even years ago in television news, but the growth in the penchant to emphasize the sensational and visual story over substance has robbed news coverage of depth, Bennett writes. The focus is more on "entertainment, disasters, accidents, and crime while reducing the coverage of environment, government activities and international affairs to make room."[2]

He cites a *Columbia Journalism Review* study from 2008: "Even as the presidential election campaign began to heat up, 22% of the cable news coverage was devoted to the death of celebrity Anna Nicole Smith, compared to 11% devoted to election coverage."[3]

Case Study: "Trumped Up" Coverage in the 2016 Presidential Campaign

The 2016 Republican presidential primary campaign took initial shape predictably, with a cadre of well-known, established candidates: former Florida governor Jeb Bush, US senators Marco Rubio and Lindsey Graham, New Jersey governor Chris Christie, Wisconsin governor Scott Walker, and Ohio governor John Kasich. There was a group from the more conservative wing of the Republican Party, including Louisiana governor Bobby Jindal and Texas senator Ted Cruz. Then there were candidates from previous elections back for another try, including former Texas governor Rick Perry, former US senator Rick Santorum, and former Arkansas governor and Fox News personality Mike Huckabee. Joining these hopefuls were three candidates who had never held political office: one-time Hewlett-Packard chief operating officer Carly Fiorina, pediatric neurosurgeon Ben Carson, and New York real estate mogul and reality television personality Donald Trump.

The nearly universal assumption was that the more established, well-known candidates, with their solid fund-raising structures and records of service in elected office,

continues

Case Study: continued

would quickly bubble to the top and focus the public's attention on just two or three realistic contenders.

But no one had counted on the "Trump Effect": Donald Trump's outsized persona and penchant for saying outrageous things. Before he entered the race, the "would he or wouldn't he run" conjecture that is such a customary part of a modern media-oriented candidacy was carried daily and nightly on network and cable television for weeks. When Trump finally did announce that he was running, on June 16, 2015, his forty-five-minute announcement became one of the biggest media events of the summer, covered start to finish on all cable channels. According to the Trump campaign, the speech generated the highest Google search volume associated with any presidential candidate.[4]

In the speech, which *Politico* called, among other things, "discursive, pugnacious, bizarre and most entertaining,"[5] Trump described his vision of "Making America Great Again." His statements about illegal immigration generated the loudest and hottest reactions. Trump said that as soon as he was elected president, the United States would immediately begin to deport all of the estimated 11 million undocumented aliens residing in the country, including "Dreamers," children of illegal immigrants brought to the United States when small who had grown up and gone to school here. "When Mexico sends its people, they're not sending their best. They're sending people that have lots of problems, and they're bringing those problems with [them]. They're bringing drugs. They're bringing crime. They're rapists. And some, I assume, are good people."

From that point on, Trump's rallies were broadcast start to finish on all cable channels and featured prominently on network newscasts. That he offered few or no specifics on his ambitious goals for the country did not measurably deter the public's interest—or his ability to command near saturation broadcast coverage. Through the summer, it became a nearly nightly report: "What did Trump say today?"

Matt Bai, national political columnist for Yahoo Politics, wrote, "By now, it's clear there's a powerful symbiosis between Trump and the media. We need him for the narrative power, for the clicks and debate ratings and sheer fascination factor. He needs us for the' free publicity and the easy, evocative foil."[6]

One after another of the more-established, well-funded candidates withered away and dropped out of the race, unable to sustain the necessary fundraising and spending to compete for the public's attention with the ubiquitous Trump, who had not had to spend a dollar on advertising because he so dominated news coverage.

Media watchdog Media Matters for America kept tabs on how much airtime Donald Trump got in the first three months of his campaign. MSNBC mentioned him 29,584 times; CNN, 19,289 times; and Fox News, 12,563 times. Media Matters calculated that Trump news coverage amounted to about ten hours and twenty minutes of airtime, the equivalent of 1,240 thirty-second prime-time ads.[7] That amount of visibility in paid advertising would have cost the Trump campaign between $37 million and $55 million. According to the Tyndall Report, which monitors the network news programs, Trump had been on the ABC, NBC, or CBS evening news programs for 234 minutes in 2015, amounting to more than $23 million in free airtime. That is more than all other candidates combined.[8] Yet on those same television networks and cable channels, political analysts and pundits continued to be perplexed at the "staying power" of the Trump campaign until his electoral victory on November 8, 2016.

Decline in Depth of News Coverage

The impact of change in print news media has led to the demise of numerous major newspapers across the country. The subscriber base and, along with it, advertising revenue have nosedived. Some publications have been consolidated. Many major cities that historically had two or more newspapers with competing and often opposing points of view—Chicago, Dallas, Denver, Honolulu, Houston, San Francisco, Seattle—now have only one. Many surviving newspapers have shrunk to "see-through" status. You can read them front to back but never be sure you really know what's going on in the world. Or, in many cases, newspapers have simply disappeared. According to the Pew Research Center's Journalism Project, total weekday print newspaper circulation dropped from 62.3 million in 1990 to 45.6 million in 2013.[9] Over that same period, according to Nielsen Online, newspaper online readership rose to nearly 75 million, with 3.7 billion page views.[10]

This evolution has affected the nature and focus of media coverage of the actions of government and political campaigns, including the media's commitment to in-depth news reportage. Capitol bureaus in state after state and Washington, DC, have been cut or allowed to shrink more slowly through attrition. The Associated Press, arguably the nation's foremost news-gathering organization since 1846, is a shell of what it used to be. United Press International, a major force in news coverage for nearly 110 years, barely exists anymore. According to Pew research, full-time professional newsroom employment declined 6.4 percent in 2012 alone: Gannett cut about 400 jobs in one year; the Tribune Company cut 700. Major newspapers, newspaper groups, syndicates, and broadcast bureaus have slashed staff to the point that one or two reporters are scrambling to cover Congress, the White House, or the entire federal government for dozens of papers or television stations in different states, all with their own individual interests and issue focuses.

With the atrophy of attention to in-depth government and political news coverage has come the inevitable loss of institutional knowledge as generations of "old hands" retire or seek more stable employment. Kennedy School professor Thomas E. Patterson writes in *Informing the News* that many of today's reporters simply don't know enough about what they're covering, which leads to news stories that "give equal weight to facts and biased opinion, stir up small controversies, and substitute infotainment for real news." "Even when they get the facts right," Patterson says, "they often misjudge the context in which they belong." He proposes a move toward knowledge-based journalism. "Unless journalists are more deeply informed about the subjects they cover, they will continue to misinterpret them and to be vulnerable to manipulation by their sources."[11]

The exodus of experienced reporters and writers is tragic and apparent. At least as important as the loss of content knowledge, though perhaps more subtle, is the loss of "the long view" in news reporting. Journalists who have been around for a while tend to develop a longer perspective. They are better able to put actions and events into context because they have more likely seen them before. Today, many reporters and analysts seem to function entirely in the present and future tenses. They focus on using today's news to predict what will happen in six months or in the next election nearly a year away, rather than analyzing events from a historical perspective.

Case Study: Premature Prognostication

In October 2013, with the terribly botched rollout of the Obama administration's Healthcare.gov website, it looked as though the entire Affordable Care Act could be dead as a mackerel. Republicans in Congress, who had opposed every aspect of the health-care reform effort since it became part of the Obama agenda, were gleefully proclaiming the end of Obamacare.

The new law had an uphill battle for gaining anything resembling public acceptance anyway. As of mid-2014, according to nonpartisan media analysis by Kantar Media's Campaign Media Analysis Group (CMAG), nearly $445 million had been spent across the country on political tele-

continues

Case Study: continued

vision advertising mentioning the health-care program during the previous four years. Attack ads, aimed either at Obamacare or attacking Democrats who had supported passage of the law in 2010, outnumbered positive ads by more than 15 to 1. Kantar estimated that $418 million had been spent on negative spots.[12]

Despite the opposition, and as mechanically botched and poorly managed as the public rollout of the Affordable Care Act was, the program got up and running. Opponents then insisted that the health insurance program would never come close to the seven million initial sign-ups originally forecast by the Congressional Budget Office. Their dire prediction was immediately picked up by the news media and became the focus of stories and commentary.

When the actual enrollment figure topped eight million, opponents went very quiet and the media focus changed quickly. Opponents began to predict that few of the people who did sign up would actually pay for their new policies, which meant the program would be hollow. Once again, their spin was featured widely in the media. But when major health insurance companies testified in congressional hearings that between 80 and 90 percent of the new enrollees had already made their initial policy payments, opponents again went quiet and the media focus changed again.

Veteran news reporters have seen premature judgments made before, and they are not as likely to start making unconditional pronouncements of their own based on a single poll or the spin from one political agenda. But with the shrinkage in traditional news media outlets and the loss of many of these seasoned reporters, we are likely to continue hearing and reading stories and commentary with precipitous statements about what will happen that lack historical perspective and turn out in the end to be wrong.

News Media Bias

Loud accusations of news media bias are a time-honored US political tradition. Sometimes the accusations have been well founded; sometimes not. Journalism has followed a bumpy path throughout our history.

On occasion, the federal government has created its own definition of bias and taken steps to prohibit it. For example, in 1798, Congress passed the Alien and Sedition Acts, prohibiting publication of "false, scandalous, or malicious writing" against the government. It was a crime to express public opposition to any law or presidential act. The law lasted three years. In 1861, President Abraham Lincoln accused several newspapers in border states of pro-Confederate bias and closed them down.

In the nineteenth and early twentieth centuries, newspapers largely reflected the opinions of their publishers. Many large cities had competing publications with radically differing views, and they openly supported and promoted one political party or another. In the 1890s, "yellow journalism," as practiced by William Randolph Hearst and Joseph Pulitzer in their New York City papers, included banner headlines and stories that were fabricated for sensational impact. Some of their "news" coverage helped push the United States into the Spanish-American War.

A slow move toward professionalizing journalism followed. Reporters were expected to be objective or at least base their stories on facts. A publication's editorials could and would continue to reflect the views and opinions of the publisher, but a separation was established between news and editorial, which became and has remained the standard for newspapers. Television news, which started to replace newspapers as the dominant information medium in the 1960s, particularly during the Vietnam War, rarely expressed an opinion or editorial position and prided itself on its objectivity.

Despite good intentions, accusations of media bias from both sides have seldom abated. During the civil rights movement in the early 1960s, there were accusations that television networks, all headquartered in New York City, were biased against white Southerners and actively favored "racial mixing." A few television

stations in southern states refused to air such highly rated programs as *I Spy* and *Star Trek* because of their racially mixed
casts.

In 1969, Vice President Spiro Agnew publicly denounced the
"nattering nabobs of negativism" in the media who opposed the
Vietnam War. With the ascension of Newt Gingrich and the
Republican Revolution in 1994, harsh criticism of the "liberal"
news media became and has remained part of the conservative
orthodoxy.

Cable television as a political medium exploded in 1996,
when billionaire Rupert Murdoch hired former Republican political strategist and NBC television executive Roger Ailes to create
the Fox News Channel as a conservative alternative to CNN and
MSNBC. Today, Fox News has a larger audience than either CNN
or MSNBC, and it is largely viewed by Democrats as "mission
control" for the conservative message machine. It is not unusual
for the same messages, in the same words and phrases seen and
heard on Fox News and on talk radio, to appear in the news pages
of the *Washington Examiner*, in the news pages of the *New York
Post* and the editorial pages of the *Wall Street Journal* (both also
owned by Murdoch), on websites such as Red State and the
Drudge Report, and eventually in Republican congressional
debates and public statements.

MSNBC continues to be the voice of the progressive agenda,
and to a large extent the Democratic Party. MSNBC commentators, though, are frequently critical of Democratic politicians,
including President Obama, for not being progressive enough or
for being ineffective. Small wonder, then, that public opinion
surveys indicate that fewer and fewer Americans have confidence in the mass media "to report the news fully, accurately,
and fairly." A more detailed discussion of the impact of "biased
media" on our political system and on society at large is
included in Chapter 11.

Suffice it to say that for political and government communicators, dealing with cable news outlets can be like walking
through a minefield. As long as they know where the tripwires
are and keep their eyes open, they'll probably be okay. That
means they have to consider who the viewers are for the various

cable channels, and they must remember that even the most innocent sounding question can blow them up if they don't answer carefully.

Conclusion

> **Principle 9:** One of the most effective ways to reach a lot of people with the same message at the same time is still through the news media.

The relationship of public officials, candidates, and interest groups with the news media has undergone colossal transformation over the past 235 or so years. That relationship will continue to change and evolve along with the roles and operations of both sides, driven by changes in society and technology. Yet the basic foundation of the relationship will continue to be their mutual need for each other.

Notes

1. Gadi Wolfsfeld, *Making Sense of Media and Politics: Five Principles in Political Communication* (New York: Routledge, 2011).

2. W. Lance Bennett, *News: The Politics of Illusion*, 9th ed. (Chicago: University of Chicago Press, 2012), 24.

3. Ibid.

4. "Donald Trump," Know Your Meme, http://knowyourmeme.com /memes/people/donald-trump (accessed June 8, 2016).

5. Adam B. Lerner, "The 10 Best Lines from Donald Trump's Announcement Speech," *Politico*, June 16, 2015, http://www.politico .com/story/2015/06/donald-trump-2016-announcement-10-best-lines -119066.

6. Matt Bai, "Trump and the Media, Made for Each Other," Yahoo Politics, December 24, 2015, https://www.yahoo.com/news/trump-and -the-media-made-1327700756660278.html.

7. Media Matters for America, December 23, 2015, https://www .mediamatters.org/blog/2015/12/23/the-2015-fox-primary-its-trump-and -then-everyon/207659.

8. "Tyndall Report: Year in Review, 2015," http://tyndallreport.com /yearinreview2015/.

9. "Key Indicators in Media & News," Pew Research Center Journalism and Media, March 26, 2014, http://www.journalism.org/2014/03/26/state-of-the-news-media-2014-key-indicators-in-media-and-news/.

10. Ibid.

11. Thomas E. Patterson, *Informing the News* (New York: Vintage Books, 2013).

12. Kantar Media CMAG, http://us.kantar.com/public-affairs/politics/2013/2014-political-media-projections/.

11

Communication in an Age of Partisanship

Principle 10: Being a political communicator in today's highly partisan environment is like working near the mouth of a volcano. The challenge is doing your job well without falling in.

Chapter 2 described ten steps advanced in 1994 by then Speaker Newt Gingrich to establish the use of more confrontational and divisive political campaign strategies and tactics in the everyday conduct of government and political business. That style has been sustained for the past twenty-plus years, leading to the partisan congressional gridlock that seems to prevent the legislative branch of the US government from doing much of anything.

The win-at-all-costs, take-no-prisoners approach has led to one of the most significant social transformations in the last fifty years, not just in government and politics, but in the American public's perception and trust in the news media, its attitudes toward the country's elected leaders and the institutions of government, and, perhaps most significantly, its attitudes toward each other. With increasing partisanship, large segments of the public have become less and less tolerant of other large segments of the public who hold divergent views and opinions.

For decades, the two political parties in key states tried to cast the partisan divide in cement by redrawing state legislative districts to favor the party in power. For years, Democrats redrew the boundaries of legislative districts following the US Census every ten years, ostensibly to make sure that districts were adjusted to reflect population shifts. But it was really more to protect their incumbents from challengers and to promote the election of more Democrats.

More recently, with a Republican majority in Congress and state capitols, those lines have been redrawn with a vengeance to promote the election of the most conservative Republicans to state legislatures. The partisan legislatures produced by this redistricting have redrawn the lines for congressional districts to create Republican House districts.

In fact, in Texas in 2003, Republicans, under the leadership of former House majority leader Tom Delay, couldn't wait for the decennial census to reshape congressional districts, and with a strong majority in the legislature they didn't have to. Congressional districts were redrawn in the middle of a decade for the first time in US history.

For Austin, Texas, the result was a game changer. According to 2014 population estimates, Austin is the nation's eleventh largest city, with 912,791 residents. It had been the anchor of the Tenth Congressional District for decades, once represented by Lyndon B. Johnson. Austin is also a Democratic stronghold in a bright red Republican state. Tom Delay's mid-decade redistricting divided Austin and surrounding Travis County among six other congressional districts, accounting for no more than 27 percent in any of them. One district was anchored 90 miles away in San Antonio, another nearly 200 miles from Austin in Houston, and another 200 miles away in Fort Worth. A city that has always voted heavily Democratic is now represented in Congress by five Republicans and one Democrat.

Has partisan redistricting been effective? In the 2012 general election, 1.7 million more people voted for Democratic congressional candidates than for Republicans, yet Republicans maintained a thirty-three-seat majority in the US House of Representatives.

And, according to the April 4, 2013 *Cook Political Report*, 2012 was "the first time since 1960 that the winner of the presidential election did not win the popular vote in a majority of congressional districts. Obama, the Democrat, 'won' 209 districts while the Republican, former Governor Romney, 'won' 226."[1] Yet President Obama won reelection by nearly five million votes nationwide.

Partisanship and Political Communication

This brand of partisanship certainly creates opportunities for political messages, but they tend to be divisive and negative messages, attacking the other party's elected officials, agendas, and candidates. Everything is seen through a lens of partisan advantage. Every word and phrase is calculated to divide. Members of Congress used to run on what they had accomplished. Now, they run as much on what they have thwarted.

Although a highly partisan environment can create opportunities for communication, it can also limit them. Sometimes, it makes any attempt to talk seriously and honestly about issues that affect people's lives very difficult, even to the point of preventing representatives from supporting issues and policies they actually favor.

Case Study: Small Business Association Loan Legislation

In 2009, a membership survey of the National Small Business Association found that 40 percent of its members were forced to use high-interest credit cards to meet routine operating expenses. In the wake of the country's near-total financial collapse, banks were sitting on deposits and had virtually stopped business lending, even to those with established lines of credit. The credit cutoff made running a small business difficult and starting or expanding a business virtually impossible.

continues

Case Study: continued

I was the lead for my boss in developing legislation to increase the size of small business loans guaranteed by the US Small Business Administration (SBA) from $2 million to $5 million. This would make needed working capital more accessible for the country's small businesses at little or no cost to the taxpayer.

I set out to find cosponsors for the bill, Democrats and Republicans, thinking that we would have a rare bipartisan message opportunity. After all, it would help the small businesses that created 64 percent of new jobs in the US economy. And everybody—Republicans and Democrats alike—supported job creation.

I had Democrats lining up to sign on as cosponsors for the bill. I called the office of every Republican member of the House Small Business Committee and House Financial Services Committee, those closest to the issue. I spoke with legislative staff of fourteen members of the former and more than thirty members of the latter about the bill, inviting their bosses to sign on. While everyone I spoke with thought the legislation was great and badly needed, not one could agree to cosponsor it. It was an issue that both sides talked up all the time, but Republican members of the House could not sign on or visibly support the legislation because it was introduced by a Democrat.

Without Republican support, the bill failed in the House. In addition to losing the chance to help America's small businesses when they really needed help, how many opportunities for great political messaging about an actual accomplishment did members of Congress lose because of partisanship?

Fortunately for the nation's small businesses, the Senate counterpart bill passed and came directly to the House floor for a vote without needing to go through the House committee process. The bill was subsumed into a larger piece of legislation, passed handily, and became law.

Partisanship and the Media

As noted in Chapter 10, public opinion surveys indicate that fewer and fewer Americans have confidence in the mass media "to report the news fully, accurately, and fairly." In 2013, according to the Gallup Organization, 59 percent of the public thought the news media was biased, 46 percent thought mass media was too liberal, and 13 percent thought it was too conservative. The perception of bias was highest among respondents who identified themselves as conservatives: 78 percent. Of those who identified themselves as liberal, 44 percent and also believed the media was biased, as did 50 percent of moderates. Only about 36 percent overall viewed mass media reporting as "just about right." Gallup reports that in every year since 2007, fewer Americans trust the media. And, interestingly, in every year since 2002, more Americans think the media show more liberal bias than conservative bias, which could simply indicate that the conservative message about media bias has been more effective than those of liberals or moderates.[2]

Not surprisingly, perceptions of media bias are magnified when the focus is cable news, particularly Fox News Channel and MSNBC. In 2014, the Pew Research Center released "Political Polarization in the American Public," an in-depth survey of public attitudes about political polarization, interviewing more than 10,000 people. Initial results from the research show that the public's perception of FOX News Channel and MSNBC is deeply divided along partisan lines.[3]

Both networks are highly regarded by people who share the network's respective political perspectives and roundly hated by people who do not. Significantly, though, Fox is viewed positively by 74 percent of people who consider themselves consistent conservatives and negatively by 5 percent. Yet MSNBC is viewed favorably by only 45 percent of consistent liberals and 38 percent of those "with mixed ideological views." Nearly half the liberals offered no opinion of MSNBC at all.

There seems to be a great deal more agreement among each group about the opposite group's favorite network. Fox News is viewed unfavorably by 73 percent of the consistent liberals. MSNBC is viewed negatively by 71 percent of the consistent conservatives.

Natalie Jomini Stroud, professor of communications studies at the University of Texas, has focused on the impact of increasingly partisan attitudes about the media and media use—where people get their information—and the larger effects on our political system and society. In *Niche News: The Politics of News Choice*, she writes that the traditional assumption that a monolithic news media transmits a single agenda is belied by findings that different patterns of media exposure are related to different issues being identified as most important.[4] Stroud says the ideological and partisan divide in cable news has greatly increased the degree of selective exposure among the public. More people who are politically aligned with one party or ideology or the other choose to get more, most, or even all of their information from news sources that agree with or reinforce their views. Based on extensive and varied research, she finds that such selective exposure strengthens preexisting beliefs: "Partisan selective exposure produces more polarized attitudes, higher levels of political participation and differences in which issues are judged to be the most important."

Has a growing preference for selective media exposure, relying on media outlets that "lean" the way we believe and reinforce our preexisting views, had an impact on the larger public? On the media itself? On our political and governing processes? Stroud reminds us that the media are commercial enterprises and subject to market pressures, and as more media options become available to consumers, each media outlet is forced to compete for a smaller niche audience. "If political partisanship persists as a viable segmentation strategy, news outlets may target their news to attract audiences with specific political leanings. If the market demands partisan news, the media will supply partisan news. There are quite clear relationships between the political leanings expressed by media outlets and the political leanings of the audience."[5]

Has political polarization made the media more partisan? Or has the partisan media added to the polarization of the public? According to the 2014 Pew Research Center public opinion survey,

The overall share of Americans who express consistently conservative or consistently liberal opinions has doubled over the past two decades from 10% to 21%. And ideological thinking is now much more closely aligned with partisanship than in the past. As a result, ideological overlap between the two parties has diminished: Today, 92% of Republicans are to the right of the median Democrat, and 94% of Democrats are to the left of the median Republican.[6]

Yet Stroud concludes that partisan media outlets actually contribute to the political process. "This research finds that like-minded media exposure contributes to political participation. Partisans using like-minded media are more active in politics. They seem to be motivated and energized by partisan media." Despite what some studies have claimed about partisan media dumbing down the partisans, Stroud writes, "I found no evidence that partisan media exposure reduces political knowledge."[7]

Stroud's research suggests, then, that partisan media outlets such as MSNBC and Fox News Channel are essentially very expensive pep squads for their respective teams, not there to provide unvarnished fact or objective analysis, but more to impart selected bits of information, generally with a point of view, and ultimately to fire up the troops.

Case Study: Partisan Media and Motivated Reasoning

The effect of partisan media on elections and the political process continues to be investigated by communication researchers, but it is safe to conclude that our partisan media environment heightened the political polarization going into the 2012 presidential election. Rarely had the electorate felt quite so strongly about one side or the other. According to Gary Jacobson of University of California–San Diego,

> Partisan divisions among ordinary Americans, after steadily widening for several decades, reached new extremes during Barack Obama's presidency. The electorate that

continues

Case Study: continued

returned Obama to the White House in 2012 was more polarized along party lines than any in at least six decades. Voters displayed the highest levels of party-line voting, lowest levels of ticket splitting, and widest partisan difference in presidential approval ever documented in American National Election Studies (ANES) going back to 1952.[8]

Why have things gotten even more polarized? Jacobson observes, "Widening partisan divisions in the public have coincided with the proliferation of partisan news and opinion outlets enabled by the spread of cable television, talk radio, and the internet, raising the obvious question of how these two phenomena might be related." This has led to a society, media researchers tell us, in which people tend to listen to talk radio and watch cable television "news" not to get information as much as to affirm what they already believe.[9]

Not only did the media on both sides continue to demonize the opposing candidates and agendas in the 2012 election, but they turned up the volume beyond even a pretense of objective coverage. In what may have been the most bizarre demonstration of motivated reasoning, or at least believing what you want to believe (see Chapter 4), Jacobson chronicles a group of seasoned Washington political writers and commentators who were simply unable to accept electoral data and preelection polling that was forecasting the 2012 Obama victory. These were die-hard conservatives who had been constant critics of the Obama administration and the Democratic political agenda, but they were far from cub reporters or political neophytes. They included Michael Barone, Glenn Beck, Ann Coulter, former House Speaker Newt Gingrich, Charles Krauthammer, William Kristol, Dick Morris, Peggy Noonan, Karl

Rove, and George Will. All these political stalwarts had predicted an impressive Romney win, and they apparently had a real problem accepting that Barack Obama won a second term by five million votes and a 332 to 206 electoral college màjority. Karl Rove, in fact, performed an election night live television meltdown on Fox News when Ohio's results showed a decisive and critical Obama victory.

Media Elites and the "Lame-Stream" Media

The conservative campaign of constant attacks and references to the liberal media, media elites, and East Coast media elites—including Sarah Palin's "lame-stream media" label—accelerated in the early 1990s, and the media reacted to that campaign. This interaction led to changes in the way the news media covers politics and the actions of government. The unrelenting attacks on the news media accomplished their mission. More reporters and editors have become timid about what they cover and how they cover it. The constant fear of being labeled liberal has caused some mainstream media outlets to pull their punches—either to decide not to cover certain actions or events that might open them to accusations of liberal bias, or, more typically, to water down their coverage. In the interest of "balance," reporters more often seek out opposing viewpoints and give them equal weight, even if the opposing viewpoint lacks credibility or factual basis.

For example, to revisit an issue discussed in Chapter 5, approximately 97 percent of the world's climate scientists agree that marked and measurable increases in the release of greenhouse gases are causing warming that is beginning to have a destructive impact. Yet coverage of this phenomenon is frequently balanced with the views of climate-change deniers who base their claims on the work of scientists serving political actors who tend to view climate-change remedies as an egregious demonstration of government overreach that will bring on burdensome regulations. In some cases, the scientists are paid by the industries that produce and emit greenhouse gases, toxic chemicals, and other pollutants. Such "balance," not based on credibile information or the weight of scientific evidence, demeans the authority and authenticity of climate-change warnings simply because a reporter or editor fears being labeled biased or liberal.

The Impact of Partisanship on US Society

In concert with its finding that Americans have become more consistent in their ideological beliefs and more partisan, the June 2014 Pew Research Center report found that both sides have become more intractable on economic issues and the role of government. Overall, the prospects for rapprochement appear bleak: "The level of antipathy members of each party feel toward the opposing party has surged over the past two decades. Not only do greater numbers of those in both parties have negative views of the other side, those negative views are increasingly intense. And many go so far as to say that the opposing party's policies threaten the nation's well-being."[10] Antipathy toward the opposite party is particularly strong among active voters.

The study also found that both conservatives and liberals, but especially conservatives, increasingly limited their social circles to people who shared their views: "35% of Americans say 'most of my close friends share my views on government and politics,' while 39% say 'some of my friends share my views, but many do not.' In comparison, "among consistent conservatives, roughly twice as many say most of their close friends share their views as do not (63% vs. 30%)."[11]

There is, however, a ray of hope for anyone who thinks the country might be better off if we were a bit less partisan: "While the left and the right may speak louder in the political process, they do not necessarily drown out other elements of the public entirely. And this may be one reason why, even in lower-turnout primaries, the more ideological candidates do not always carry the day."[12]

Conclusion

> **Principle 10:** Being a political communicator in today's highly partisan environment is like working near the mouth of a volcano. The challenge is doing your job well without falling in.

The nearly toxic partisan atmosphere in our national government has drastically changed the tone of political communication—and not just in election campaigns. Both sides in Congress now tend to express every thought in sharply parochial terms, framing issues to advance their party's position and agenda rather than seeking actual solutions to national problems and challenges. It's all about winning for one side or the other.

Inevitably, this trend has trickled down to state governments. The words and actions of governors and legislatures have shown that state officials can be as narrowly and bitterly partisan as anyone in Washington. And it has metastasized into local governments as well. We see and hear candidates for city council and other local offices running on national platforms. In a county in Texas, there is a candidate whose signs proclaimed that he was a "Conservative for Sheriff." There was no Conservative Party on the ballot, so I'm guessing he was a Republican, but I wonder what conservative sheriffs do that moderate sheriffs, or even liberal sheriffs, don't do. Do they approach law enforcement in a different way? Do they only enforce laws they deem conservative? Do they wear wingtips instead of cowboy boots? It's a small, but telling example of how deeply partisanship is becoming embedded in our institutions of government.

What this means is that political communicators—whether they are working for an elected official, trying to get someone elected to office, or conveying a message to the public about an issue—are likely going to become part of a partisan messaging machine. I think the best we can hope for is that, as they craft political messages, they will maintain some sense of perspective and avoid crossing the line into dishonest communication. Chapter 13 discusses dishonest political communication in detail.

Notes

1. *Cook Political Report*, April 4, 2013, www.cookpolitical.com.

2. Elizabeth Mendes, "In U.S., Trust in Media Recovers Slightly From All-Time Low," Gallup Organization. September 19, 2013, http://www .gallup.com/poll/164459/trust-media-recovers-slightly-time-low.aspx.

3. Pew Research Center, "Political Polarization in the American Public" (Washington, DC: June 2014).

4. Natalie Jomini Stroud, *Niche News: The Politics of News Choice* (New York: Oxford University Press, 2011), 172.

5. Ibid.

6. Pew Research Center, "Political Polarization in the American Public."

7. Stroud, *Niche News*, 176.

8. Gary Jacobson, "Partisan Media and Electoral Polarization in 2012: Evidence from the American National Election Study," paper prepared for delivery at the Conference on American Gridlock: Causes, Characteristics, and Consequences, Center for Congressional and Presidential Studies, the American University, Washington, DC, May 9, 2014.

9. Ibid.

10. Pew Research Center, "Political Polarization in the American Public."

11. Ibid.

12. Ibid.

12

Crisis Communication

Principle 11: In politics and government, something bad is bound to happen. The smart thing is to be as ready as possible when a crisis hits.

Crises Are Inevitable

At some point, every public or private organization will need to respond to an internal crisis or external bad news that threatens the reputation, stability, success, or, in extreme instances, the actual survival of the organization. The world's dependence on technology opens up almost endless possibilities for digital disaster, such as system breakdowns, hacking, leaks, or careless or embarrassing messages or videos.

For political communicators, the key to weathering a crisis lies in preparation. This chapter begins by describing a few crises in which communicators failed to rise to the occasion and then offers guidelines for preparing to handle a crisis effectively.

Case Study: Healthcare.gov Rollout

Few public policy events have been as ripe for problems as the 2013 rollout of Healthcare.gov, the website to allow people to shop and enroll for health insurance under the Affordable Care Act, or Obamacare. Few new programs had as many moving and interdependent parts. Few government programs had ever been more opposed, criticized, condemned, and disparaged as the health-care reform measure passed by Congress in 2010. As a result, few, if any, new product rollouts ever had so many people rooting for failure.

With the attention of every politically conscious American on the process, the assumption was that the Obama administration would take every possible step, checking and rechecking, to make sure all the bugs were worked out and that everything would go smoothly. But, as former Texas governor, now secretary of energy, Rick Perry once said, "Oops."

In Chapter 10, I described the rollout as mechanically botched and poorly managed, and it was both. Serious technical problems plagued the Healthcare.gov website. But just as problematic for the White House and Obamacare supporters was a failure in effective crisis communication in the face of devastating and effective political attacks from Republicans. Rather than one highly credible spokesperson conveying very specific information about what was being done to fix the problems, the public heard vague accounts of "technical surges" and assurances that "the best and brightest" were working on solutions. The administration's point person for Healthcare.gov, Health and Human Services Secretary Kathleen Sibelius (who some cynical Washington observers thought might be asked to commit ritual suicide on live television), continued to respond to specific questions with general responses.

The Holmes Report, a respected public relations news website, listed the rollout in its top 2013 crises. In the analysis, the Holmes Report said, "The best course of action would have been to immediately take ownership of the problem and present a unified singular voice to address user and public concerns. A more emotionally resonant approach would have also helped. Opposition ads often focused, to dramatic effect, on the issues being suffered by regular Americans. The Democratic Party, meanwhile, favored a dry, fact-based tone."[1]

Amazingly, after such a spectacular stumble out the door, Healthcare.gov appears several years later to be a success. Enrollments and paid-healthcare subscribers continue to outstrip estimates, and research indicates that the eight million new customers in the first year seemed to be able to navigate the website with no problems. Nevertheless, for a time the big winners in the debacle were those who criticized President Obama as an inept manager and levied an unending stream of allegations about the entire health-care program.

Despite the terrible start, Obamacare and its Healthcare.gov website have proved popular with the public. The launch of this major component in health-care reform was infinitely more difficult owing to ineffective management of the technical processes and poor communication when problems began to occur. The episode gave credence to criticism about the administration's ineptitude and provided opponents with lots of ammunition. As the Holmes Report concluded, "The main lesson to be learned through this case is that it is always harder to regain trust than it is to preserve it."[2]

As suggested in Chapter 3, congressional Republicans have usually been more artful at framing policy issues and more disciplined in communicating a persuasive and consistent message to the public than Democrats. But not always. There have been periods, sometimes extended, when Republicans in Congress couldn't stop tripping over themselves on political messaging.

Case Study: Majority Bumbling

The Republican Party, or GOP, faced a two-year parade of messaging challenges in 2004–2006 and handled none of them well. The problems actually began earlier, shortly after the 1998 midterm election. House Speaker Newt Gingrich had been forced to step down when, despite his absolute assurances of a GOP victory, House Republicans lost five seats. Gingrich had also been badly tarnished by a reprimand from the House for ethics violations and the revelation of serial philandering at the same time he was leading an impeachment effort against President Bill Clinton for the same thing.

The Republican conference's unanimous choice for Gingrich's successor was Bob Livingston, a leader in the Clinton impeachment effort. But when it came to light that he too had illicit affairs, he resigned from Congress. Ultimately, Illinois representative Dennis Hastert was elected Speaker of the House in 1999. Hastert was never a mesmerizing orator and took a much lower profile in the media than his predecessor.

For the first few years of the new millennium, nearly all communication coming out of Washington dealt with the terror attacks of 9/11, the US response in Afghanistan, and the ensuing decision to invade Iraq. And nearly all public messages emanated from the White House.

Then in 2004, a series of ethics questions surfaced about House majority leader Tom DeLay, including financial dealings with former Republican operative and lobbyist Jack Abramoff, who had been convicted of bribery, corruption, and mail fraud. The House Ethics Committee admonished DeLay for repeatedly providing large financial contributors with direct access to decisionmakers and for the misuse of federal resources to try to track down political enemies in Texas. Nicknamed "the Hammer" for his success in using threats, enticements, and intimidation to produce the necessary votes to pass legislation, DeLay wound up stepping down as majority leader and ultimately retiring from Congress in June 2006 after his indictment by a Texas grand jury for criminal conspiracy and money laundering.

Republican fortunes and their ability to tell a compelling story to the American public continued to decline. In 2004, after several years of war in Iraq, the existence of Saddam Hussein's weapons of mass destruction (WMD)—the justification for US invasion—had proved to be complete fiction (see Chapters 2 and 4).

In November 2004, George W. Bush eked out reelection with 50.7 percent of the vote, the smallest winning margin in history for an incumbent president. Even with his victory, the GOP gained only three seats in the House.

Less than two years later, in September 2006, news stories broke that Representative Mark Foley (R-FL) had been sending sexually suggestive instant messages and e-mails to teenaged boys who were former House pages and had physical contact with several. Foley resigned within weeks, but the scandal created major problems for House Republicans. The scandal deepened as stories emerged that Foley's behavior had been going on for several years and that a number of Republican leaders had known about the situation and reported it to the Speaker, who had taken no action. The Republican message to the public was a series of accusations, denials, and claims of bad memory about who knew what when.

A former senior Republican communication staffer described an October 2006 meeting in the Speaker's office:

> Looking back, the briefing was probably meant to encourage Republican press secretaries to keep our heads and continue fighting, but it was really devoid

continues

Case Study: continued

of any substance. We were expecting to hear about the path forward; how to save our bosses from losing (and us from losing our jobs). Maybe poll numbers would be involved. Maybe a way to mitigate the damage would be presented. Or maybe they would just level with us and tell us, "Hey, we know this is a tough time, but we've got to keep fighting if we want to have a shot at holding on to the House." Several dozen press secretaries were jammed into the Speaker's office. We waited to hear the game plan. Why else would we be summoned to the Speaker's office?

Instead, we were cheerfully told that we had a good story to tell! We were going to go out and talk about what Republicans were doing to fight high gas prices (even though prices were soaring)! The economy was good (though polling showed people didn't believe it)! After about five minutes, we were told to get back to business.

Unfortunately, the briefing had the opposite of the desired effect. Staffers went back to their desks and immediately started dialing reporters inside the Capitol, telling them, "The House GOP leadership has no plan!"[3]

Speaker Hastert's inability to convey a positive "we're in control" message was symbolized by his news conference to talk about the scandal, held—amazingly—with a cemetery in the background. It generated many wry observations about Republican prospects in the election.

The observations were prophetic. In the November 2006 midterm election, Democrats picked up thirty-one seats and won a majority in the House for the first time in twelve years. Nancy Pelosi of California was the first woman to be elected Speaker of the House in history.

While the vagaries of digital technology and mechanical systems can turn even the most carefully planned operation into a catastrophe, many more communication crises result from human factors like stunningly bad judgment: someone in your organization does or says something incredibly stupid, or someone in your organization did or said something incredibly stupid years ago and it just popped up on YouTube. Sometimes the news media digs up bad news or something that can be made to look bad. Sometimes an opponent uses the news media to make a damaging assertion. But more often, the wound is self-inflicted.

Case Study: Susan G. Komen Race for the Cure

The nonprofit Susan G. Komen for the Cure was founded in 1982 and named for a thirty-six-year-old breast cancer victim. The foundation funds research and community services aimed at preventing and ultimately curing the disease. Through 2010, Komen had spent nearly $1.5 billion for breast cancer education, research, advocacy, health services, and social support programs in the United States and through partnerships in more than fifty countries. The foundation may be best known for sponsoring annual Race for the Cure events across the country to raise awareness and contributions for their efforts.

A major focus of the Komen foundation is working "through national and state-level advocacy coalitions to protect federal funding for breast cancer screening and research and to advance breast health and cancer care," and for years, one of the organizations funded by the foundation was the Planned Parenthood Federation of America (PPA).

Planned Parenthood is one of the largest health-care providers for women, men, and young people and the nation's largest provider of sex education. Through its

continues

Case Study: continued

affiliates, PPA operates more than 800 health centers throughout the United States, providing health and reproductive services to women, including treatment for sexually transmitted diseases, contraception and abortion services, nearly 500,000 Pap tests for cervical cancer, and more than half a million breast exams each year. Planned Parenthood has received federal funds for these services since 1970. In 2013, it received more than $540 million, but importantly, PPA is forbidden by law from using any of the federal funds for abortions, which comprise approximately 3 percent of its services.

In 2012, Karen Handel joined the Komen foundation as a top executive. Handel had run for governor of Georgia in 2010 on a largely antiabortion platform. In January 2013, the Komen board decided to drop Planned Parenthood from its list of grant recipients, claiming that Planned Parenthood was under investigation by Congress for using federal funds for abortion. Rather than reveal the decision, the board decided to keep their heads down and wait until Planned Parenthood announced it. The Komen board's decision was immediately deemed to be a transparent attempt by the new executive to placate antiabortion forces, and all hell broke loose.

Within months, the Komen foundation experienced a 22 percent drop in contributions and corporate sponsorships. Participation for its events fell off, and with it, revenue from participation and sponsorships. Revenues from Race for the Cure and three-day events dropped 19 percent, from about $258 million to $208 million. Total revenue, including race fees and contributions, fell 18 percent in the same period, from $399 million to $325 million. Revenues and participation slowly recovered, but it took more than a year.

"The Komen Foundation's fall from grace isn't the result of a communications problem; it is the direct result of a policy and strategy problem, exacerbated by a fundamental misjudgment of the priorities of its constituents," said Carreen Winters, executive vice president at MWW, one of the nation's leading business communication firms. "The moral of the story: no amount of communications can fix a policy or strategy problem."[4]

The second major mistake was the decision to duck. Communication may not be able to fix a policy and strategy problem, but it can cut the losses. Komen's failure to take charge of communication from the outset allowed Planned Parenthood and others to define the situation.

What's important is how communication is handled. But what's even more important is that it *is* handled. The fundamental concept is this: information flow during a crisis must be managed. *Managed*, in this sense, does not mean sitting on information or hiding facts, and it absolutely does not mean trying to mislead the media or the public. Leaving the information to chance or attempting to stop the information flow are perilous courses. The news media have time and space to fill. If they get no information from the organization, they will go elsewhere and they will find something to fill the space or time, even if it is rumor, accusation, or speculation.

Managing Crisis Communication: Be Prepared

Crisis information management is the process of making affirmative decisions about what facts and information should be shared, when, how, by whom, and to whom. The process begins with a detailed crisis management plan that should be followed every time. Every staff member should become familiar with the plan and his or her likely role in its execution. Here are some practical steps in a crisis communication process:

- The organization should have a crisis communication plan in place, even if it's informal. A plan lets an organization respond in a fast and organized manner so everything isn't taken over by the crisis.

- Staff should know how decisions will be made about how to respond, what to say, who should say it, and in what format (news conference, press release, interview, off-the-record, background).

- Who will deal with the media should be established ahead of time.

- If the organization has a communications team, it should assign specific roles, figuring out who should handle particular activities during a crisis and making sure each is trained. The same person can't be on Twitter, writing a press release, talking to bloggers, e-mailing supporters, and answering questions from reporters at the same time.

- The communicators have to manage information flow. They shouldn't try to stop it. Something will go on the air, in the newspaper, and on the Internet. The important question is whether it will have their side of the story.

- The response to every crisis should be released in the same news cycle it was raised. In today's online world, this is more important than ever.

- If communicators have news that is bad for the organization, they should get it out fast and get it out completely.

- They must maintain message discipline.

- The communication team should have an opportunity to rehearse—to map out some of the most likely crisis scenarios and discuss them. It's unlikely that any of them will be exactly the same as the crisis that occurs, but it will give the team a chance to work together in such situations and build confidence.

- In a political campaign, it's just as likely that the opponent will have a crisis situation emerge. How will that be handled? There should be a plan of attack when it happens. The effective communicator needs to be ready to get the entire campaign on message before the other side can respond.

- The team has to monitor media coverage so they know what's being said and written, when the crisis is over, and what the next steps ought to be.

- They need to decide if any opportunities for positive coverage have been created.

- In addition to the news media, with whom do they need to communicate? Nearly every organization has stakeholders; campaigns have contributors.

- Do the finance people need to get on the phone to calm big donors—and maybe raise money to deal with the crisis?

- Does the field team need to be reaching out to prominent supporters to spread the message? A crisis is no time to disappear.

- Communicators need to explain themselves truthfully and fully. They should let supporters know everything and let them know how to help. If the organization is truthful with them, they will most likely continue to support it. If they sense even an ounce of hogwash in a story, the organization will lose all credibility.

- Remember: If supporters aren't hearing about the crisis from the organization, they're hearing about it from someone else.

Any attempt to take on the media, to argue or fight back, should be very carefully thought through and undertaken only if it's really important. If you decide to push back, know beforehand what you want from the media.

- Correction?

- Retraction?

- Follow-up story?

- Guest editorial?

- Letter to the editor?

Remember that the media's willingness to listen and negotiate depends a lot on your organization or campaign's relationship with the reporter approached or the media in general.

Case Study: A Little Preparation Can Pay Off

This account is not about an issue of national significance, but it illustrates the value of looking down the road toward potential crises and asking, "What would we do if . . . ?"

Congressional offices operate through a rather arcane accounting and purchasing system to keep track of the Member's Representation Allowance (MRA), the monthly budget for staff salaries, travel, computers, office rental back home, and any other expenses. Most offices have a professional accounting person to manage or oversee the MRA process.

In 2007, the House Business Office determined that a senior employee in our congressional office had been stealing money for several years by double billing, creating fake invoices, and covering it up to the tune of about $200,000. Among her mistakes was mailing deposits to her personal bank account in Alexandria, Virginia, across the river. That made it interstate theft and a federal offense, and the Federal Bureau of Investigation got involved. The matter was very low key, however, and no mention of it was made to the press.

As soon as the shock wore off, we realized we needed to have some sort of statement from the congressman ready just in case the story made it into the media. We were glad we did.

Weeks later, an enterprising Associated Press reporter happened to see the employee's name and the nature of her offense on the federal court docket in Alexandria. He called for details, and I confirmed the basics of the situation. When he asked to speak to the congressman, I told him the boss was in the district, but that we had a pre-pared statement, which I sent him immediately. That's what ran (names omitted).

Statement of Rep. _____ on the plea bargain of _____.
_____ was an employee who attempted to take advantage of the office accounting system for personal gain. However, the system includes built-in safeguards and Ms. _____ was caught. She will now have to accept the consequences for her actions, including restitution to the US House/US government, so there will be no loss of public funds. Our office has fully recovered, is back on firm financial footing, and in full operation.

Crisis Communication in the Digital World

Operating in today's digital world adds additional responsibilities and urgencies to the crisis communication process. The following steps are offered by Phil Neiman, vice president at the Social Media Council:

- The first step that any campaign or organization can take is to get involved and stay involved in the online community.

- Have an active Facebook group and be engaged on Twitter. If you have a strong presence before a crisis, you will have built-in community support when you need it. If you're only getting on when you're having the crisis, you will be forced to build support and explain your story at the same time. An army of Facebook fans and Twitter followers helping spread your message is much more powerful than your team going at it alone.

- Establish relationships with local/national bloggers (comment on their posts, link to their stories, and treat them like members of the press). Just like your social communities, you need to reach out to bloggers before you need their help.

- Figure out which bloggers are on your side, which bloggers will give a balanced opinion, and which bloggers don't support you. Establish a strong relationship with the first two, and know how to avoid the third. For your die-hard supporters, ask them to be on your crisis response team and have a special distribution list for them. Even blogs with small readership will help keep your story on the front page of Google and will help get it out to other active social media users. For the blogs that you know will take a balanced approach to reporting a story, treat them just like press. Give them the story, give them quotes, and if possible, access to a spokesperson.

- Establish a strong, engaged e-mail distribution list. You have a list of people who want to support you, and a lot of them have already invested time, money, or both. They have a huge investment in seeing you succeed, so let them help. Stats show that more than 60 percent of the entire online population are involved in social communities. That means that you have a list of people who can spread the word faster and wider than you can alone. Cultivate that list, educate them, share information, and ask them to share it with others. When you need them most, provide them with the whole story and let them know how they can share it.

Conclusion

Principle 11: In politics and government, something bad is bound to happen. The smart thing is to be as ready as possible when a crisis hits.

In case after case, the number of organizations—governmental, political, nonprofit, and business—that have been caught totally off guard and unprepared for a crisis situation is astounding. Wise managers and communication professionals know they can rarely predict what will occur and what specific response will be required. But they also know that they need to have a process in place to deal with crises when they do occur, a plan that will tell them how they are going to make decisions so the organization can respond and act promptly.

Notes

1. "The Top 12 Crises of 2013: Part 1," The Holmes Report, February 9, 2014, http://www.holmesreport.com/long-reads/article/the-top-12-crises-of-2013-part-1.

2. Ibid.

3. Conversation with Republican communication director, Washington, DC, 2011.

4. Carreen Winters, executive vice president, MWW, quoted in "The Top 12 Crises of 2012: Part 1," The Holmes Report, February 3, 2013, https://www.holmesreport.com/long-reads/article/the-top-12-crises-of-2012-part-1

13

The Ethical Line in
Political Communication

Principle 12: Ultimately, whether political communicators
are ethical or not is completely up to them.

George Orwell wrote, "Political language is designed to make lies
sound truthful and murder respectable." He's correct — sometimes.
Orwell took a very dark view of politics and political communication. However, although it's true that nearly all political communication is intended to persuade, there are ethical limits on how
far the communicator can go beyond a starting point of neutral,
fact-based arguments that present both sides of an issue in cold,
objective terms. The communicator has to know where those limits are because many of the same techniques common in effective
political communication are also characteristic of spin and propaganda. In fact, many of these techniques are included in public
relations training and education.

Spin

Spin essentially means you accentuate the positive and don't mention the negative. Americans see and hear spin every day. Every good sales pitch or television commercial is spin. In politics and public affairs, spin is usually a pejorative term for a biased portrayal of an event or situation in one's own favor. Used as such, the term implies disingenuous, deceptive, manipulative tactics. Politicians are often accused of spin by their opponents, who are also busy doing their own spinning.

Spin and Persuasion

Why do politicians spin? Because they're selling. Politics is about the distribution of resources, and its practitioners frequently have diametrically opposed points of view about what to do with those resources. Most political communication takes place in a world of competing ideas, priorities, and agendas—a world in which winning is the goal. This doesn't mean honest political communicators shouldn't try to persuade, that they shouldn't try to marshal the most compelling and convincing arguments to win people over.

Is "spin-free" political communication even possible? Possible perhaps, but extremely unlikely, and it would be unbelievably dull and passionless. Imagine a political debate over ideology, public policy, and spending priorities in which the opposing debaters said nothing to persuade the audience to support their viewpoint. If you think voter participation is low now, imagine what it would be if no politician ever spoke with zeal and conviction. Imagine how much interest and participation in our political system there would be if no one ever stirred or motivated people on an issue.

It's the abuse—the overreliance on persuasion over substance— that weakens the public's belief and trust in their leaders and institutions. Building public support through spin without substance is destructive because eventually, inevitably, the lack of substance will be exposed. Like a hollow sales pitch, it's all hype. The public will feel betrayed—promises of performance have been made and not kept—and there will be a backlash.

Case Study: Senator Harry Reid's Great Uncle Remus

US Senate Democratic leader Harry Reid (D-NV) has described a great-great-uncle, Remus Reid, who was hanged for horse stealing and train robbery in Montana in 1889. In fact, the only known photograph of Remus Reid shows him standing on the gallows in Montana territory. On the back of the picture is the inscription: "Remus Reid, horse thief, sent to Montana Territorial Prison 1885, escaped 1887, robbed the Montana Flyer six times. Caught by Pinkerton detectives, convicted and hanged in 1889."

A professional genealogy researcher contacted Senator Reid's office to see if he had a biographical sketch of his notorious relative. Here's what she received:

> Remus Reid was a famous cowboy in the Montana Territory. His business empire included acquisition of valuable equestrian assets and intimate dealings with the Montana railroad. Beginning in 1883, he devoted several years of his life to government service, finally taking leave to resume his dealings with the railroad. In 1887, he was a key player in a vital investigation run by the renowned Pinkerton Detective Agency. In 1889, Remus passed away during an important civic function held in his honor when the platform upon which he was standing collapsed.

It should be noted that either there were an amazing number of horse thieves named Remus in the late nineteenth-century, or it is just such a great example of spin that it inspired similar accounts of Remus Rodham, a forefather of former secretary of state Hillary Rodham Clinton, and Remus Stevens, a progenitor of former senator Ted Stevens. There were also ancestors of former president George W. Bush (Chadsworth Bush, hanged in 1889), former vice president Joe Biden (Robert Biden, also hanged in 1889), former vice president Al Gore (Gunther Gore, hanged in

1889), and even of Canadian political leader Stephanie Dion (Robert Dion, also hanged in 1889). At the very least, 1889 was a very bad year to be a horse thief.

Spin Techniques

There are two basic kinds of spin: defensive and offensive. Defensive spin tries to recast or redefine an unfavorable set of circumstances to encourage people to view them in a more favorable light. Offensive spin is an attack, often using anger, to immobilize opponents who are trying to capitalize on embarrassing circumstances. The tactic can also be used to try to immobilize the news media and make it "uncomfortable" for them to ask tough questions. A politician might say, "I can't believe you'd ask that kind of question," or "I'm not going to dignify that sort of smear with a response."

Here are some commonly used spin techniques:

- *Cherry-picking:* The use of individual cases or facts that appear to confirm a particular position while ignoring a significant portion of related cases that may contradict it.

- *Counterattack:* Impugning the reliability, credibility, motivation, or even the ethics or morals of a source without addressing the fact alleged by the source.

- *Euphemisms:* Using words or expressions intended to be less offensive, disturbing, or troubling to the listener than the word or phrase it replaces. Nowhere is this more commonly practiced than in Department of Defense and military communication. In Iraq, roadside bombs became *improvised explosive devices*, torture was *physical persuasion*, kidnapping someone and turning them over to someone else for torture was *extraordinary rendition*, and ending US military involvement in Iraq was an *exit strategy*.

- *Misdirection or deflection:* Politicians will sometimes answer the question they want rather than the question asked. They might do it directly: "That's not the question we should be talking about. The real issue is. . . ." Or they may ignore the question entirely.

- *Nondenial denial:* An apparent denial that sounds clear-cut and definite but is ambiguous and not a denial at all — in other words, something made to sound like a denial without actually being one. One example would be characterizing a statement as "ridiculous" or "absurd" without specifically saying it's not true. Another would be, as with offensive spin, "We are not going to dignify that with a response."

- *Sound bite:* A short phrase or sentence that captures the essence of what the speaker is trying to say. They help the politician and political communicator focus the news media's attention on parts of a speech or statement that advance the overall message. Don't feel sorry for the news media for having to wade through all these sound bites. They love them. The best news footage contains at least one.

- *Staying "on message":* Everyone sings from the same sheet music. It limits questions and focuses attention on a narrow discussion favorable to the communicators. How many times have you heard multiple spokespeople on one side or another say exactly the same thing, even using the same words and phrases?

- *Timing:* Communicators frequently delay the release of bad news until periods of low news coverage, such as late nights or weekends, or they schedule events that might generate bad publicity the same way. Doing so gives journalists less time to pursue the story, and the Friday night television audience and Saturday morning newspaper readership are smaller than at other times. This timing has become so commonplace at the White House that it's called "taking out the trash." Many highly controversial issues are brought to the floor of Congress on Friday afternoon or evening, such as the Prescription Drug bill in November 2003. The legislation specifically prohibited the federal government from negotiating with drug manufacturers for better prices.

Propaganda

For many people, the word *propaganda* brings to mind some of the most cruel and repressive regimes in history: Adolph Hitler's Nazi Germany, the Soviet Union under Joseph Stalin, Maoist China, and North Korea under Kim Jong-un today. The notion of propaganda reeks of dictatorships and mind control on a massive scale. But propaganda is not only a tool for totalitarian regimes, and it does not die out when they do. It is alive and well in the United States, among other places, and it continues to be widely used because it serves a variety of purposes. Some are positive and beneficial; some are not.

Propaganda seeks to change the way people understand an issue or situation to suit a particular interest. The aim is to directly influence people's opinions rather than communicate facts. Propaganda shares many techniques with advertising. In fact, advertising really is a form of propaganda that promotes a certain product or service. But the word *propaganda* usually refers to political or governmental uses.

Government propaganda may be positive, like a public information campaign that encourages seatbelt use or urges people not to smoke. But there is a negative side. In 2004, the nonpartisan Government Accountability Office (GAO) identified "covert propaganda" used by our own government. It referred to television programs, video news releases, and endorsements from columnists that did not disclose they were paid government messages produced by at least twenty different federal agencies.

The GAO considered this covert propaganda because point-of-view messages were masquerading as objective information. News outlets are not expected to be mouthpieces for the government. Advertising presents an issue in the best possible light, to persuade rather than inform. We know ads are trying to sell us something, but if the audience believes what they are watching is a news item, the message is likely to be accepted as such. Federal law now specifically mandates that any government-generated message appearing in the format of a news item must disclose that it is a paid message.

The narrower and more dangerous use of propaganda employs deliberately false or misleading information that furthers a political cause or interest. The propagandist tries to change the way people understand an issue or situation in ways that are desirable to the interest group.

What sets this sort of propaganda apart from other forms of advocacy is the willingness of the propagandist to manipulate people through deception and confusion rather than persuasion and understanding. And what separates this kind of propaganda from more straightforward persuasion is the subtle, often insidious ways the message attempts to manipulate the public's opinion. For example, propaganda often includes calculated attempts to evoke strong emotions by suggesting illogical or nonexistent relationships.

In moving public opinion to support a US invasion of Iraq, the George W. Bush administration continuously paired Iraqi president Saddam Hussein and al-Qaeda as if they were fraternal twins, although no link between the bloody dictator and the terrorist organization was ever established. Such rhetorical linking is a classic propaganda technique.

Other familiar forms of propaganda include what appear to be legitimate, two-way news interviews that are completely staged productions, or "town hall" meetings that are tightly controlled in every aspect.

Here are a few other classic propaganda techniques:

- *Appeal to authority:* Appeals to authority cite the endorsement of prominent figures to support a position, idea, argument, or course of action.

- *Appeal to fear:* This appeal seeks to build support by instilling fear in the general population. An example would be the Bush administration's claims that Saddam Hussein possessed and was prepared to use weapons of mass destruction, discussed in Chapter 3.

- *Association:* Association projects positive or negative qualities of a person, entity, object, or value onto another to make the second more acceptable or less credible. It is often used to transfer blame from one member of a conflict to another. For example, in his January 29, 2001, State of the Union speech, President Bush grouped Iran, North Korea, and Iraq in an "axis of evil," claiming that all three were aiding and abetting terrorism and developing weapons of mass destruction. Iraq, in fact, had no weapons of mass destruction and no known ties to terrorist organizations. But including them in the axis helped rally support for the US invasion.

- *Astroturfing:* Used frequently today, this technique tries to create the impression of a spontaneous, grassroots organization that is actually a front for a business, industry, or interest group, such as a "citizen" group to save coal mining jobs that turns out to be a coal industry effort. Consumers for Cable Choice actually received their funding from telecommunications companies Verizon and AT&T.

- *Bandwagon effect:* These appeals attempt to persuade the target audience that "everyone" is taking a certain course of action and that audience members should also do so for that reason. Congressional Democrats and Republicans both frequently tell us what the American people want, which happens to be what each political group wants.

- *Common man:* The "plain folks" or "common man" approach attempts to convince the audience that the propagandist's positions reflect the common sense of the public.

- *Direct order:* A direct order uses images and words to tell the audience exactly what actions to take, often using authority figures to give the order. Remember the iconic Uncle Sam "I want you" posters?

- *Glittering generalities:* Glittering generalities seek approval without giving any reason for it. They use intense, emotionally appealing words or phrases that are closely associated with highly valued concepts and beliefs. They carry conviction without information and appeal to such emotions as love of country or desire for peace, freedom, or glory and honor.

- *Intentional vagueness:* Generalities are kept deliberately vague so that the audience can supply its own interpretations. The intention is to move the audience by use of undefined phrases without analyzing their validity or attempting to determine their reasonableness or application. "Our economy has been slowed down and millions of American jobs lost because of too many government regulations."

- *Inevitable victory:* This approach invites those who aren't already on the bandwagon to join everyone else on the road to certain victory. This also helps keep those on the bandwagon from getting off.

- *Obtain disapproval:* The opposite approach to the bandwagon effect, this method tries to persuade a target audience to disapprove of an action or idea by suggesting that the idea is popular with groups the audience fears or disapproves of.

- *Oversimplification:* Oversimplification offers favorable generalities that provide simple answers to complex social, political, economic, or military problems. "Spending more on protecting our environment can help all Americans lead healthier lives."

- *Rationalization:* Individuals or groups may use favorable generalities to rationalize questionable acts or beliefs. Vague and pleasant phrases are often used to justify such actions or beliefs. "Negative news coverage of President Trump is simply the result of biased media."

- *Scapegoating:* This technique assigns blame to an individual or group for a problem they are not really responsible for. The aim may be to redirect guilt away from responsible parties or to distract attention from the need to fix the problem.

- *Slogans:* A slogan is a brief, striking word or phrase that may include labeling and stereotyping. If good ideas can be made into honest slogans, they should be, as good slogans are self-perpetuating.

- *Stereotyping or labeling:* Stereotypes or labels attempt to arouse prejudices in an audience by identifying the object as something the audience fears, hates, or otherwise finds undesirable. "Donald Trump's primary appeal is to White southerners without college educations" or "Most of the drug problem in the United States is the result of people crossing our southern border illegally."

- *Testimonials:* Testimonials are quotations, in or out of context, cited to support or reject a given policy, action, program, or personality. They exploit the reputation or role (expert, respected public figure, etc.) of the individual making the statement, who might be an expert, a respected public figure, or the like. Secretary of State Colin Powell's presentation on Iraq's "weapons of mass destruction" at the United Nations used his reputation to give credence to the claims.
- *Virtue words:* These are words in the value system of the target audience that tend to produce a positive image when attached to a person or issue. Peace, happiness, security, wise leadership, and freedom, for example, are virtue words.

Lies

Lies are not spin. But the pervasive use of spin by politicians, its tacit acceptance by the media, and, to a large extent, its acceptance by the public have created an environment that tempts political communicators to dress up flat-out lies as spin.

Liar used to be one of the most powerful words in our language. Calling someone a liar has led to untold shouting matches, slapped faces, punched noses, duels, and lawsuits—and probably the occasional war. Being called a liar or accused of lying used to be a grievous insult. Being caught in a lie brought many public careers to a screeching halt. Not anymore.

Historic Political Lies

Today, lying has somehow become okay in many quarters, especially in politics and government. Telling an outright lie in political debates or discussion over national policy seems to be acceptable. A US senator can tell a bald-faced lie on the floor of the Senate and it's fine. Congressional leaders can hold endless news conferences and lie their heads off, and they're said to be exercising strong leadership. Candidates for the highest offices in the nation can tell whopper after whopper and no one seems to take offense. Often, no one even calls them on it.

• When President Richard Nixon said in 1973, "There can be no whitewash at the White House," that wasn't spin. It was a lie.

• When President Bill Clinton said in 1998, "I did not have sexual relations with that woman," that wasn't spin. It was a lie.

• When Senator John Kyl (R-AZ) said in an April 8, 2011, speech on the Senate floor that abortion services "were well over 90 percent of what Planned Parenthood does," that wasn't spin. It was a lie. He was off by 87 percent. His office's stunning response to criticism of his misstatement was, "It was not intended to be a factual statement."

• When 2016 Republican presidential candidate Senator Ted Cruz (R-TX) sent an urgent message to potential Iowa Republican caucus-goers that fellow Republican Ben Carson had just pulled the plug on his campaign, and suggested that Carson supporters should caucus for him instead, that was a lie. Carson never announced he was ending his campaign. When Cruz said he got the information from a CNN story, that too was a lie. CNN never reported that Carson was quitting.

• When Democratic presidential candidate and former secretary of state Hillary Clinton claimed in a January 20, 2016, speech in Burlington, Iowa, that she was "the only candidate in the 2016 campaign for president who had laid out a detailed plan to defeat ISIS," that was a lie. In fact, at least seven other Republican and Democratic candidates had offered plans of five to eighteen specific points.

• When Republican candidate Donald Trump said in a town hall gathering in Norwalk, Iowa, also on January 20, 2016, that "Mexico can afford to build a wall because the country's trade deficit with America is billions of dollars," that was a lie. The trade deficit refers to the fact that Americans spend more on products from Mexico than Mexicans spend on US products. It has nothing whatsoever to do with finding money to build a wall.

Where Are the Consequences?

Politicians get away with lying for three reasons: media timidity, party loyalty, and low expectations. How often do we hear, see, or read a news story in which a reporter questions the veracity of a public official's statement to the official's face? How often have you seen a journalist with the nerve to take issue with some totally fallacious utterance? How often have you heard questions like, "Excuse me, Senator, but doesn't the record show that . . . ?" or "But Congresswoman, didn't you actually vote against . . . ?" or "Don't all available public opinion surveys show overwhelmingly that what the American people really want is . . . ?" It happens occasionally, but not enough.

Many lies are told to stir the pot of partisan loyalty, either to fire up the base or, sometimes, for the opposite reason: to keep them temporarily tranquilized so they don't rise up like a swarm of hornets and sting anyone who happens to be close. This is done with the knowledge that many people will believe the most outrageous lies because they want to believe them—because the lies are congruent with what they already accept.

The third reason our national political dialogue has degenerated into a contest of ideological prevarication is that a large proportion of the population doesn't expect politicians to tell the truth. This is hardly new. People have written off politicians as liars since the infant days of the republic. But it's still a bit disheartening to admit that we simply don't expect any better from the people we elect to public office.

Case Study: Scaling New Heights in Mendacity

Among many significant changes in the process and practice of political communication during the 2016 presidential general election was an apparent new level in false statements by the candidates on both sides. Democrat Hillary Clinton and Republican Donald Trump said things that ranged from not quite true to completely false. But never in our nation's history has there been such a torrent of outright lies.

One major departure in the 2016 election was the absolutely unprecedented willingness of major news publications, such as the *New York Times*, to use the word *lie* in stories and even headlines concerning candidates' misstatements. This led to extraordinary changes in the very nature of the election news coverage. For example, two organizations—the Pulitzer Prize–winning PolitiFact.com, run by editors and reporters from the *Tampa Bay Times*, an independent newspaper in Florida, and FactCheck.org, a project of the Annenberg Public Policy Center of the University of Pennsylvania—were working overtime to parse candidates' public statements, compare those statements with documented facts and records, and render judgments about whether the statement was truthful or a lie.

Table 13.1 shows a summary by PolitiFact of the veracity of President Donald Trump's statements five months into his administration, while Table 13.2 shows the PolitiFact scorecard for Democrat Hillary Clinton over the course of her candidacy.

Table 13.1 Donald Trump's PolitiFact Scorecard (through June 2017)

Rating	Number of Statements	Percentage
True	20	5
Mostly True	50	12
Half True	61	15
Mostly False	87	21
False	134	32
Pants on Fire[a]	65	16

Source: "Comparing Hillary Clinton, Donald Trump on the Truth-O-Meter," PolitiFact, http://www.politifact.com/truth-o-meter/lists/people/comparing-hillary-clinton-donald-trump-truth-o-met/ (accessed June 26, 2017).

Note: a. PolitiFact assigns its "Pants on Fire" rating if they determine that "the statement is not accurate and makes a ridiculous claim."

continues

Case Study: continued

Table 13.2 Hillary Clinton's PolitiFact Scorecard (through June 2017)

Rating	Number of Statements	Percentage
True	72	24
Mostly True	76	26
Half True	69	23
Mostly False	41	14
False	29	10
Pants on Fire[a]	7	2

Source: "Comparing Hillary Clinton, Donald Trump on the Truth-O-Meter," PolitiFact, http://www.politifact.com/truth-o-meter/lists/people/comparing-hillary-clinton-donald-trump-truth-o-met/ (accessed June 26, 2017).

Note: a. PolitiFact assigns its "Pants on Fire" rating if they determine that "the statement is not accurate and makes a ridiculous claim."

Numerous journalists and pundits have decried what they term "post-truth politics." In an editorial entitled "Art of the Lie," the *Economist* magazine suggested that, "post-truth politics is more than just an invention of whining elites who have been outflanked. The term picks out the heart of what is new: that truth is not falsified or contested, but of secondary importance."[1]

Is this the future of political communication? When White House senior advisor Kellyanne Conway was pushed on NBC's *Meet the Press* on January 22, 2017, to explain untrue public statements about the size of the inaugural crowd by Trump press secretary Sean Spicer, she said, "He gave 'alternative facts.'"

We used to rely on the news media to patrol the borders of truth and fact and to sound the alarm when someone in government or politics crossed the line. Unfortunately, with the dramatic changes in the media and the reporters who cover politics (see Chapter 10), politicians have learned that they can lie with impunity.

Fewer reporters today have the institutional memory to know when a politician is telling a lie or the tenure to feel secure in calling the politician on it. I've been told several times over the past few years by reporters on the Hill that being the "honesty police" is the job of PolitiFact and FactCheck, not them.

Conclusion

Principle 12: Ultimately, whether political communicators are ethical or not is completely up to them.

What separates propaganda, spin, and lying from honest political discourse, more than anything else, is the intent of the communicator. And intent is governed, more than anything else, by that communicator's ethics.

Of course, it's not that simple. Most communicators work for someone else. That someone else is the driving force and has the final say on whether or not unethical communication is used or attempted. It therefore falls to the communicator to decide if he or she consents to participate in unethical communication. If the communicator cannot dissuade the decisionmaker from proceeding, then the choice is clear: go along or walk away. In the broader perspective, if there is little or no accountability or consequence for misleading or outright dishonest communication, it will continue. Unethical political communication will continue as long as the public allows it.

Notes

1. "Post-truth Politics: Art of the Lie," *Economist*, September 10, 2016.

Suggested Readings

Ansolabehere, Stephen, and Shanto Iyengar. *Going Negative: How Political Advertisements Shrink and Polarize the Electorate*. New York: Free Press, 1995.

Bennett, W. Lance. *News: The Politics of Illusion*. 9th ed. Chicago: University of Chicago Press, 2012.

Bennett, W. Lance, Regina Lawrence, and Steven Livingston. *When the Press Fails: Political Power and the News Media from Iraq to Katrina*. Chicago: University of Chicago Press, 2007.

Bonk, Kathy, Emily Tynes, Henry Griggs, and Phil Sparks. *Strategic Communications for Nonprofits: A Step-by-Step Guide to Working with the Media*. 2nd ed. San Francisco: Jossey-Bass, 2008.

Brader, Ted. *Campaigning for Hearts and Minds: How Emotional Appeals in Political Ads Work*. Chicago: University of Chicago Press, 2006.

Casey, Maura, and Barbara Mantz Drake, eds. *Beyond Argument: A Handbook for Opinion Writers and Editors*. 2nd ed. Association of Opinion Journalists, 2010.

Daly, John. *Advocacy: Championing Ideas and Influencing Others*. New Haven, CT: Yale University Press, 2011.

Denton, Robert E., Jr., ed. *The 2012 Presidential Campaign: A Communication Perspective*. Lanham, MD: Rowman and Littlefield, 2014.

Dionne, E. J., Jr. *Our Divided Political Heart*. New York: Bloomsbury USA, 2012.

Draper, Robert. *Do Not Ask What Good We Do: Inside the U.S. House of Representatives*. New York: Free Press, 2012.

Eilperin, Juliet. *Fight Club Politics: How Partisanship Is Poisoning the House of Representatives*. Lanham, MD: Rowman and Littlefield, 2006.

Fiorina, Morris P. *Culture War? The Myth of a Polarized America*. 3rd ed.
    New York: Longman, 2011.
Fitch, Bradford. *Media Relations Handbook for Agencies, Associations,
    Nonprofits and Congress*. Alexandria, VA: TheCapitol.Net, 2004.
Geer, John G. *In Defense of Negativity: Attack Ads in Presidential Cam-
    paigns*. Chicago: University of Chicago Press, 2006.
Graber, Doris. *Mass Media and American Politics*. 8th ed. Washington, DC:
    CQ Press, 2010.
Iyengar, Shanto. *Media Politics: A Citizen's Guide*. 3rd ed. New York: W. W.
    Norton, 2016.
Jackson, Brooks, and Kathleen Hall Jamieson. *Unspun: Finding Facts in a
    World of Disinformation*. New York: Random House, 2007.
Kurtz, Howard. *Spin Cycle: How the White House and the Media Manipu-
    late the News*. New York: Touchstone, 1998.
Lehrman, Robert. *The Political Speechwriter's Companion: A Guide for
    Writers and Speakers*. Washington, DC: CQ Press, 2009.
Luntz, Frank I. *Words That Work: It's Not What You Say, It's What People
    Hear*. New York: Hyperion, 2007.
Mann, Thomas E., and Norman J. Ornstein. *The Broken Branch: How Con-
    gress Is Failing America and How to Get It Back on Track*. Oxford:
    Oxford University Press, 2006.
———.*It's Even Worse Than It Looks: How the American Constitutional Sys-
    tem Collided with the New Politics of Extremism*. New York: Basic
    Books, 2012.
Marcus, George E., W. Russell Neuman, and Michael MacKuen. *Affective
    Intelligence and Political Judgement*. Chicago: University of Chicago
    Press, 2000.
Mooney, Chris. *The Republican Brain: The Science of Why They Deny
    Science—and Reality*. Hoboken, NJ: Wiley, 2012.
Mutz, Diana C., Paul M. Sniderman, and Richard A. Brody, eds. *Political
    Persuasion and Attitude Change*. Ann Arbor: University of Michigan
    Press, 1996.
Neuman, W. Russell, George Marcus, Ann Crigler, and Michael Mackuen,
    eds. *The Affect Effect: Dynamics of Emotion in Political Thinking and
    Behavior*. Chicago: University of Chicago Press, 2007.
Pasquier, Martial, and Jean-Patrick Villeneuve. *Marketing Management and
    Communications in the Public Sector*. New York: Routledge, 2012.
Pelosi, Alexandra. *Sneaking into the Flying Circus: How the Media Turn
    Our Presidential Campaigns into Freak Shows*. New York: Free Press,
    2005.
Perloff, Richard M. *The Dynamics of Political Communication: Media and
    Politics in the Digital Age*. New York: Routledge, 2014.
———. *Political Communication: Politics, Press, and Public in America*.
    Mahwah, NJ: Lawrence Erlbaum Associates, 1998.
Popkin, Samuel L. *The Reasoning Voter: Communication and Persuasion in
    Presidential Campaigns*. 2nd ed. Chicago: University of Chicago Press,
    1994.

Powell, Larry, and Joseph Cowart. *Political Campaign Communication: Inside and Out*. 2nd ed. New York: Routledge, 2013.

Roman, Kenneth, and Joel Raphaelson. *Writing That Works: How to Write Memos, Letters, Reports, Speeches, Resumes, Plans, and Other Papers That Say What You Mean—and Get Things Done*. New York: Harper and Row, 1981.

Stimson, James A. *Tides of Consent: How Public Opinion Shapes American Politics*. Cambridge: Cambridge University Press, 2004.

Stonecipher, Harry W. *Editorial and Persuasive Writing*. 2nd ed. Mamaroneck, NY: Hastings House, 1990.

Stroud, Natalie Jomini. *Niche News: The Politics of News Choice*. Oxford: Oxford University Press, 2011.

Theriault, Sean M. *The Gingrich Senators: The Roots of Partisan Warfare in Congress*. Oxford: Oxford University Press, 2013.

———.*Party Polarization in Congress*. Cambridge: Cambridge University Press, 2011.

Thurber, James A., and Candice J. Nelson. *Campaigns and Elections American Style*. 4th ed. Boulder, CO: Westview Press, 2014.

Trent, Judith S., Robert Friedenberg, and Robert E. Denton, Jr. *Political Campaign Communication: Principles and Practices*. 8th ed. Lanham, MD: Rowman and Littlefield, 2016.

Tuman, Joseph S. *Political Communication in American Campaigns*. Thousand Oaks, CA: Sage Publications, 2008.

Westen, Drew. *The Political Brain: The Role of Emotion in Deciding the Fate of the Nation*. New York: PublicAffairs, 2007.

Wolfsfeld, Gadi. *Making Sense of Media and Politics: Five Principles in Political Communication*. New York: Routledge, 2011.

Zaller, John R. *The Nature and Origins of Mass Opinion*. Cambridge: Cambridge University Press, 1992.

Index

Abercrombie, Neil, 225
abortion: congressional lies about,
    277; as issue-symbol, 99–100;
    Planned Parenthood education,
    258
Abramoff, Jack, 254
academic research, 3–4
accessibility accommodation, 21–23
activists: targeting the message, 109
Adams, John, 179
ad-blockers, 202–203
AdExchanger Politics, 202–203
advertising: congressional framing
    wars, 53–54; continuing
    importance of paid advertising,
    157–158; elements in print media,
    175–177; 527 committees, 180;
    importance in political
    communication, 9, 157;
    importance of emotional appeal,
    166–169; LBJ's "Daisy" ad, 73–
    74, 169–170; means-end theory,
    63; media communication
    planning, 130–131; negative ads,
    177–183; news media's
    relationship, 10–11; Obama
    campaign's data collection, 197–
    199; online ad-blockers, 202–203;
    online campaign advertising,

191–192; print media reinforcing
    the message, 175–177;
    propaganda techniques and, 272;
    radio, 162; reelecting a deceased
    candidate, 172–173; role of focus
    groups, 118–119; same-sex
    marriage as issue-symbol, 101–
    102; use of humor, 173; use of
    repetition, 42–44; visual and
    audio imagery, 174. *See also*
    attack advertising; television
advocacy communication:
    importance of research, 106;
    organizations and messages, 36;
    settings for, 18; targeting the
    advocacy message, 36–37. *See
    also* issue advocacy
affective intelligence, 167
Affordable Care Act (ACA): framing
    elections, 61, 64; Healthcare.gov
    rollout, 233–234, 252–253; issue-
    symbols, 98; the partisan divide,
    33–34; partisan history of health-
    care legislation, 93–94; partisan
    use of research to support goals
    of, 119–120; Romneycare origins,
    87; simplification of message
    language, 69
Afghanistan: War on Terror, 85

use of, 119–120; the future of
public opinion research, 124–126;
HELP ME! model, 128–129;
importance in political
communication, 8, 83, 105;
importance of communication
planning, 132–133; for message
development, 107–108; the
message police, 120–121;
qualitative, 117–119; quantitative,
110–117; speechwriters' fact
checking, 151; value in preparing
political messages, 79–81; voter
identification, 121–122
respect between media and political
communicators, 220
response rates in public polling, 115–
116
*Retail Is Detail: A Retailer's
Playbook for Beating Walmart*
(Scott and Hawkins), 193
rhetorical devices in speechwriting,
149
Rice, Condolleeza, 51
Roe v. Wade, 99
Roman Empire, 2
Romney, Mitt: editorial
endorsements, 223; framing the
midterm elections, 62; issue-
symbols, 98; the media priming
effect, 46; partisan news media in
the 2012 election, 246–247; poor
political oratory, 143;
Romneycare, 86–87; television
advertising, 161; voter
demographics, 125
Roosevelt, Franklin D., 68, 112,
136–137, 228
ROPE (Research-Objectives-
Program-Evaluation), 128
Roper Poll, 112
Rove, Karl, 247
Rubio, Marco, 204, 229
Rumsfeld, Donald, 68–69
rush letters, 191

same-sex marriage, 34, 56–58, 100–
102

San Bernadino shooting, 90–91
Santorum, Rick, 229
Scalia, Antonin, 59
scapegoating as propaganda
technique, 275
Scherer, Michael, 197–198
Schneider, Bill, 92–93
Schreiber, Darren, 77
Schuck, Peter, 181–182
Schwartz, Tony, 73–74
Science Applications International
Corporation (SAIC), 25–27
Science journal, 47
Scott, Bill, 193
selling, politics as, 268
*The Sentimental Citizen, Emotion in
Democratic Politics* (Marcus),
167
September 11, 2001, 51, 85, 254
settings for political communication,
17
sex education, 257–259
sexual scandals, 255–256
Shapiro, Robert, 49
Shaw, Donald, 45
Sibelius, Kathleen, 252
simile and metaphor, 149
simplifying language, 68
Skutnik, Lenny, 70
slogans, 41, 275
small business loans, 241–242
Smith, Thomas, 42
social media, 10; campaigns
combining Internet and traditional
communication media, 206–207;
congressional framing wars, 53–
54; LinkedIn, 200; Obama's
campaign data collection, 198–
199; online issue advocacy, 209–
210; policy communication
through, 207–209; political
advertising, 158; primary sites,
200; Trump's use of, 203–206;
user demographic, 201–202. *See
also* Facebook; Twitter
Social Security reform, 34
Socrates, 2
sound bites as spin technique, 271

About the Book

From developing effective messages to working with the news media, from writing speeches to tweeting, from crisis communication to the ethics of political communication, and everything in between, *Political Communication in Action* takes the reader step by step through the process.

This approachable new text:

- Covers both theory and real-world practice

- Uses examples and case studies to illustrate key concepts

- Shows what aspects of the process look like when done well, and when done poorly

- Addresses public affairs and advocacy communication, as well as political campaigns

- Explores changes emerging from the 2016 elections

Uniquely, it provides a tour of the communication process as it actually works: in political campaigns, in government from City Hall to Congress and the White House, and in advocacy organizations.

David L. Helfert has more than four decades of experience working in the field of political communication, including service in the Clinton administration (1994–2000) and as communications director for a congressional committee and two congressmen (2001–2010). He has taught political communication at Johns Hopkins University, American University, and Texas State University, and he has been a regular lecturer at the US Naval Academy.